DISCOVERING PSYCHOLOGY:
A Guide to Active Study

to accompany

Psychology
David G. Myers

Richard O. Straub

University of Michigan, Dearborn

Worth Publishers, Inc.

DISCOVERING PSYCHOLOGY: A Guide to Active Study
by Richard O. Straub
to accompany
Myers: Psychology

Printed in the United States of America.
ISBN: 0-87901-312-5
Fourth printing, April 1988

Worth Publishers, Inc.
33 Irving Place
New York, New York 10003

Preface

This Study Guide is designed for use with *Psychology* by David G. Myers. It is intended to help you evaluate your understanding of the text material, and then to review any problem areas. "How to Manage Your Time Efficiently and Study More Effectively" (p. v) gives detailed instructions on how to use the Study Guide for maximum benefit. It also offers additional study suggestions based on principles of time management, effective notetaking, evaluation of exam performance, and an effective program for improving your comprehension while studying from textbooks.

I would like to thank all the students at the University of Michigan, Dearborn, and Hope College who used this Study Guide in its preliminary form and provided such insightful and useful suggestions.

Richard O. Straub
January 1986

How to Manage Your Time Efficiently and Study More Effectively

How effectively do you study? Good study habits make the job of being a college student much easier. Many students who *could* succeed in college fail or drop out, because they have never learned to manage their time efficiently. Even the best students can usually benefit from an in-depth evaluation of their current study habits.

There are many ways to achieve academic success, of course, but your approach may not be the most effective or efficient. Are you sacrificing your social life, or your physical or mental health, in order to get As on your exams? Good study habits result in better grades *and* more time for other activities.

EVALUATE YOUR CURRENT STUDY HABITS

To improve your study habits, you must first have an accurate picture of how you currently spend your time. Begin by putting together a profile of your present living and studying habits. Answer the following questions by writing yes or no on each line.

_____ 1. Do you usually set up a schedule to budget your time for studying, recreation, and other activities?

_____ 2. Do you often put off studying until time pressures force you to cram?

_____ 3. Do other students seem to study less but get better grades?

_____ 4. Do you usually spend hours studying one subject, rather than dividing that time between several subjects?

_____ 5. Do you often have trouble remembering what you have just read in a textbook?

_____ 6. Before reading a chapter in a textbook, do you skim through it and read the section headings?

_____ 7. Do you try to predict exam questions from your lecture notes and reading?

_____ 8. Do you usually attempt to paraphrase or summarize what you have just finished reading?

_____ 9. Do you find it difficult to concentrate very long when you study?

_____ 10. Do you often feel that you studied the wrong material for an exam?

Thousands of college students have participated in similar surveys. Students who are fully realizing their academic potential usually respond as follows: (1) yes, (2) no, (3) no, (4) no, (5) no, (6) yes, (7) yes, (8) yes, (9) no, (10) no.

Compare your responses with those of successful students. The greater the discrepancy, the more you could benefit from a program to improve your study habits. The questions are designed to identify areas of weakness. Once you have identified your weaknesses, you will be able to set specific goals for improvement and implement a program for reaching them.

MANAGE YOUR TIME

Do you often feel frustrated because there isn't enough time to do all the things you must and want to do? Take heart. Even the most productive and successful people feel this way at times. But they establish priorities for their activities and learn to budget their time. There's much in the saying "If you want something done, ask a busy person to do it." A busy person *knows* how to get things done.

If you don't now have a system for budgeting your time, develop one. Not only will your academic performance improve, but you will also find more time in your schedule for other activities. And you won't have to feel guilty about "taking time off," because all your obligations will be covered.

Establish a Baseline

As a first step in preparing to budget your time, keep a diary for a few days to establish a summary, or baseline, of the time you spend in studying, socializing, working, and so on. If you are like many students, much of your "study" time is nonproductive; you may sit at your desk and leaf through a book, but the time is actually wasted. Or you may procrastinate. You are always getting ready to study, but you rarely do.

Besides revealing where you waste time, the diary will give you a realistic picture of how much time to allot for meals, commuting, and other fixed activities. In addition, careful records should indicate the times of the day when you are consistently most productive. A sample time-management diary is shown in Table 1.

Table 1 Sample Time-Management Diary

Monday		
Behavior	Time Completed	Duration Hours: Minutes
Sleep	7:00	7:30
Dressing	7:25	:25
Breakfast	7:45	:20
Commute	8:20	:35
Coffee	9:00	:40
French	10:00	1:00
Socialize	10:15	:15
Videogame	10:35	:20
Coffee	11:00	:25
Psychology	12:00	1:00
Lunch	12:25	:25
Study Lab	1:00	:35
Psych. Lab	4:00	3:00
Work	5:30	1:30
Commute	6:10	:40
Dinner	6:45	:35
TV	7:30	:45
Study Psychology	10:00	2:30
Socialize	11:30	1:30
Sleep		

Prepare a similar chart for each day of the week. When you finish an activity, note it on the chart and write down the time it was completed. Then determine its duration by subtracting the time the previous activity was finished from the newly entered time.

Plan the Term

Having established and evaluated your baseline, you are ready to devise a more efficient schedule. Buy a calendar that covers the entire school term and has ample space for each day. Using the course outlines provided by your instructors, enter the dates of all class lectures, exams, term paper deadlines, and other important academic obligations. If you have any long-range personal plans (concerts, weekend trips, etc.), enter the dates on the calendar as well. Keep your calendar up-to-date and refer to it often. I recommend carrying it with you at all times.

Develop a Weekly Calendar

Now that you have a general picture of the school term, develop a weekly schedule that includes all of your activities. Aim for a schedule that you can live with for the entire school term. A sample weekly schedule, which incorporates the following guidelines, is shown in Table 2.

Table 2 Sample Weekly Schedule

Time	Mon.	Tues.	Wed.	Thurs.	Fri.	Sat.
7–8	Dress Eat	Dress Eat	Dress Eat	Dress Eat	Dress Eat	
8–9	Psych.	Study Psych.	Psych.	Study Psych.	Psych.	Dress Eat
9–10	Eng.	Study Eng.	Eng.	Study Eng.	Eng.	Study Eng.
10–11	Study French	Free	Study French	Open Study	French	Study Stats.
11–12	French	Study. Psych. Lab.	French	Open Study	French	Study Stats.
12–1	Lunch	Lunch	Lunch	Lunch	Lunch	Lunch
1–2	Stats.	Psych. Lab.	Stats.	Study or Free	Stats.	Free
2–3	Bio.	Psych. Lab.	Bio.	Free	Bio.	Free
3–4	Free	Psych.	Free	Free	Free	Free
4–5	Job	Job	Job	Job	Job	Free
5–6	Job	Job	Job	Job	Job	Free
6–7	Dinner	Dinner	Dinner	Dinner	Dinner	Dinner
7–8	Study Bio.	Study Bio.	Study Bio.	Study Bio.	Free	Free
8–9	Study Eng.	Study Stats.	Study Psych.	Open Study	Open Study	Free
9–10	Study	Study	Study	Open	Free	Free

This is a sample schedule for a student with a 16-credit load and a 10-hour-per-week part-time job. Using this chart as an illustration, make up a weekly schedule, following the guidelines outlined here.

1. Enter your class times, work hours, and any other fixed obligations first. *Be thorough.* Using information from your time-management diary, allow plenty of time for such things as commuting, meals, laundry, and the like.

2. Set up a study schedule for each course. The study habits survey and your time-management diary will direct you. The following guidelines should also be useful.

(a) Establish regular study times for each course. The 4 hours needed to study one subject, for example, are most profitable when divided into shorter periods spaced over several days. If you cram your studying into one 4-hour block, what you attempt to learn in the third or fourth hour will interfere with what you studied in the first 2 hours. Newly acquired knowledge is like wet cement: it needs some time to "harden" to become memory.

(b) Alternate subjects. The type of interference just mentioned is greatest between similar topics. Set up a schedule in which you spend time on several *different* courses during each study session. Besides reducing the potential for interference, alternating subjects will help to prevent mental fatigue with one topic.

(c) Set weekly goals to determine the amount of study time you need in order to do well in each course. This will depend on, among other things, the difficulty of your courses and the effectiveness of your methods. Many professors recommend studying at least 2–3 hours for each hour in class. If your time diary indicates that you presently study less time than that, do not plan to jump immediately to a much higher level. Increase study time from your baseline by setting weekly goals [see (4)] that will gradually bring you up to the desired level. As an initial schedule, for example, you might set aside an amount of study time for each course that matches class time.

(d) Schedule for maximum effectiveness. Tailor your schedule to meet the demands of each course. For the course that emphasizes lecture notes, schedule time for a daily review soon after the class. This will give you a chance to revise your notes and clean up any hard-to-decipher shorthand while the material is still fresh in your mind. If you are evaluated for class participation (for example, in a language course), allow time for a review just *before* the class meets. Schedule study time for your most difficult (or least motivating) courses during times when you are the most alert and distractions are fewest.

(e) Schedule open study time. Emergencies, additional obligations, and the like could throw off your schedule. And you may simply need some extra time periodically for a project or for review in one of your courses. Schedule several hours each week for such purposes.

3. After you have budgeted time for studying, fill in slots for recreation, hobbies, relaxation, household errands, and the like.

4. Set specific goals. Before each study session, make a list of specific goals. The simple note "7–8 pm: study psychology" is too broad to ensure the most effective use of your time. Formulate your daily goals according to what you know you must accomplish during the term. If you have course outlines with advance assignments, set systematic daily goals that will allow you, for example, to cover fifteen chapters before the exam. And be realistic: Can you actually expect to cover a 78-page chapter in one session? Divide large tasks into smaller units; stop at the most logical resting points. When you complete a specific goal, take a 5- or 10-minute break before tackling the next goal.

5. Evaluate how successful or unsuccessful your studying has been on a daily or weekly basis. Did you reach most of your goals? If so, reward your-self immediately. You might even make a list of 5 to 10 rewards to choose from. If you have trouble studying regularly, you may be able to motivate yourself by making such rewards contingent on completing specific goals.

6. Finally, until you have lived with your schedule for several weeks, don't hesitate to revise it. You may need to allow more time for chemistry, for example, and less for some other course. If you are trying to study regularly for the first time and are feeling burned out, you probably have set your initial goals too high. Don't let failure cause you to despair and abandon the program altogether. Accept your limitations and revise your schedule so that you are studying only 15 to 20 minutes more each evening than you are used to. The point is to *identify a regular schedule with which you can achieve some success.* Time management, like any skill, must be practiced to become effective.

TECHNIQUES FOR EFFECTIVE STUDY

Knowing how to put study time to best use is, of course, as important as finding a place for it in your schedule. Here are some suggestions that should enable you to increase your reading comprehension and improve your notetaking. A few study tips are included as well.

Using SQ3R to Increase Reading Comprehension

How do you study from a textbook? If you are like many students, you simply read and reread in a *passive* manner. Studies have shown, however, that most students who simply read a textbook cannot remember more than half the material 10 minutes after they have finished. Often, what is retained is the unessential material rather than the important points upon which exam questions will be based.

This Study Guide is designed to facilitate, and allow you to assess, your comprehension of the important facts and concepts in *Psychology* by David Myers. It employs a program known as SQ3R (*Survey, Question, Read, Recite,* and *Review*).

Once you have learned this program, you can improve your comprehension of any textbook. Research has shown that students using SQ3R achieve significantly greater comprehension of textbooks than students reading in the more traditional passive manner.

Survey Before reading a chapter, determine whether the textbook or the study guide has an outline or a list of objectives. Read this material and the summary at the end of the chapter. Next, read the textbook chapter fairly quickly, paying special attention to the major headings and subheadings. This survey will give you an idea of the chapter's contents and organization. You will then be able to divide the chapter into logical sections in order to formulate specific goals for a more careful reading of the chapter.

In this Study Guide, the *Chapter Overview* summarizes the major topics of the textbook chapter. This section also provides a few suggestions for approaching topics you may find difficult.

Question You will retain material longer when you have a use for it. If you look up a word's definition in order to solve a crossword puzzle, for example, you will remember it longer than if you merely fill in the letters as a result of putting other words in. Surveying the chapter will allow you to generate important questions for which the chapter will provide answers. These questions correspond to "mental files" into which knowledge will be sorted for easy access.

As you survey, jot down several questions for each chapter section. One simple technique is to generate questions by rephrasing a section heading. For example, the "Imprinting" head could be turned into "What is imprinting?" Good questions will allow you to focus on the important points in the text. Examples of good questions are those that begin as follows: "List two examples of." "What is the function of?" "What is the significance of?" Such questions give a purpose to your reading. Alternatively, you may formulate questions based on the chapter outline.

The *Guided Study* section of this Study Guide provides the types of questions you might formulate while surveying each chapter. This section is actually an extremely detailed set of objectives covering the points made in the text.

Read When you have established "files" for each section of the chapter, review your first question, begin reading, and continue until you have discovered its answer. If you come to material that seems to an-

swer an important question you don't have a file for, stop and write down the question.

Using this Study Guide, read the chapter one section at a time. First, preview the section by skimming it, noting headings and boldface terms. Next, study the appropriate section objectives in the *Guided Study*. Then, as you read the chapter section, search for the answer to each objective.

Be sure to read and look at everything. Don't skip photo or art captions, graphs, or marginal notes. In some cases, what may seem vague in the text will be made clear by a simple graph. Keep in mind that it is not uncommon for test questions to be drawn from this type of supplementary material.

Recite When you have found the answer to a question, close your eyes and mentally recite the question and its answer. Then *write* the answer next to the question. It is important that you recite an answer in your own words rather than the author's. Don't rely on your short-term memory to repeat the author's words verbatim.

In responding to the objectives, pay close attention to what is called for. If you are asked to identify or list, do just that. If asked to compare, contrast, or do both, you should focus on the similarities (compare) and differences (contrast) between the concepts or theories. Answering the objectives carefully not only will help you to focus your attention on the important concepts of the text, but will also provide excellent practice for essay exams.

Recitation is an extremely effective study technique, recommended by many learning experts. In addition to increasing reading comprehension, it is useful for review. Trying to explain something in your own words clarifies your knowledge, often by revealing aspects of your answer that are vague or incomplete. If you repeatedly rely upon "I know" in recitation, you really *may not know.*

Recitation has the additional advantage of simulating an exam, especially an essay exam; the same skills are required in both cases. Too often, students study without ever putting the book and notes aside, which makes it easy for them to develop false confidence in their knowledge. When the material is in front of you, you may be able to *recognize* an answer, but will you be able to *recall* it later, when you take an exam that does not provide these retrieval cues?

After you have recited and written your answer, continue with your next question. Read, recite, and so on.

Review When you have answered the last question on the material you have designated as a study goal, go back and review. Read over each question and your written answer to it. Your review might also include a brief written summary that integrates all of your questions and answers. This review need not take longer than a few minutes, but it is important. It will help you retain the material longer and will greatly facilitate a final review before the exam.

In this Study Guide, the *Chapter Review* section contains fill-in questions, which are to be completed after you have finished reading the text and written answers to the objectives. The correct answers appear in the margin next to the questions. Generally, your answer should exactly match that in the margin (as in the case of important terms, theories, or people). In some cases, the answer is not a term or name, so a word close in meaning will suffice. Using your hand, or a strip of paper, cover the correct answers and complete each sentence. Verify each answer by uncovering the correct one. You should go through the review several times before taking an exam, so it is a good idea to mentally fill in the answers until you are ready for a final pretest review. Textbook page references are provided with each section title, in case you need to review any of the material.

Also provided to facilitate your review are two *Progress Tests* that include multiple-choice questions and, where appropriate, matching or true–false questions. These tests are *not* to be taken until you have read the chapter, written answers to the objectives, and completed the Chapter Review. Correct answers, along with the relevant text page numbers, are provided at the end of the chapter. If you miss a question, review the text pages to understand why. The progress tests do not test every aspect of a concept, so you should treat an incorrect answer as an indication that you need to review the concept.

Five *Sample Essay Questions* are included after Progress Test 2. In some cases, these questions closely reflect a chapter objective. In others, the question may ask you to integrate information in an unusual way, or to apply your knowledge to a novel situation. Responding to these questions is an effective study method, especially if you are likely to be tested with essay questions.

In this Study Guide, two additional sections are provided to enrich your understanding of the textbook material.

Applying Psychology

Focus on Psychology This section expands upon the text coverage. Each chapter contains two such sections of the Study Guide, the ''Focus'' sections will text material, provocative issues for you to think about, or relevant research articles. In addition to serving as refreshing study breaks from the other sections of the Study Guide, the ''Focus'' sections will enrich your understanding of the textbook's material by applying it to new information. Integrating the textbook material with this new information is an excellent way for you to learn by actively participating, rather than by merely repeating information from the text.

Projects The chapter concludes by describing a demonstration or experiment relevant to the text material. In some cases, the projects will be replications of famous psychology experiments; in others, they are stimulating projects for learning more about yourself. Your instructor may choose to assign these projects, or you may find them rewarding to conduct on your own. In some cases, you will be asked simply to fill out a questionnaire; in others, you will need to prepare materials, obtain subjects, and so on. This study aid is also based on the principle that people learn more by actively participating than by listening, or repeating information. In addition, carrying out these projects will give you first-hand experience with many of the research methods used by psychologists.

One final suggestion: Incorporate SQ3R into your time-management calendar. Set specific goals for completing SQ3R with each assigned chapter. Keep a record of chapters completed and reward yourself for being so conscientious. Initially, it takes more time and effort to ''read'' using SQ3R, but with practice, the steps will become automatic. More important, you will comprehend significantly more material and retain knowledge longer than passive readers do.

Taking Lecture Notes

Are your class notes as useful as they might be? One way to determine their worth is to compare them with those taken by other good students. Are yours as thorough? Do they provide you with a comprehensible outline of each lecture? If not, then the following suggestions might increase the effectiveness of your notetaking.

1. Keep a separate notebook for each course. Use $8\frac{1}{2} \times 11$-inch pages. Consider using a ring binder that would allow you to revise and insert notes while still preserving lecture order.

2. Take notes in the format of a lecture outline. Use roman numerals for major points, letters for supporting arguments, and so on. Some instructors will make this easy by delivering organized lectures and, in some cases, by outlining their lectures on the board. If a lecture is disorganized, you will probably want to revise your notes soon after the class.

3. As you take notes in class, leave a wide margin on one side of each page. After the lecture, expand or clarify any shorthand notes while the material is fresh in your mind. Use this time to write important questions in the margin next to notes that answer them. This will facilitate later review and will allow you to anticipate similar exam questions.

EVALUATE YOUR EXAM PERFORMANCE

How often have you received an exam grade that did not do justice to the effort you spent preparing for the exam? This is a common experience that can leave students feeling bewildered and abused. "What do I have to do to get an A?" "The test was unfair!" "I studied the wrong material!!"

The chances of this happening are greatly reduced if you have an effective time-management schedule and use the study techniques described here. But it can happen, even to the best-prepared student. It is most likely to occur on your first exam with a new professor.

Remember that there are two main reasons for studying. The first is to learn for your own general academic development. Many people believe that such knowledge is all that really matters. Of course, it is possible, though unlikely, to be an expert on a topic without achieving commensurate grades, just as one can, occasionally, earn an excellent grade without truly mastering the course material. During a job interview or in the workplace, however, your A in Fortran won't mean much if you can't actually program a computer.

In order to keep career options open after you graduate, you must both know the material *and* maintain competitive grades. In the short run, this means performing well on exams, which is the second main objective in studying.

Probably the single best piece of advice to keep in mind when studying for exams is to *try to predict exam questions.* This means ignoring the trivia and focusing on the important questions and their answers (with your instructor's emphasis in mind).

A second point is obvious. How well you do on exams is determined by your mastery of *both* lecture and textbook material. Many students (partly because of poor time management) concentrate too much on one at the expense of the other.

To evaluate how well you are learning lecture and textbook material, analyze the questions you missed on the first exam. Many instructors review exams during class, but if yours does not, you can easily do it yourself. Divide the questions into two categories: those drawn primarily from lectures and those drawn primarily from the textbook. Determine the percentage of questions you missed in each category. If your errors are evenly distributed and you are satisfied with your grade, you have no problem. If you are weaker in one area, you will need to set future goals for increasing and/or improving your study of that area.

Similarly, note the percentage of test questions drawn from each category. Although most exams cover *both* lecture notes and the textbook, the relative emphasis of each may vary from instructor to instructor. While your instructors may not be entirely consistent in making up future exams, you may be able to tailor your studying for each course by placing *additional* emphasis on the appropriate area.

Exam evaluation will also point out the types of questions your instructor prefers. Does the exam consist primarily of multiple-choice, true–false, or essay questions? You may also discover that an instructor is fond of wording questions in certain ways. For example, an instructor may rely heavily on questions that require you to draw an analogy between a theory or concept and a real-world example. Evaluate both your instructor's style and how well you do with each format. Use this information to guide your future exam preparation.

Important aids, not only in studying for exams but also in determining how well prepared you are, are the Progress Tests provided in this Study Guide. If these tests don't include all of the types of questions your instructor typically writes, make up your own practice exam questions. Spend extra time testing yourself with question formats that are most difficult for you. There is no better way to evaluate your preparation for an upcoming exam than by testing yourself under the conditions most likely to be in effect during the actual test.

A FEW PRACTICAL TIPS

Even the best intentions for studying sometimes fail. Some of these failures occur because students attempt to work under conditions that are simply not conducive to concentrated study. To help ensure the success of your self-management program, here are a few suggestions that should assist you in reducing the possibility of procrastination or distraction.

1. If you have set up a schedule for studying, make your roommate, family, and friends aware of this commitment, and ask them to honor your quiet study time. Close your door and post a "Do Not Disturb" sign.

2. Set up a place to study that minimizes potential distractions. Use a desk or table, not your bed or an extremely comfortable chair. Keep your desk and the walls around it free from clutter.

3. Do nothing but study in this place. It should become associated with studying so that it "triggers" this activity, just as a mouth-watering aroma elicits an appetite.

4. Never study with the television on or with other distracting noises present. If you must have music in the background (in order to mask dorm noises, for example), play soft instrumental music. Don't pick vocal selections; your mind will be drawn to the lyrics.

5. Study by yourself. Other students can be distracting or can break the pace at which *your* learning is most efficient. In addition, there is always the possibility that group studying will become nothing more than a social gathering. Reserve that for its own place in your time schedule.

6. Avoid studying in too many places. If you need a place besides your room, find one that meets as many of these requirements as possible. Find a place, for example, in the library stacks.

If you continue to have difficulty concentrating for very long, try the following suggestions.

7. Study your most difficult or most challenging subjects first, when you are most alert.

8. Start with relatively short periods of concentrated study. If your attention starts to wander, get up immediately and take a break. It is better to study effectively for 15 minutes and then take a break than to fritter away 45 minutes out of an hour's study time. Gradually increase the length of your study periods, using your attention span as an indicator of successful pacing.

SOME CLOSING THOUGHTS

I hope that these suggestions not only help make you more successful academically but also enhance the quality of your college life in general. Not having the necessary skills makes any job a lot harder and more unpleasant than it has to be. Let me repeat my warning not to attempt to make too drastic a change in your lifestyle immediately. Start by establishing a few realistic goals, then gradually shape your performance to the desired level. Good habits require time and discipline to develop. Once established, they can last a lifetime.

Contents

PART ONE   FOUNDATIONS OF PSYCHOLOGY **1**

         Chapter 1   **Introducing Psychology** **3**
         Chapter 2   **Biological Roots of Behavior** **17**

PART TWO   DEVELOPMENT OVER THE LIFE-SPAN **35**

         Chapter 3   **Infancy and Childhood** **37**
         Chapter 4   **Adolescence and Adulthood** **49**
         Chapter 5   **Gender** **61**

PART THREE   EXPERIENCING THE WORLD **71**

         Chapter 6   **Sensation** **73**
         Chapter 7   **Perception** **86**
         Chapter 8   **States of Consciousness** **98**

PART FOUR   LEARNING AND THINKING **113**

         Chapter 9   **Learning** **115**
         Chapter 10   **Memory** **128**
         Chapter 11   **Thinking and Language** **141**
         Chapter 12   **Intelligence** **152**

PART FIVE   MOTIVATION AND EMOTION **165**

         Chapter 13   **Motivation** **167**
         Chapter 14   **Emotion** **182**

PART SIX   PERSONALITY, DISORDER, AND WELL-BEING **195**

         Chapter 15   **Personality** **197**
         Chapter 16   **Psychological Disorders** **214**
         Chapter 17   **Therapy** **231**
         Chapter 18   **Health** **246**

PART SEVEN   SOCIAL BEHAVIOR **263**

         Chapter 19   **Social Influence** **265**
         Chapter 20   **Social Relations** **279**

APPENDIX A   **Statistical Reasoning in Everyday Life** **294**

PART ONE

FOUNDATIONS
OF PSYCHOLOGY

CHAPTER 1

Introducing Psychology

CHAPTER OVERVIEW

Psychology's historical development and current activities lead us to define the field as the science of behavior and mental processes. Chapter 1 discusses the development of psychology and the range of behaviors and mental processes being investigated by psychologists in each of the various specialty areas. In addition, it explains how psychologists employ the methods of observation, correlation, and experimentation in order to describe, predict, and understand behavior. Chapter 1 concludes with a discussion of several commonly discussed issues concerning psychology, including the ethics of laboratory experiments, the relevance of animal research, and whether psychological theories are dangerous or simply based on common sense.

Chapter 1 should not be too difficult for you. There are not very many difficult terms or theories to remember. The chapter does discuss a number of concepts and issues that will reappear in later chapters. Pay particular attention to the section "Psychology's Methods and Aims." Make sure you understand the experimental method, especially the difference between independent and dependent variables, and the importance of control conditions.

GUIDED STUDY

The text chapter should be studied one section at a time. Before you read, preview each section by skimming it, noting headings and boldface items. Then read the appropriate section objectives from the following outline. Keep these objectives in mind, and as you read the chapter section, search for the information that will complete each one. You may wish to write out answers for each objective as soon as you finish reading that section of the chapter.

What Is Psychology? (pp. 4–8)

1. Briefly describe the historical roots of psychology and identify the first psychologists.

2. Explain how psychology has been defined historically and give its current definition.

3. Discuss the importance of internal and external factors in behavior and describe how psychology's emphasis on each factor has varied historically.

4. Identify several aspects of behavior that each of the following study.

a. physiological psychologists

b. developmental psychologists

c. experimental psychologists

d. personality and social psychologists

e. clinical psychologists

5. Explain and contrast the following perspectives on behavior and mental processes.

a. biological perspective

b. psychoanalytic perspective

c. behavioral perspective

d. humanistic perspective

e. cognitive perspective

Scientific Attitudes and Theories (pp. 9–10)

6. Discuss the importance of skepticism and humility in scientific inquiry.

7. Explain the differences between theories and hypotheses.

Psychology's Methods and Aims (pp. 10–14)

8. Describe the following observation techniques.

a. case study

b. survey method

c. random sample

d. naturalistic observation

9. Explain what it means when there is a correlation between two events and why correlation does not prove causation.

10. Describe the following elements of an experiment.

a. control condition

b. experimental condition

c. independent variable

d. dependent variable

Commonly Asked Questions about Psychology (pp. 15–18)

11. Discuss why psychologists *intend* laboratory experiments to present a simplified and artificial reality.

12. Identify two reasons why psychologists study animals.

13. Describe the "I-knew-it-all-along" phenomenon.

14. Discuss whether psychology is potentially dangerous.

CHAPTER REVIEW

When you have finished reading the chapter, complete the sentences that follow. Using your hand or a strip of paper, cover the correct answers in the margin and fill in each blank. Verify your answer by uncovering the correct one. As you proceed, evaluate your performance for each chapter section. *Do not continue with the next section until you understand why each margin term is the correct answer.* If you need to, review or re-read the appropriate chapter section in the text before continuing.

1. Psychology is the science that seeks to answer questions about how people _____, _____, and _____.

think; feel; act

What Is Psychology? (pp. 4–8)

2. The historical roots of psychology include the fields of _____ and _____.

philosophy; physiology

3. The first psychology laboratory was founded in the year _____ by Wilhelm _____.

1879; Wundt

4. Some early psychologists include Pavlov, who pioneered the study of _____; the personality theorist _____; Piaget, who studied _____; and _____, the author of one of the first psychology texts.

learning
Freud; children;
James

5. Although psychology is now growing rapidly in other countries, in the last few decades it has flourished more in the _____ _____ than in any other country.

United States

6. In its earliest years, psychology was first defined as the science of _____ life.

mental

7. This definition focused on sensations, feelings, and thoughts—experiences in consciousness that are _____ (internal/external).

internal

8. From about 1920 until 1960, psychology in America was redefined as the science of _____.

behavior

9. This definition placed the focus of psychology on _____ (internal/external) behaviors that could be observed.

external

10. The author of the text defines psychology as the science of _____ and _____ processes.

behavior; mental

11. The Greek philosopher who has been called the first psychologist is _____.

Aristotle

12. The Greek philosopher who assumed that character and intelligence are inherited is _____.

Plato

13. The Greek philosopher who argued that external factors are more important in human behavior is _____.

Aristotle

14. In the seventeenth century, external factors were emphasized by _____, while internal factors were emphasized by _____.

Locke
Leibniz

15. Among professional psychologists, approximately _____ work in the mental health fields.

one-half

16. Most of the remaining psychologists are involved in conducting basic or applied _____.

research

17. Psychologists who explore the links between biology and behavior are known as _____ psychologists.

physiological

18. Developmental psychologists study the _____, _____, and _____ changes that occur throughout the life cycle.

physical
mental; social

19. Research psychologists who study sensation, learning, motivation, and similar areas are called _____ psychologists.

experimental

20. Psychologists who study how individuals are influenced by enduring, inner factors are called _____ psychologists.

personality

21. Psychologists who study how people influence and are influenced by other people are called _____ psychologists.

social

22. Psychologists who assess and treat people with psychological difficulties are called _____ psychologists.

clinical

23. Most clinical psychologists have attended graduate school and earned the _____ degree.

Ph.D.

24. Mental health professionals who have earned an M.D. are called _____.

psychiatrists

25. Psychologists who study hereditary influences on behavior, how messages are transmitted within the brain, and similar phenomena are following the _____ perspective on behavior.

biological

26. The _____ perspective assumes that behavior is the product of unconscious drives. This perspective builds on the ideas of _____.

psychoanalytic

Freud

27. Psychologists who study the mechanisms by which observable responses are acquired in particular environments are following the _____ perspective.

behavioral

28. Psychologists who emphasize our capacities to choose our own life patterns and to grow to higher levels of maturity are following the _____ perspective. This subfield of psychology arose as a reaction against the _____ perspective.

humanistic

psychoanalytic

29. The _____ perspective explores how the mind processes and retrieves information.

cognitive

Scientific Attitudes and Theories (pp. 9–10)

30. Scientific inquiry involves a set of _____ and an effort to construct _____ that predict facts.

attitudes

theories

31. Testable predictions that allow a scientist to evaluate a theory are called _____.

hypotheses

Psychology's Methods and Aims (pp. 10–14)

32. Three basic methods in psychology are _____, _____, and _____.

observation

correlation; experimentation

33. These methods help achieve three aims of psychology: _____, _____, and _____.

description; prediction; understanding

34. The method in which one individual is studied in depth in order to reveal general principles of behavior is the _____ _____ method.

case study

35. One personality psychologist who regularly used this method was _____.

Freud

36. The research method in which a group of people is questioned about their behavior is the _____ method.

survey

37. One researcher who used this method to study sexual behavior was _____.

Kinsey

38. In order to ensure that a sample of respondents is representative of the population at large, a _____ sample of people is defined.

random

39. In such a sample, every person _____ (does/does not) have an equal chance of being included.

does

40. The method in which people are directly observed in their natural environments is called _____ _____.

naturalistic observation

41. The case study, survey, and naturalistic observation methods do not explain behavior; they simply _____ it.

describe

42. When changes in one event are accompanied by changes in another, there is a _____ between them.

correlation

43. A common error is to assume that a correlation between two events implies that one _____ the other.

causes

44. To study cause-and-effect relationships, psychologists conduct _____.

experiments

45. In an experiment, two conditions are generally present: the _____ condition and the _____ condition.

experimental; control

46. In the experiment that tested the theory of animal magnetism, the tree that was magnetized constituted the _____ condition.

experimental

47. Testing the effects of a tree that had not been magnetized constituted the _____ condition.

control

48. The factor being studied and manipulated in an experiment is called the _____ _____.

independent variable

49. The factor being measured, which may vary during the experiment, is called the _____ _____.

dependent variable

50. One way to minimize any preexisting differences between people who are assigned to different groups in an experiment is to _____ _____ them to the various conditions.

randomly assign

Commonly Asked Questions about Psychology (pp. 15–18)

51. Laboratory experiments in psychology are sometimes criticized as not reflecting reality by being _____.

artificial

52. In laboratory experiments, psychologists are concerned not with the actual behaviors that occur, but with the underlying _____.

principles

53. Repeating an experiment to check on the reliability of the results is called _____.

replication

54. The tendency to perceive an outcome as more obvious and predictable after it has occurred is called the _____-_____-_____-_____ phenomenon.

I-knew-it-all-along

FOCUS ON PSYCHOLOGY:
A CAREER IN PSYCHOLOGY

Preparing for a career in psychology usually requires training that leads to a graduate degree. To earn the degree of Doctor of Philosophy (Ph.D.), students complete a four- to six-year program, at the end of which they must design and conduct an original research report. Although the Ph.D. is required for many jobs in psychology, the degree of Master of Arts (M.A.) is sufficient for others, such as teaching at some community colleges or becoming a school psychologist. The M.A. degree program typically requires one or two years of training beyond the undergraduate curriculum.

The figure on page 9 indicates the percentage of psychologists who work in various settings and fields of specialization (Boneau and Cuca, 1974). Traditionally, most Ph.D.s accepted teaching or research positions at universities and four-year colleges. Since the 1970s, however, the rate at which new Ph.D.s have been conferred has increased faster in psychology than in any other field. At the same time, college and university enrollments have declined, and this decline is expected to continue through the 1980s (Syverson, 1982). As this decline continues, psychologists are increasingly employed in nonacademic settings such as government agencies.

Training in psychology can, of course, provide benefits other than employment. Many of the findings of psychologists have obvious practical applications, such as improving how you study, helping you to understand the ways that groups influence a person's behavior, or helping you to eliminate undesirable habits. As a student of psychology, you may also develop the objective and skeptical eye of the behavioral scientist. This will help you evaluate information reported in popular magazines, newspapers, and on

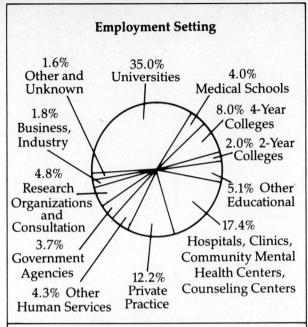

Employment Setting

- 1.6% Other and Unknown
- 35.0% Universities
- 4.0% Medical Schools
- 1.8% Business, Industry
- 8.0% 4-Year Colleges
- 2.0% 2-Year Colleges
- 4.8% Research Organizations and Consultation
- 5.1% Other Educational
- 3.7% Government Agencies
- 17.4% Hospitals, Clinics, Community Mental Health Centers, Counseling Centers
- 4.3% Other Human Services
- 12.2% Private Practice

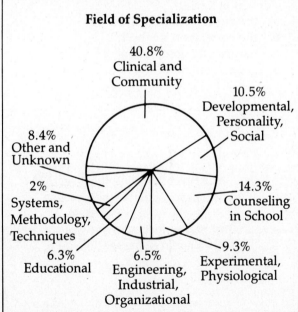

Field of Specialization

- 40.8% Clinical and Community
- 10.5% Developmental, Personality, Social
- 8.4% Other and Unknown
- 2% Systems, Methodology, Techniques
- 14.3% Counseling in School
- 6.3% Educational
- 6.5% Engineering, Industrial, Organizational
- 9.3% Experimental, Physiological

Sources: Boneau, C. A., and Cuca, J. M. (1974). An overview of psychology's human resources: Characteristics and salaries from the 1972 APA survey. *American Psychologist, 29*, 821–840. Copyright © American Psychological Association. Reprinted with permission of the publisher and author.

Syverson, P. D. (1982). *Summary report 1981: Doctoral recipients from United States universities.* Washington, D.C.: National Academy Press.

television. Developing this perspective will make you a more objective and better-informed citizen and consumer.

PROGRESS TEST 1

Circle your answers to the following questions and check them with the answer key at the end of this chapter. Be sure to consult the appropriate pages of the text to understand the correct answer for any missed question.

Multiple-Choice Questions

1. Psychology is defined as the:
   a. study of mental phenomena.
   b. study of conscious and unconscious activity.
   c. study of behavior.
   d. science of behavior and mental processes.

2. After studying the behavior of a victim of a gunshot wound, a psychologist concludes that the brain region destroyed was important to memory. Which method of observation was used?
   a. case study
   b. survey
   c. correlation
   d. experimentation

3. In an experiment to determine the effects of exercise on motivation, exercise is the:
   a. control condition.
   b. intervening variable.
   c. independent variable.
   d. dependent variable.

4. In order to determine the effects of a new drug on memory, one group of subjects is given a pill that contains the drug. A second group is given a sugar pill that does not contain the drug. This second group constitutes the:
   a. random sample.
   b. experimental condition.
   c. control condition.
   d. test group.

5. Integrated sets of principles that help explain and predict facts are called:
   a. hypotheses.
   b. variables.
   c. control conditions.
   d. theories.

6. A psychologist studies the play behavior of third-grade children by watching groups during recess at school. Which method is being used?
a. correlation
b. case study
c. experimentation
d. naturalistic observation

7. One issue in psychology concerns the relative influence of genetic predispositions, biological drives, and other influences on behavior that are:
a. internal.   c. variable.
b. external.   d. unchanging.

8. The seventeenth-century philosopher who believed that the mind is blank at birth is:
a. Plato.   c. Leibniz.
b. Aristotle.   d. Locke.

9. Which psychological perspective emphasizes the interaction of the brain and body in behavior?
a. biological   c. behavioral
b. cognitive   d. psychoanalytic

10. A professor constructs a questionnaire to determine how students at the university feel about nuclear disarmament. Which of the following techniques should be used in order to survey a random sample of the student body?

a. Every student should be sent the questionnaire.
b. Only students majoring in psychology should be asked to complete the questionnaire.
c. Only persons living on campus should be asked to complete the questionnaire.
d. From an alphabetical listing of all students, every tenth person should be asked to complete the questionnaire.

11. Which of the following psychologists would be most likely to study the effects of fraternity membership on an individual member's behavior?
a. clinical psychologist
b. developmental psychologist
c. personality psychologist
d. social psychologist

12. Which of the following methods is the most useful in uncovering cause-and-effect relationships in behavior?
a. the survey method
b. the correlation method
c. naturalistic observation
d. experimentation

Matching Items

Match each subfield and psychological perspective with its defining feature.

_____ **1.** physiological psychology
_____ **2.** developmental psychology
_____ **3.** experimental psychology
_____ **4.** personality psychology
_____ **5.** social psychology
_____ **6.** clinical psychology

_____ **7.** psychiatry
_____ **8.** psychoanalytic perspective
_____ **9.** behavioral perspective
_____ **10.** humanistic perspective
_____ **11.** cognitive perspective

a. concerned with the study of behavior throughout the life cycle
b. emphasis on a person's capacity to grow to higher levels of fulfillment
c. concerned with research on sensation, learning, motivation, and similar behaviors
d. medical field concerned with psychological disorders

e. assumes that behavior springs from unconscious drives
f. concerned with the mechanisms by which observable responses are acquired
g. concerned with the exploration of the links between biology and behavior

h. concerned with how the mind processes, retains, and retrieves information

i. concerned with how people influence other people

j. concerned with how enduring, inner factors influence behavior

k. concerned with the assessment and treatment of people with psychological difficulties

FOCUS ON PSYCHOLOGY:
SCIENCE AND PSEUDOSCIENCE

As the text indicates, psychology is based on the traditional methods of scientific inquiry, including careful observation and objective experimental testing of hypotheses. Theories and fields of inquiry based on nonscientific premises are called *pseudoscience* ("false science"). Advocates of such theories point out that what is accepted as "scientific" changes over time, and compare themselves to individuals such as Galileo and Pasteur, who were once ridiculed by the scientific community for their beliefs.

Like all fields, the study of human behavior has given rise to a number of pseudoscientific theories. In the nineteenth century, Franz Joseph Gall advanced the theory of *phrenology,* based on the principle that the shape and size of specific parts of the brain indicate specific personality traits. In his theory of the *bicameral mind,* Princeton psychologist Julian Jaynes proposes that, before the second millennium B.C., the right hemisphere of the human brain was the mechanism by which gods directed the behavior of our ancestors. The enduring appeal of psychological pseudoscience is illustrated by the belief of millions in *astrology,* which is based on the premise that celestial events influence human behavior.

Radner and Radner (1982) have found that pseudoscientific theories often have a similar pattern. They start with stories or myths from ancient times, formulate a hypothesis that explains them, and point to the myth as providing evidence for the hypothesis. Or the theory is based on evidence that is great in quantity, but anecdotal or unreliable in nature. Another mark of pseudoscience is the searching out of unexplained mysteries, such as those that led to the theories of UFOs, ESP, Bigfoot, and the Bermuda Triangle. One hallmark of scientific inquiry is that a theory is not supported simply by virtue of its providing *some* explanation of an unexplained phenomenon. Pseudoscientists also attempt to gain support by arguing that the principles on which their theory is based are already accepted by the scientific community. Astrologers, for example, point out that the influence of certain celestial events on the earth (such as the moon's effect on tides) is already established. The *biorhythm* fad is another pseudoscience that has attempted to appear consistent with an established phenomenon. According to this theory, a 33-day intellectual clock, a 28-day emotional clock, and a 23-day physical clock influence a person's behavior. Although *biological* rhythms that have shorter cycles do exist (for example, the sleep and menstrual cycles), there is no evidence for biorhythms.

Why are some pseudoscience theories so appealing? One reason is that the average person has no training in the methods of scientific inquiry, and is not in a position to evaluate "evidence" advanced in support of new theories. A second possible reason is that many people simply prefer to believe that the ultimate responsibility for their own lives is not in their hands, but in other forces such as biorhythms or heavenly bodies.

Even if this is the only psychology course you take in college, after completing it you should be a much more sophisticated skeptic of pseudoscientific fads that disguise themselves as science.

PROGRESS TEST 2

Progress Test 2 should be completed during a final chapter review. Do so after you thoroughly understand the correct answers for the Chapter Review and Progress Test 1.

Multiple-Choice Questions

1. The first psychology laboratory was established by _____ in the year _____.

 a. Leibniz; 1910
 b. Wundt; 1879
 c. Wundt; 1910
 d. Leibniz; 1879

2. If eating saturated fat and the likelihood of cancer are correlated, which of the following is true?

 a. Saturated fat causes cancer.
 b. People who are prone to develop cancer prefer foods containing saturated fat.
 c. A separate factor links the consumption of saturated fat to cancer.
 d. None of the above is necessarily true.

3. In an experiment to determine the effects of attention on memory, memory is the:

 a. control condition.
 b. intervening variable.
 c. independent variable.
 d. dependent variable.

4. The group that receives the treatment of interest in an experiment is the:

 a. test group.
 b. random sample.
 c. experimental condition.
 d. control condition.

5. Which of the following best describes the "I-knew-it-all-along" phenomenon?

 a. Events seem more predictable before they have occurred.
 b. Events seem more predictable after they have occurred.
 c. A person's intuition is usually correct.
 d. A person's intuition is usually not correct.

6. The procedure in which all potential subjects in an experiment have an equal chance of being selected is called:

 a. variable controlling.
 b. random sampling.
 c. representative sampling.
 d. stratification.

7. Two historical roots of psychology are the disciplines of _____ and _____.

 a. philosophy; chemistry
 b. physiology; chemistry
 c. philosophy; physiology
 d. philosophy; physics

8. Which of the following individuals is also a physician?
 a. clinical psychologist
 b. experimental psychologist
 c. psychiatrist
 d. counseling psychologist

9. Why are animals frequently used in psychology experiments?

 a. The processes that underlie behavior in animals and humans are often similar.
 b. Animal behavior is generally simpler to understand.
 c. Animals are worthy of study for their own sake.
 d. For all of the above reasons.

10. The Greek philosopher who believed that intelligence was inherited is:
 a. Aristotle.
 b. Plato.
 c. Locke.
 d. Leibniz.

11. Which psychological perspective is concerned with the ways in which the mind processes and retains information?
 a. neuroscience perspective
 b. psychoanalytic perspective
 c. behavioral perspective
 d. cognitive perspective

12. According to the text:
 a. because laboratory experiments are artificial, any principles discovered cannot be applied to everyday behaviors.
 b. theories of behavior are of no use to psychology.
 c. psychology's theories simply reflect common sense.
 d. psychology is a science.

Matching Items

_____ 1. hypothesis
_____ 2. theory
_____ 3. independent variable
_____ 4. dependent variable
_____ 5. experimental condition
_____ 6. control condition
_____ 7. case study
_____ 8. survey
_____ 9. replication
_____ 10. random assignment
_____ 11. experiment

a. an in-depth observational study of one individual
b. the variable being manipulated in an experiment
c. the variable being measured in an experiment
d. the "treatment-absent" condition in an experiment
e. a testable prediction
f. repeating an experiment with different subjects
g. the process in which subjects are selected by chance for different groups
h. an integrated set of principles that organizes observations
i. the research method in which the effects of one or more variables on behavior are tested
j. the "treatment-present" condition in an experiment
k. the research method in which a representative sample of individuals is questioned

SAMPLE ESSAY QUESTIONS

1. Discuss the development of psychology and how the definition of psychology has changed historically.

2. Describe the methods of observation and correlation; identify the differences between a cause-effect relationship and a correlation.

3. Describe a typical experiment and explain the concept of control in experimentation.

4. Explain the differences among psychologists, psychiatrists, and clinical psychologists.

5. Discuss the value of theory in science and whether psychology's theories merely reflect common sense.

PROJECT:
EVALUATING RESEARCH CLAIMS IN ADVERTISING

Many television networks and advertising agencies employ psychologists to evaluate the validity of product performance claims based on marketing research. Here are examples of claims you may be familiar with: "Kids using our toothpaste had 90 percent fewer cavities"; "Beer drinkers prefer our brand two to one." Analyze an actual television or magazine advertisement that claims that the product yields superior performance, or is preferred to that of another company. Evaluate the research in terms of the issues raised in the text. (1) How were the subjects selected for the experiment? Do they constitute a representative, unbiased sample of the population to which the results are being generalized? (2) Are appropriate comparison or control groups present? (3) Are the conditions of testing applicable to real-world conditions? (4) Are there any potential sources of confounding variables that could account for the results, irrespective of the treatment of interest? (5) Are the results significantly greater than would be expected if chance were the only factor operating?

Another way of testing the claims of such advertising is to conduct some tests of your own. Find a friend who claims that he or she can tell the difference between certain soft drinks or brands of beer and states a strong preference for one of them. Before conducting the experiment, make the following preparations. Collect a bottle of the brand preferred and of three other brands. Pour about four ounces of each into separate containers that are identical. Label the four A, B, C, and D, and refer to them as such throughout the experiment. When you are ready to begin, blind-fold your subject (to prevent the person from identifying the drink by its color) and allow the subject to sample each of the four brands one at a time, indicating which is his or her favorite brand. Allow the subject to sample as much of each brand as desired before choosing. You should also provide the subject with water to clear his or her palate between samples. Test your subject two or three times, presenting the different brands being sampled in a different order each time (ABCD, CBAD, etc.).

Questions to Consider

1. Was your subject able to tell the difference between the various brands?

2. Was your subject's preference consistent?

3. How could you change the conditions of the experiment in order to influence the subject's choice? You may wish to test your hypothesis by changing the conditions and repeating the experiment with a new subject.

WHERE TO LOOK FOR MORE INFORMATION

Nessel, J. (1982, May). Understanding psychological man: A state of the science report. *Psychology Today.*

Eleven psychologists discuss the most significant work in psychology during the past decade.

James, W. (1983). *The principles of psychology.* Cambridge, Mass.: Harvard University Press (first published in 1890).

A paperback reprint of a classic—one of the first psychology textbooks.

Radner, D., and Radner, M. (1982). *Science and unreason.* Belmont, Calif.: Wadsworth.

A fun book in which the authors refute a number of popular pseudoscientific myths.

Robinson, D. N. (1981). *An intellectual history of psychology.* New York: Macmillan.

A very readable discussion of the historical roots of psychology.

To get a first-hand idea of what psychology is all about, browse through the psychology section of your library. Look at research-oriented journals such as *Psychological Bulletin, The American Psychologist,* and *The Journal of Personality and Social Psychology.* Ask your librarian to explain the use of *Psychological Abstracts.* These volumes index and summarize articles published in major journals. A number of popular magazines also publish articles of interest to psychologists. These include *Psychology Today, Science Digest,* and *Omni.*

ANSWERS

PROGRESS TEST 1

Multiple-Choice Questions

1. d (p. 5)
2. a (p. 10)
3. c (p. 13)
4. c (p. 13)

5. d (p. 9)
6. d (p. 11)
7. a (p. 6)
8. d (p. 6)

9. a (p. 7)
10. d (p. 11)
11. d (p. 7)
12. d (p. 12)

Matching Items

1. g (p. 6)
2. a (p. 6)
3. c (p. 7)
4. j (p. 7)

5. i (p. 7)
6. k (p. 7)
7. d (p. 7)
8. e (p. 7)

9. f (p. 7)
10. b (p. 7)
11. h (p. 8)

PROGRESS TEST 2

Multiple-Choice Questions

1. b (p. 4)
2. d (p. 12)
3. d (p. 13)
4. c (p. 13)

5. b (p. 17)
6. b (p. 11)
7. c (p. 4)
8. c (p. 7)

9. d (p. 16)
10. b (p. 6)
11. d (p. 8)
12. d (p. 5)

Matching Items

1. e (pp. 9–10)
2. h (p. 9)
3. b (p. 13)
4. c (p. 13)

5. j (p. 13)
6. d (p. 13)
7. a (p. 10)
8. k (p. 10)

9. f (p. 15)
10. g (p. 13)
11. i (p. 12)

CHAPTER 2

Biological Roots of Behavior

CHAPTER OVERVIEW

The biological roots of behavior include natural selection, which acts on genetic diversity to favor organisms best equipped to survive and reproduce. Genes contain the architectural plans that direct development. Under the direction of the brain, the nervous and endocrine systems coordinate a variety of voluntary and involuntary behaviors.

The brain consists of three regions: the brainstem, the limbic system, and the cerebral cortex. Knowledge of the workings of the brain has increased with advances in neuropsychological methods. Studies of split-brain patients have also given researchers a great deal of information about the specialized functions of the brain's right and left hemispheres.

Many students find the technical material in this chapter difficult to master. Not only are there many terms for you to remember, but you must also know the organization and function of the various divisions of the nervous system. Learning this material will require a great deal of rehearsal. Working the chapter review several times, drawing and labeling brain diagrams, and mental recitation of terms are all useful techniques for rehearsing this type of material.

GUIDED STUDY

The text chapter should be studied one section at a time. Before you read, preview each section by skimming it, noting headings and boldface items. Then read the appropriate section objectives from the following outline. Keep these objectives in mind and, as you read the chapter section, search for the information that will complete each one. You may wish to write out answers for each objective as soon as you finish reading that section of the chapter.

Natural Selection (pp. 24–27)

1. Explain how evolution acts on genetic diversity in the evolution of a trait.

2. Explain the central idea of the theory of sociobiology.

3. Discuss why sociobiology is controversial and identify the reasons for criticisms of it.

The Nervous System (pp. 27–32)

4. Outline and label the various divisions of the nervous system.

5. Compare and contrast the general functions of the central and peripheral divisions of the nervous system.

6. State and contrast the general functions of the somatic and autonomic divisions of the nervous system.

7. Identify the functions of the sympathetic and parasympathetic divisions of the nervous system.

8. Describe and compare the functions of sensory neurons, motor neurons, and interneurons.

9. Outline the mechanisms of a simple reflex.

10. Identify the components of a typical neuron and explain the function of each.

11. Describe how information is transmitted across a synapse.

12. Explain the all-or-none response and the concept of threshold in a neuron.

13. State the behavioral significance of the following neurotransmitters.

a. ACh

b. Serotonin

c. Norepinephrine

d. Dopamine

e. Endorphin

The Brain (pp. 32–52)

14. Identify the general functions and evolutionary significance of the brainstem, limbic system, and cerebral cortex.

15. Describe each of the following techniques for studying brain function.

a. Clinical observation

b. Lesioning

c. The electroencephalogram

d. CAT scan

e. PET scan

16. State the functions of the following structures of the brainstem.

a. Medulla

b. Cerebellum

c. Thalamus

d. Reticular activating system

17. State the function of the following limbic structures.

a. Amygdala

b. Hypothalamus

18. Sketch the cerebral cortex and label the four lobes.

19. List the major functions of the lobes of the cerebral cortex.

a. Frontal

b. Occipital

c. Temporal

d. Parietal

20. Describe the effects of electrical stimulation of the somatosensory cortex and the motor cortex.

21. State the functions of association areas of the cortex.

22. Identify the functions of Broca's area, Wernicke's area, and the angular gyrus in using language.

23. Describe the aphasia that results from injury to Broca's area and Wernicke's area.

24. Describe split-brain surgery and how it is used to study hemispheric specialization.

25. Contrast the usual functions of the right and left cerebral hemispheres.

26. Describe several techniques by which left/right hemisphere functions are studied in the normal brain.

27. Explain how, through plasticity and reorganization, the brain may recover from injury.

The Endocrine System (p. 52)

28. Explain the functions of the hormones secreted by the pituitary and adrenal glands of the endocrine system.

Genes and Behavior (pp. 52–55)

29. Distinguish the functions of genes, chromosomes, and DNA in heredity.

30. Explain what is at issue in the nature-nurture question.

31. Discuss the value (and limitations) of selective breeding research.

32. State how identical and fraternal twins differ and why they are useful in studies of heritability.

CHAPTER REVIEW

When you have finished reading the chapter, complete the sentences that follow. Using your hand or a strip of paper, cover the correct answers in the margin, and fill in each blank. Verify your answer by uncovering the correct one. As you proceed, evaluate your performance for each chapter section. *Do not* *continue with the next section until you understand why* *each margin term is the correct answer.* If you need to, review or re-read the appropriate chapter section in the text before continuing.

1. The human species is called _____ _____ .

homo sapiens

2. The theory that linked the brain's functions to various bumps on the skull was _____ .

phrenology

3. This theory was proposed by _____ .

Gall

Natural Selection (pp. 24–27)

4. Charles Darwin proposed the process of _____ _____ to account for the origin of species.

natural selection

5. Most species tend to produce _____ (more/less) offspring than their environment can support.

more

6. Natural selection refers to the tendency of the environment to favor organisms that possess inheritable traits that best allow them to survive and _____ .

reproduce

7. According to the theory of _____ , the fundamental motive for behavior is to pass on genes.

sociobiology

8. According to this theory, females tend to be _____ (more/less) cautious than males in choice of a mate.

more

9. Critics of sociobiology are concerned that the theory may perpetuate stereotypes and double standards in society by providing _____ explanations for differences in behavior.

genetic

10. One problem with sociobiology is that it provides convincing explanations that are made only _____ _____ _____ .

after the fact

11. A second problem is that, while sociobiology implies that universal behavior patterns should be _____ (common/uncommon), there is generally great _____ (similarity/diversity) in behavior.

common

diversity

12. Compared with the behavior of other species, human behavior is determined more by _____ (genes/learning).

learning

13. In general, the more complex an organism's nervous system, the _____ (more/less) its behavior is fixed genetically, and the _____ (more/less) adaptable it is.

less

more

14. The circuitry of the body consists of billions of nerve cells, or
_____.

neurons

15. In different animals these cells _____ (are/are not) very much alike.

are not

16. The brain and spinal cord comprise the _____ nervous system.

central

17. The neurons that link the brain and spinal cord to the rest of the body form the _____ nervous system.

peripheral

18. The division of the peripheral nervous system that directs movements of the skeletal muscles is the _____ division.

somatic

19. These movements are usually under _____ control.

voluntary

20. Involuntary, self-regulating responses are controlled by the _____ nervous system.

autonomic

21. The body is made ready for action by the _____ division of the autonomic nervous system.

sympathetic

22. The division of the autonomic nervous system that produces relaxation is the _____ division.

parasympathetic

23. Information arriving in the central nervous system from the body travels in afferent, or _____, neurons.

sensory

24. The central nervous system sends instructions to the body's muscles by means of efferent, or _____, neurons.

motor

25. A third class of neurons, the _____, intervene between sensory and motor neurons.

interneurons

26. Automatic, inborn responses to stimuli are called
_____.

reflexes

27. The paths traveled by these responses are composed of _____ (one/many) sensory and motor neuron(s).

one

28. The extensions of a neuron that receive impulses from other neurons are the _____.

dendrites

29. The extensions of a neuron that transmit information to other neurons are the _____.

axons

30. Axons are generally much _____ (longer/shorter) than dendrites.

longer

31. Identify the major parts of the neuron diagrammed below:

a. _____ b. _____

c. _____

    (a)

    (b)   (c)

dendrites; cell body; axon

32. Compared to electricity, neural impulses travel at speeds that are much _____ (faster/slower).

slower

33. In order to trigger a nerve impulse, a stimulus must be greater in intensity than the neuron's _____ .

threshold

34. Increasing the stimulus above this level _____ (will/will not) increase the strength or speed of the nerve impulse.

will not

35. This phenomenon is called an _____-_____-_____ response.

all-or-none

36. The gap between two neurons is called a _____ .

synapse

37. The chemical messengers that convey information across synapses are called _____ .

neurotransmitters

38. Neurotransmitters unlock "gates" on receptor sites, allowing electrically charged _____ to enter the neuron.

ions

39. Neurotransmitters may _____ (increase/decrease/both increase and decrease) the likelihood of a neuron firing.

both increase and decrease

40. A neurotransmitter that appears to be important in motor control is _____ .

ACh

41. The poison curare, which causes total paralysis of the body's muscles, _____ (facilitates/disrupts) ACh transmission.

disrupts

42. A neurotransmitter involved in the regulation of temperature and sleep is _____ .

serotonin

43. A neurotransmitter that affects mood and arousal is _____ .

norepinephrine

44. A neurotransmitter that affects attention and complex body movements is _____ .

dopamine

45. Naturally occurring painkillers in the brain are called _____ .

endorphins

The Brain (pp. 32–52)

46. The oldest technique for studying the brain involves
_____ _____ of patients with brain
injuries or diseases.

clinical observation

47. Damage to one side of the brain will affect the _____
side of the body.

opposite

48. Researchers have investigated brain function by selective destruction of brain tissue; this is called a brain _____.

lesion

49. A recording of the electrical activity of the whole brain is called an
_____.

EEG or
electroencephalogram

50. A three-dimensional X ray of the brain is called a _____
_____.

CAT scan

51. The technique for measuring the brain's consumption of glucose is
called the _____ _____.

PET scan

52. The first part of the brain to evolve controlled basic survival functions such as _____, _____, and
_____.

sleeping; breathing;
feeding

53. Brain evolution in mammals resulted in increased capacities for
_____ and _____.

emotion; memory

54. In the highest mammals, the brain's ability to _____
_____ and act with foresight evolved.

process information

55. The brain can be divided into three regions corresponding to the
stages of evolution: the _____, the _____
_____, and the _____
_____.

brainstem; limbic
system; cerebral cortex

56. At the base of the brain, where the spinal cord enters the skull, lies
the _____, which controls _____
and _____.

medulla; breathing;
heartbeat

57. At the rear of the brainstem lies the _____. Its
major function is _____ control and coordination of
_____ movement.

cerebellum
muscular
voluntary

58. Like the higher brain centers, the cerebellum has two
_____.

hemispheres

59. At the top of the brainstem sits the _____, which relays information from _____ neurons to the higher regions of the brain.

thalamus
sensory

60. The _____ _____ system is contained inside the brainstem and is designed to _____ the brain. Magoun discovered that electrical stimulation in this region would cause a sleeping animal to _____.

reticular activating;
arouse;

awaken

61. Between the brainstem and cerebral hemispheres is the _____ system. This system is important in the regulation of emotions and drives, such as _____, _____, _____, and _____.

limbic
fear
aggression; hunger;
sex

62. Rage or terror will result from stimulation of different regions in the _____.

amygdala

63. Below the thalamus is the _____, which regulates bodily maintenance behaviors, such as _____, _____, _____ _____ and _____ _____.

hypothalamus
hunger
thirst; body
temperature
sexual behavior

64. The hypothalamus acts chemically by secreting hormones which affect the _____ gland and by triggering activity in the _____ system.

pituitary
autonomic

65. Olds and Milner discovered that the hypothalamus also contains _____ centers, which animals will work hard to have stimulated.

pleasure

66. The most complex functions of human behavior are linked to the most developed part of the brain, the _____ _____. If this region is not functioning, the person will lapse into a _____.

cerebral
cortex
coma

67. The cortex is divided into two halves, or _____, each of which is divided into four _____.

hemispheres
lobes

68. Label these four lobes in the sketch on page 24.
a. _____ b. _____
c. _____ d. _____

frontal lobe
parietal lobe
occipital lobe
temporal lobe

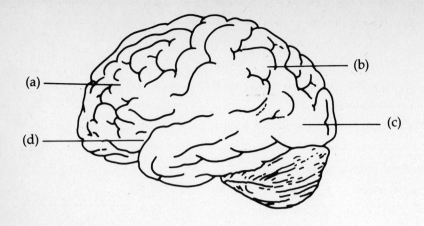

69. Fritsch and Hitzig discovered that electrical stimulation of one side of the _____ cortex resulted in movement on the opposite side of the body.

motor

70. At the front of the parietal lobe lies the _____ cortex. Stimulation of this area elicits a sensation of _____.

somatosensory

touch

71. Visual information projects to the _____ lobe at the very back of the brain.

occipital

72. Stimulation of the _____ areas in the _____ lobe might cause one to hear a sound.

auditory

temporal

73. Most brain areas are "silent" when stimulated. These _____ areas integrate information received by other regions of the brain.

association

74. Association areas in the _____ lobe are involved in making judgments and carrying out plans.

frontal

75. Brain injuries may produce an impairment in the use of language known as _____.

aphasia

76. Damage to _____ area in the _____ lobe on the _____ side of the brain impairs ability to form words.

Broca's; frontal; left

77. Impaired comprehension of language results from damage to _____ area in the left _____ lobe of the brain.

Wernicke's; temporal

78. When a person is reading, the _____ _____ translates the visual information into an _____ form.

angular gyrus

auditory

79. Because damage to it will impair language and reasoning, the _____ hemisphere came to be known as the _____ hemisphere.

left

dominant

80. In experiments with cats and monkeys, Roger Sperry separated the two hemispheres of the brain by surgically cutting the _____ _____. When this structure is severed in humans, the result is referred to as a _____ _____ .

corpus callosum;

split brain

81. The split-brain operation was originally performed to control seizures caused by _____ .

epilepsy

82. In a split-brain patient, only the _____ hemisphere will be aware of an unseen object held in the left hand. In this case, the person would not be able to _____ the object.

right

name

83. Shown a different word in the left and right portions of the visual field, a split-brain patient will say the word shown on the _____ .

right

84. Identify which hemisphere is the more important for each of the following abilities: a. Writing _____ ; b. Speaking _____ ; c. Emotion _____ ; d. Intuition _____ ; e. Facial recognition _____

left

left; right

right; right

85. As a result of hemispheric specialization, the _____ side of the face is more expressive in conveying emotion.

left

86. Hemispheric specialization is studied in the normal brain by monitoring activity levels in the form of _____ waves, _____ flow, and _____ consumption. In addition, injections may be used to _____ the hemispheres individually.

brain

blood; glucose;

anesthetize

87. In a _____ listening task, different messages are played to the left and right ears.

dichotic

88. The _____ ear, which projects mostly to the _____ hemisphere, is superior at perceiving melodies, laughing, and crying.

left

right

89. About _____ percent of people are left-handed.

ten

90. Unlike skin tissue, neurons in the CNS will not _____ .

regenerate

91. Labbe and her colleagues have found that the learning ability of rats with damaged frontal lobes increased following _____ of brain tissue from other animals.

transplants

92. Brain tissue transplants may one day be used in treating illnesses that involve degeneration of brain tissue, such as _____ disease and _____ disease.

Parkinson's
Alzheimer's

93. The phenomenon whereby undamaged brain areas take over the functions of damaged regions is called _____ .

plasticity

The Endocrine System (p. 52)

94. In addition to the nervous system, the body has another, slower communication network called the _____ system.

endocrine

95. Endocrine glands release _____ into the bloodstream.

hormones

96. During an emergency, the _____ glands become active.

adrenal

97. These glands release the hormones _____ and _____ , which prepare the body for danger.

epinephrine
norepinephrine

98. The master gland, or _____ , produces hormones that regulate other glands as well as body growth.

pituitary

99. The secretions of the pituitary are regulated by the _____ .

hypothalamus

Genes and Behavior (pp. 52–55)

100. The body's genetic plans are stored within the _____ .

chromosomes

101. In number, each person inherits _____ pairs of chromosomes.

23

102. Chromosomes are composed of thousands of structures called _____ .

genes

103. The genetic instructions are found in complex chemical molecules of _____ .

DNA

104. Psychology has long been concerned with the question of whether nurture is a more important influence on behavior than genes, or _____ .

nature

105. Most behaviors are not determined solely by nature or nurture, but by the manner in which these two factors _____ .

interact

106. An index of the extent to which differences in a trait are genetically determined is _____.

heritability

107. One technique for investigating heritability is to mate animals sharing a particular trait, using a procedure called _____ _____.

selective breeding

108. Research on heritability includes studies of twins developed from a single egg, and therefore genetically _____.

identical

109. Twins developed from different fertilized eggs and no more genetically similar than siblings are called _____.

fraternal

110. Nurture is difficult to rule out as a cause of the similarity of identical twins because such individuals usually mature in similar _____.

environments

FOCUS ON PSYCHOLOGY:
THE JUNK FOOD SYNDROME

Did you know that your eating habits may enhance or hinder the functioning of your brain? Jeffrey Bland, a professor of nutritional biochemistry, suggests: "Without a proper ratio between key vitamins and minerals on the one hand and calories on the other, brain function and behavior may be disturbed." Bland and other researchers have found that many children and adults who suffer from insomnia, excessive aggressiveness, and other behavioral problems tend to eat too many empty-calorie junk foods, and too few nutritious foods. In many such cases, the behavioral abnormalities disappear when the diet is improved.

The link between diet and brain function involves neurotransmitters. In order to manufacture neurotransmitters, such as ACh and serotonin, the brain requires certain nutrients. Serotonin, for example, is produced from tryptophan, an amino acid found in protein-rich foods. The synthesis of serotonin from tryptophan is also facilitated by the presence of vitamin B. In this manner, nutritious foods can actually raise the level of neurotransmitters in the brain. "You are what you eat" applies not only to appearance, but to the mind as well.

PROGRESS TEST 1

Circle your answer to the following questions and check them with the answer key at the end of this chapter. Be sure to consult the appropriate pages of the text to understand the correct answer for any missed question.

Multiple-Choice Questions

1. In nearly every _____, there are _____.
a. cell; 23 pairs of chromosomes
b. cell; 46 pairs of chromosomes
c. gene; 23 pairs of chromosomes
d. chromosome; 46 genes

2. You, your sister, and both parents all share a certain behavioral trait. This shows that:
a. a recessive gene controls the trait.
b. a dominant gene controls the trait.
c. the trait does not have a genetic basis.
d. a, b, or c could be true.

3. Differences in the behavioral characteristics of fraternal twins are attributed mainly to:
a. differences in their environments.
b. gender differences.
c. genetic differences.
d. environmental and genetic differences.

4. Afferent is to efferent as _____ is to _____.
a. central; peripheral
b. sensory; motor
c. motor; sensory
d. peripheral; central

5. Heart rate, digestion, and other self-regulating bodily functions are governed by the:

a. voluntary nervous system.
b. autonomic nervous system.
c. sympathetic and parasympathetic divisions of the CNS.
d. somatic nervous system.

6. The all-or-none principle states that:
a. strong stimuli cause neurons to produce stronger impulses.
b. strong stimuli cause neurons to fire less frequently.
c. strong stimuli cause neurons to fire more frequently.
d. the intensity of the neural impulse does not vary with the strength of the stimulus.

7. The pain of heroin withdrawal may be due to the fact that:
a. under the influence of heroin, the brain ceases production of endorphins.
b. under the influence of heroin, the brain ceases production of all neurotransmitters.
c. during withdrawal, the brain's production of all neurotransmitters is greatly increased.
d. heroin destroys endorphin receptors in the brain.

8. The brain research technique that involves monitoring the brain's usage of glucose is called the:
a. PET scan.
b. CAT scan.
c. EEG.
d. EMG.

9. A split-brain patient has a picture of a knife flashed to her left hemisphere and that of a fork to her right hemisphere. She will be able to:
a. identify a knife using her left hand.
b. identify a fork using her left hand.
c. identify a knife using either hand.
d. identify a fork using either hand.

10. The limbic system plays an important role in:
a. regulating emotional states.
b. linking the brain's hemispheres.
c. perceptual skills.
d. controlling the voluntary muscles.

11. A stroke leaves a patient paralyzed on the left side of the body. Which region of the brain has been damaged?
a. the reticular system
b. the limbic system
c. the left hemisphere
d. the right hemisphere

12. Generally speaking, the brains of _____ exhibit greater plasticity than those of _____.
a. adults; children
b. children; adults
c. males; females
d. females; males

13. Aphasia, in which a person loses the ability to comprehend language, results from injury to:
a. the angular gyrus.
b. Broca's area.
c. Wernicke's area.
d. frontal lobe association areas.

14. Which of the following is typically controlled by the right hemisphere?
a. language
b. learned voluntary movements
c. arithmetic reasoning
d. perceptual tasks

15. Which part of the human brain is most like that of a fish?
a. the cortex
b. the limbic system
c. the brain stem
d. the right hemisphere

Matching Items

Match each of the structures with its corresponding function.

Structures	*Functions*
_____ 1. hypothalamus	a. auditory areas
_____ 2. frontal lobe	b. visual areas

_____ **3.** parietal lobe
_____ **4.** temporal lobe
_____ **5.** reticular system
_____ **6.** occipital lobe
_____ **7.** thalamus
_____ **8.** corpus callosum
_____ **9.** cerebellum
_____ **10.** amygdala
_____ **11.** medulla

c. sensory switchboard
d. pleasure centers
e. somatosensory cortex
f. motor cortex
g. controls arousal
h. links cerebral hemispheres
i. rage and terror
j. breathing and heartbeat
k. coordination
l. taste areas
m. facial expression control
n. controls sense of smell

FOCUS ON PSYCHOLOGY:
BE STILL MY HEMISPHERE!

As noted in the text, one or the other of the two cerebral hemispheres can be anesthetized by the injection of a sedative into the brain. If it were possible for you to "deactivate" either hemisphere whenever you wanted to, would you do so? Would there be any practical advantage to having this control over your brain? In what type of situation would you "silence" the right hemisphere? The left hemisphere?

Recently, Floyd Bloom and his colleagues at the University of California at San Diego found that airflow in the right and left nostrils of the nose may affect activity in the two brain hemispheres. When the right nostril of subjects was closed, and they were forced to breathe through the left nostril, brain wave activity in the right hemisphere increased significantly. Breathing through the right nostril was followed by greater activity in the left hemisphere. The discovery of a possible link between breathing and activity in the two hemispheres has several possible applications. For example, certain disorders, such as schizophrenia, appear to be related to abnormally high or low activity levels in one or both hemispheres. It may be possible to correct such abnormal brain activity with breathing techniques, rather than with drugs.

These findings also suggest that a person may be able to exert greater control over his or her own mental activity by changing the balance of hemispheric activity in order to more effectively concentrate on a task. For example, skills that are primarily left-hemisphere functions might be improved by forcible breathing through the right nostril for a few minutes. Alterna-

tively, when a person wished to enter a "creative" mood, he or she might first breathe through the left nostril for a few minutes.

PROGRESS TEST 2

Progress Test 2 should be completed during a final chapter review. Do this test after you thoroughly understand the correct answers for the Chapter Review and Progress Test 1.

Multiple-Choice Questions

1. The theory of sociobiology:
a. attempts to apply the principles of evolution to social behavior.
b. suggests that social rather than biological factors are the most important determinants of behavior.
c. argues that the fundamental motive in human behavior is to help others.
d. has no support, since no universal behavior patterns have been demonstrated.

2. If heredity determines a particular trait, we would expect that _____ should be more similar to one another than _____ .

a. cousins; siblings
b. fraternal twins; siblings
c. children and biological parents; children and adoptive parents
d. children and adoptive parents; children and biological parents

3. Voluntary movements such as writing with a pencil are directed by:
a. the sympathetic nervous system.
b. the somatic nervous system.
c. the parasympathetic nervous system.
d. the autonomic nervous system.

4. You are able to pull your hand quickly out of a hot shower before a sensation of pain is felt because:
a. movement of the hand is a reflex wired through the spinal cord.
b. movement of the hand does not require intervention of the central nervous system.
c. the brain reacts quickly to prevent severe injury.
d. reflexes are governed by the faster autonomic nervous system.

5. Which is the correct sequence in the transmission of a neural impulse?
a. axon; dendrite; cell body; synapse
b. dendrite; axon; cell body; synapse
c. dendrite; cell body; axon; synapse
d. axon; synapse; cell body; dendrite

6. Neurotransmitters are chemicals released by _____ into spaces called

_____ .
a. dendrites; cell bodies
b. the axon terminal; synapses
c. the cell body; axons
d. the synapse; axons

7. The chemical messengers of the endocrine system are called:
a. endorphins.
b. neurotransmitters.
c. hormones.
d. enzymes.

8. A head injury results in severe disruption of sleeping. Most likely the damage occurred to the:
a. thalamus.
b. corpus callosum.
c. reticular system.
d. cerebellum.

9. For left-handed people, language is processed by:
a. both hemispheres.
b. the right hemisphere.

c. the left hemisphere.
d. either a or b.

10. In a dichotic listening experiment, the left ear will be faster than the right in processing:
a. a song's lyrics.
b. a song's melody.
c. pictures of faces.
d. spoken words.

11. Following an injury, undamaged brain areas may take over the functions of damaged areas. This phenomenon is called:
a. recombination.
b. regeneration.
c. enrichment.
d. plasticity.

12. Cortical areas that are not primarily concerned with sensory-motor or language functions are known as:
a. gray matter.
b. association areas.
c. white matter.
d. projection areas.

13. The motor cortex is in the:
a. occipital lobe.
b. temporal lobe.
c. frontal lobe.
d. parietal lobe.

14. Which of the following is typically controlled by the left hemisphere?
a. spatial reasoning
b. arithmetic reasoning
c. the left side of the body
d. perceptual skills

15. The characteristic of the human brain most related to our intelligence is:
a. its large size.
b. the high ratio of brain to body weight.
c. the size of the frontal lobes.
d. the amount of association area.

Matching Items

Match each structure or term with its corresponding function or definition.

Structure or Term	Function or Definition
_____ **1.** right hemisphere	**a.** controls speech production
_____ **2.** brainstem	**b.** arithmetic reasoning
_____ **3.** CAT scan	**c.** translates writing into sound
_____ **4.** aphasia	**d.** emotional tasks
_____ **5.** EEG	**e.** three-dimensional brain X ray
_____ **6.** Broca's area	**f.** language disorder
_____ **7.** Wernicke's area	**g.** oldest part of the brain
_____ **8.** limbic system	**h.** regulates emotions
_____ **9.** association areas	**i.** recording of brain waves
_____ **10.** left hemisphere	**j.** language comprehension
_____ **11.** angular gyrus	**k.** "silent" brain areas
	l. smallest region of brain
	m. eating disorder center
	n. converts speech into writing

In the diagrams below, the numbers refer to brain locations that have been damaged. Match each location with its probable effect on behavior.

1. _____ **a.** vision disorder
2. _____ **b.** insensitivity to touch
3. _____ **c.** motor paralysis
4. _____ **d.** hearing problem
5. _____ **e.** speech disorder
6. _____ **f.** problem in language comprehension
7. _____ **g.** lack of coordination in movement
8. _____ **h.** abnormal hunger
9. _____ **i.** split-brain
10. _____ **j.** sleep disorder
            k. loss of smell
            l. loss of taste
            m. scalp disease

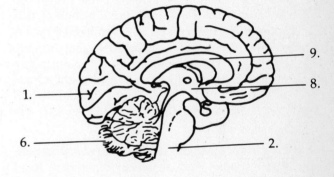

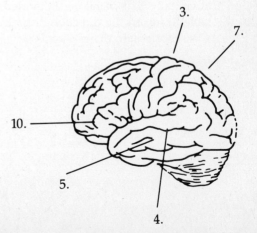

SAMPLE ESSAY QUESTIONS

1. Explain the brain processing involved in the production and comprehension of language while one is reading aloud.

2. Describe the three layers of the brain, including their structures, evolutionary significance, and general functions.

3. Discuss why the nature-nurture issue is difficult or impossible to resolve.

4. What evolutionary selection pressures might have accounted for the evolution of the brain's receptors for opiates such as morphine?

5. Describe the split-brain experiment and discuss its significance in research on hemispheric specialization.

PROJECT:

HEMISPHERIC SPECIALIZATION

Hemispheric specialization can easily be demonstrated in normal subjects. When a person is formulating an answer to a question, the direction of that person's gaze is often related to which hemisphere is processing the question. Questions that require mathematical or verbal skills tax the left hemisphere and result in the person's gazing to the right. Questions of an emotional or spatial nature are addressed by the right hemisphere and result in gazing to the left.

Below is a list of questions divided into mathematical, emotional, spatial, and analytical categories. Read each question individually to several right-handed friends. Use the table to record the direction of their initial eye gaze as they formulate the answer.

Mathematical Questions

1. What is the square root of 256?

2. Multiply 15 times 8 in your head.

3. What is 224 divided by 7?

Emotional Questions

1. How well do you and your mother get along?

2. What does love mean to you?

3. Do you feel that you are well liked?

Spatial Questions

1. On a penny, does Lincoln's head face to the right or to the left?

2. How many surfaces are there on a pyramid?

3. How would you direct someone to your house?

Analytical Questions

1. What is the most difficult course you are taking?

2. What does deciduous mean?

3. Jack is taller than Jim, and Jack is shorter than Joe. Who is the shortest?

Subject	Eye Gaze Direction			
	1	2	3	4
Mathematical 1. 2. 3.				
Emotional 1. 2. 3.				
Spatial 1. 2. 3.				
Analytical 1. 2. 3.				

Questions to Consider

1. What percentage of left-hemisphere questions produced eye gaze in the predicted direction? Right-hemisphere questions?

2. What results would you expect if you conducted this experiment with left-handed subjects? If you know some, try it.

3. Is this a good test of hemispheric specialization? Can you think of any ways the experimenter could have biased the results? How could you redesign the experiment to control for such a possibility?

WHERE TO LOOK FOR MORE INFORMATION

Bland, Jeffrey (1982, January). The junk-food syndrome. *Psychology Today*, p. 92.

A biochemical nutritionist explains why "You are what you eat."

Dawkins, Richard (1976). *The selfish gene.* New York: Oxford University Press.

Dawkins' book provides an excellent general discussion and critique of the theory of sociobiology.

Fincher, Jack, F. (1984, January). New tools for medical diagnosis. *Smithsonian, 14*(10), pp. 64–71.

An intriguing discussion of PET scans, CAT scans, and the latest marvels of medical technology.

Gazzaniga, M. S. (1967). The split brain in man. *Scientific American, 217*, pp. 24–29.

This article is a readable summary of split-brain research.

Shannahoff-Khalsa, D. (1984, September). Rhythms and reality: The dynamics of the mind. *Psychology Today*.

This article discusses the link between nasal breathing and the balance of activity in the right and left hemispheres of the brain.

ANSWERS

PROGRESS TEST 1

Multiple-Choice Questions

1. a (p. 53)	6. d (p. 30)	11. d (p. 40)
2. d (p. 53)	7. a (p. 32)	12. b (p. 51)
3. d (p. 54)	8. a (p. 34)	13. c (p. 42)
4. b (p. 28)	9. b (p. 45)	14. d (p. 47)
5. b (p. 27)	10. a (p. 37)	15. c (p. 35)

Matching Items

1. d (p. 37)	5. g (p. 36)	9. k (p. 36)
2. f (p. 40)	6. b (p. 41)	10. i (p. 37)
3. e (p. 41)	7. c (p. 36)	11. j (p. 36)
4. a (p. 41)	8. h (p. 44)	

PROGRESS TEST 2

Multiple-Choice Questions

1. a (p. 25)	6. b (p. 31)	11. d (p. 51)
2. c (p. 54)	7. c (p. 52)	12. b (p. 41)
3. b (p. 27)	8. c (p. 36)	13. c (p. 40)
4. a (p. 29)	9. c (p. 50)	14. b (p. 48)
5. c (p. 30)	10. b (p. 49)	15. d (p. 42)

Matching Items

1. d (p. 48)	5. i (p. 34)	9. k (p. 41)
2. g (p. 36)	6. a (p. 43)	10. b (p. 48)
3. e (p. 34)	7. j (p. 43)	11. c (p. 43)
4. f (p. 42)	8. h (p. 37)	

Brain Damage Diagram

1. a (p. 43)	5. d (p. 41)	9. i (p. 44)
2. j (p. 36)	6. g (p. 40)	10. e (p. 42)
3. c (p. 40)	7. b (p. 41)	
4. f (p. 43)	8. h (p. 37)	

PART TWO

DEVELOPMENT OVER THE LIFE-SPAN

CHAPTER 3

Infancy and Childhood

CHAPTER OVERVIEW

Developmental psychologists study the life cycle, from conception to death, and examine how we develop physically, cognitively, and socially. This chapter covers prenatal, infant, and childhood development. Although there are not too many terms to learn, there are quite a number of important research findings to remember. Pay particular attention to Harlow's research on social deprivation, the section on the origins of attachment, and Piaget's theory of cognitive development.

GUIDED STUDY

The text chapter should be studied one section at a time. Before you read, preview each section by skimming it, noting headings and boldface items. Then read the appropriate section objectives from the following outline. Keep these objectives in mind and, as you read the chapter section, search for the information that will complete each one. You may wish to write out answers for each objective as soon as you finish reading that section of the chapter.

Developmental Issues (pp. 64–65)

1. Explain the question: "Is development influenced more by maturation or by experience?"

2. Explain the continuity-discontinuity issue in developmental psychology.

Prenatal Development (pp. 65–66)

3. Describe the significance of X and Y chromosomes and, beginning with conception, outline the basic sequence of prenatal development.

4. State the effects on the developing fetus of the mother's nutrition and exposure to teratogens.

Infancy (pp. 66–79)

5. Discuss the effects of early experience on brain development.

6. Identify the infant's basic reflexes and perceptual abilities.

7. Explain why, from Piaget's viewpoint, "the child's mind is not a miniature model of the adult's."

8. Describe assimilation and accommodation and their importance in the development of cognitive schemas.

9. Define object permanence and describe the cognitive abilities of the sensorimotor infant.

10. Describe Harlow's research on attachment formation in monkeys.

11. Explain the importance of contact, familiarity, and responsive parenting in the development of attachment.

12. Discuss the concept of critical period in imprinting, language learning, and mother-infant bonding.

13. State the effects of deprivation of social attachments in children and monkeys.

Childhood (pp. 79–84)

14. Define egocentrism and describe the cognitive abilities of the preoperational child.

15. Explain the principle of conservation and characterize the cognitive abilities of the concrete-operational child.

16. Describe the development of the self-concept in children.

17. Contrast the effects of permissive, authoritarian, and firmly controlling parents on their children.

CHAPTER REVIEW

When you have finished reading the chapter, complete the sentences that follow. Using your hand or a strip of paper, cover the correct answers in the margin and fill in each blank. Verify your answer by uncovering the correct one. As you proceed, evaluate your performance for each chapter section. *Do not continue with the next section until you understand why each margin term is the correct answer.* If you need to, review or re-read the appropriate chapter section in the text before continuing.

Developmental Issues (pp. 64–65)

1. One perspective on development emphasizes the importance of genes in programming an orderly sequence of biological _____.

maturation

2. Psychologists who emphasize maturation tend to see development not as a continuous process, but as a sequence of predictable events that occur in _____.

stages

Prenatal Development (pp. 65–66)

3. Reproduction begins when an egg, or _____, is released by the female's _____.

ovum
ovary

4. Sperm that cause the fertilized egg to become a male carry a(n) _____ chromosome. Those that produce a female carry a(n) _____ chromosome.

Y
X

5. Fertilized human eggs are called _____.

zygotes

6. From about 2 until 6 weeks after conception, the developing human is called a(n) _____.

embryo

7. During the final stage of prenatal development, the developing human is called a(n) _____.

fetus

8. The filter through which the mother's blood, nutrients, and oxygen pass to the fetus is the _____.

placenta

9. Prenatal development is divided into three stages called _____.

trimesters

10. Many factors can interfere with prenatal growth. Premature and stillbirths may be related to the mother's being _____ during the later stages of pregnancy.

malnourished

11. Risk of a newborn being addicted, underweight, or retarded is increased if the mother is a user of heroin, nicotine, alcohol, or other substances that are called _____ .

teratogens

Infancy (pp. 66–79)

12. At birth the human nervous system _____ (is/is not) fully mature.

is not

13. In one study, rats raised in deprived environments had thinner _____ than those raised in normal environments.

cortexes

14. At birth, infants possess a number of simple responses called _____ .

reflexes

15. When an infant's cheek is touched, it will vigorously search for a nipple, which is the _____ reflex.

rooting

16. Infants pass the milestones of motor development at different rates, but the basic _____ of stages is fixed.

order/sequence

17. Maturation creates in children a readiness to walk at about the age of _____ .

1

18. Until the necessary muscular and neural maturation is complete, experience has a _____ (large/small) effect on behavior.

small

19. A newborn's sensory equipment appears to be biologically pre-wired to facilitate _____ responsiveness.

social

20. Newborns will ignore artificial sounds, but will turn in the direction of a human _____ .

voice

21. It has also been reported that newborn infants may be capable of _____ facial expressions.

imitating

22. The term for all the mental activities associated with thinking and knowing is _____ .

cognition

23. The first researcher to show that the cognitive processes of adults and children are very different was _____ .

Piaget

24. In Piaget's first stage of cognitive development, that of _____ intelligence, children experience the world through their motor activities and sensory impressions.

sensorimotor

25. This stage occurs between infancy and the age of _____ .

2

26. Children develop the ability to pretend during the stage of _____ intelligence, which occurs between the ages of _____ and _____ .

preoperational
2; 6

27. Concrete-operational intelligence begins at about the age of _____ , when children are able to think _____ about concrete things.

7
logically

28. Children begin to think hypothetically and abstractly during the stage of _____-_____ intelligence, which begins at about age _____ .

formal-operational
12

29. To organize its experiences, the developing brain constructs cognitive concepts called _____ .

schemas

30. The tendency to interpret new experiences in terms of existing knowledge is called _____ .

assimilation

31. The adaptation of old ideas to fit new situations defines the process of _____ .

accommodation

32. The development of an awareness that things continue to exist even when they have been removed from view is called _____ _____ . This awareness begins to develop at about _____ months of age.

object permanence
8

33. At about the same age a new fear, called _____ _____ , emerges.

stranger anxiety

34. Freud referred to a person's inability to remember experiences during infancy as _____ _____ .

infantile amnesia

35. It has been suggested that the first two years of an infant's life are a _____ _____ for learning language.

critical period

36. The development of a strong social bond between infant and parent is called _____ .

attachment

37. Harlow's studies of monkeys have shown that mother-infant attachment does not depend on the mother providing nourishment so much as it does her providing _____ comfort.

contact

38. Lorenz discovered that young birds would follow almost any object if it were the first moving thing they observed. This phenomenon is called _____ .

imprinting

39. Some pediatricians and researchers speculate that humans may have a critical period in attachment formation when mother-infant _____ is most likely to occur.

bonding

40. Critical periods for attachment in monkeys and humans probably _____ (are/are not) as well-defined as in birds.

are not

41. In terms of psychological benefits to the infant, breast feeding _____ (does/does not) appear to convey an advantage over bottle feeding.

does not

42. Recent studies of fathers as primary caregivers suggest that father-mother differences in nurturant behaviors _____ (are/are not) biologically fixed.

are not

43. According to Erikson, infants form a lifelong attitude of either basic _____ or _____, depending on the nature of their early attachment experiences.

trust; mistrust

44. Harlow found that monkeys reared in social isolation showed either extreme fear or increased _____ when first placed with other monkeys.

aggression

45. Upon reaching sexual maturity, most of these monkeys were not able to _____ normally.

mate

46. Most abusive parents _____ (were/were not) themselves abused as children.

were

47. Research has shown that foster children placed in homes before the age of 16 months _____ (could/could not) form new attachments without permanent emotional scars.

could

48. Sroufe has found that infants who are securely attached at 12 to 18 months of age are more socially _____ than insecure children.

competent

Childhood (pp. 79–84)

49. Both physical growth and brain development tend to slow down in children after the age of _____.

2

50. The last areas of the brain that develop are the _____ areas of the cortex, which are involved in thinking, memory, and language.

association

51. Researchers have found that children rated by their teachers as the most socially assertive and competitive are also the most physically _____.

active

52. Preschoolers are often unable to perceive things from another person's point of view. This type of behavior is called _____.

egocentrism

53. Preschoolers often find that negative instructions are _____ (easier/more difficult) to follow than positive instructions.

more difficult

54. During Piaget's _____ stage, children are unable to perform important mental operations, such as reversing information.

preoperational

55. During this period they _____ (are/are not) able to comprehend that substances remain the same even when their appearances change. This ability is called _____.

are not

conservation

56. Between 7 and _____ years of age, children are in Piaget's period of _____ _____. During this stage children _____ (are/are not) capable of reasoning abstractly.

12
concrete operations
are not

57. List some characteristics of children who have formed a positive self-image: _____, _____, _____, _____, _____.

confidence; independence
optimism; assertiveness
sociability

58. Children generally have a stable self-image by the age of _____.

8 or 10

59. Parents who make few demands of their children and who tend to submit to their children's desires are identified as _____ parents.

permissive

60. The parent who imposes rules and expects blind obedience is exhibiting the _____ style of parenting.

authoritarian

61. Setting and enforcing standards after some discussion with their children is the approach taken by _____ _____ parents. Studies have shown that these children will tend to be the happiest and have the highest _____-_____.

firmly controlling

self-esteem

FOCUS ON PSYCHOLOGY:
YOU AND YOUR PARENTS

Parental influence on the social, cognitive, and emotional development of children has been a favorite research topic of developmental psychologists. Here are several issues to start you thinking about your own upbringing and how it has affected your behavior.

Birth Order. First-born children tend to have higher IQs, be more conservative, more concerned about social approval, and more achievement-oriented than later-born children. Although birth order interacts with other factors, such as family size and how close the children are in age, many researchers believe that first- and later-born children are raised and socialized in different ways. For example, parents typically raise their first child in an environment that is stricter and more encouraging of achievement than that of second- or third-born children. What other differences would you expect in the upbringing of first- and later-born children? What is your birth order? Compare your upbringing with that of your brothers and sisters. Note any behavioral differences. Take a survey of your friends. Are there any consistent effects of birth order?

Parental Discipline. The text identifies three types of parenting styles and discusses their effects on the social development of children. *Permissive parents* make few demands and tend to submit to the wishes of their children. *Authoritarian parents* dictate rules and expect blind obedience. *Firmly controlling parents* set and enforce rules after discussion with their children. How would you characterize your parents and upbringing? What behavioral effects of this upbringing can you identify in yourself? How might you be different had you been raised by other parents? How do you and your parents differ from close friends and their parents?

Parental Malpractice. In recent years, several children have attempted to sue their parents for parental malpractice. For example, a son sued his parents for $350,000, claiming that their neglect of him as a child was responsible for his psychological problems. To what extent should parents be held legally accountable for the way their children turn out? Under what circumstances would you decide such a case in favor of the child?

PROGRESS TEST 1

Circle your answer to the following questions and check them with the answer key at the end of this chapter. Be sure to consult the appropriate pages of the text to understand the correct answer for any missed question.

1. Piaget's theory is primarily concerned with
_____ development.
a. motor
b. social
c. biological
d. cognitive

2. In Piaget's stage of concrete-operational intelligence, the child acquires an understanding of the principle of:
a. conservation.
b. deduction.
c. attachment.
d. object permanence.

3. Egocentrism is characteristic of which developmental stage?
a. sensorimotor intelligence
b. preoperational intelligence
c. concrete-operational intelligence
d. formal-operational intelligence

4. Which parenting style usually produces children having the greatest confidence and self-esteem?
a. permissive
b. authoritarian
c. firmly controlling
d. There is no evidence of a correlation between these two factors.

5. If a mother is severely malnourished during the last third of her pregnancy:
a. the placenta will replace any missing nutrients.
b. the effects will not be as damaging as those resulting from malnutrition earlier in the pregnancy.
c. the risk of a premature birth or a stillbirth is increased.
d. mother-infant bonding will be delayed.

6. During which stage of cognitive development do children acquire object permanence?
a. sensorimotor
b. preoperational
c. concrete operations
d. formal operations

7. The rooting reflex occurs when:
a. a baby's foot is tickled.
b. a newborn's mouth is touched.
c. a newborn hears a loud noise.
d. a light is flashed in a newborn's eyes.

8. Harlow's studies of attachment in monkeys showed that:
a. nourishment was the single most important factor.

b. a cloth mother produced the greatest attachment response.

c. whether a cloth or a wire mother was present mattered less than the presence or absence of other infants.

d. attachment in monkeys is based on imprinting.

9. The process by which schemas are adapted to fit new experiences is called:

a. accommodation.

b. assimilation.

c. conservation.

d. convergence.

10. Biological growth processes that are *not* influenced by experience are the result of:

a. conservation.

b. continuity.

c. centrism.

d. maturation.

11. The phenomenon in which young birds follow the first moving object they observe is called:

a. imprinting.

b. bonding.

c. assimilation.

d. accommodation.

12. The developmental theorist who suggests that children develop an attitude of basic trust or mistrust is:

a. Piaget.

b. Erikson.

c. Kohlberg.

d. Freud.

13. Developmental theorists who emphasize learning tend to see development as a:

a. sequence of stages, not necessarily in one particular order.

b. sequence of stages, in one particular order.

c. slow, continuous shaping process.

d. slow, discontinuous shaping process.

14. Whether a male or female is produced at conception is determined by:

a. the X or Y chromosome contributed by the father's sperm.

b. the X or Y chromosome contributed by the mother's egg.

c. the mother's age.

d. the father's age.

15. Research with Hopi Indian children who are bound to cradleboards during much of their first year showed that:

a. age of walking was determined primarily by learning rather than by maturation.

b. learning to walk in these children was delayed only one to two months.

c. these children learned to walk at a significantly earlier age than children who were not restrained.

d. walking occurred at about the same age as in unrestrained children.

FOCUS ON PSYCHOLOGY:
TERATOLOGY

Not too long ago, the placenta was believed to protect a growing fetus from health hazards (teratogens) such as drugs, disease, and household chemicals. Scientists now know this belief is false. It is important to emphasize that the relationship between particular teratogens and birth defects is not completely predictable. A variety of other factors, including nutrition, the mother's age, and the child's birth order may interact with a particular teratogen in producing birth defects. In addition, the effects of a particular teratogen will depend on the time of exposure. Developing organs are usually the most vulnerable. For this reason, the first trimester of a pregnancy (when many organs are in the formative stage) is often considered a critical period. Table 4.1 lists a few of the many teratogens that have been identified.

Table 4.1. Teratogens

Type of Hazard	Potential Effects on Fetus
Environmental	
Pollution (carbon monoxide, mercury), pesticides, food additives, X rays	physical deformity, retardation, birth defects in animals, massive doses lethal
Disease	
syphilis	liver, bone, brain damage
rubella	blindness, deafness,
diabetes	circulatory, respiratory problems
smallpox, measles, mumps	fetus may become infected

Table 4.1 (continued)

Type of Hazard	Potential Effects on Fetus
Drug use	
alcohol	physical deformity, retardation (fetal alcohol syndrome)
heroin	addiction at birth, death
nicotine	premature birth, low weight, cardiac problems
barbiturates	asphyxiation, brain damage

PROGRESS TEST 2

Progress Test 2 should be completed during a final chapter review. Do this test after you thoroughly understand the correct answers for the Chapter Review and Progress Test 1.

1. Assimilation refers to:
a. the application of existing schemas to new experiences.
b. the modification of schemas to fit new experiences.
c. the progression of a child through the various stages of cognitive development.
d. the bonding of mother and infant.

2. Which of the following statements about child abuse is correct?
a. Most abused children come from high-income families.
b. Most abuse occurs to children between 10 and 15 years old.
c. Most abusive parents were abused children.
d. Most abused children have firmly controlling parents.

3. Cognitive concepts that are used to organize experiences are called:
a. operations.   c. schemas.
b. loci.   d. transformations.

4. The development of stranger anxiety coincides with the mastery of the concept of:
a. conservation.   c. equilibrium.
b. egocentrism.   d. object permanence.

5. The primary social response of infancy is:
a. self-concept.   c. attachment.
b. peer identity.   d. gender identity.

6. Developmental theorists who emphasize the importance of maturation see development as a:
a. sequence of predictable stages.
b. slow, continuous shaping process.
c. completely unpredictable process.
d. sequence of stages, not necessarily in a predictable order.

7. An authoritarian child-rearing style involves:
a. discipline through give-and-take discussion.
b. love without discipline.
c. neither love nor discipline.
d. discipline that demands unquestioning obedience.

8. Which is the correct sequence of stages in Piaget's theory of cognitive development?
a. sensorimotor, preoperational, concrete operational, formal operational
b. sensorimotor, concrete operational, preoperational, formal operational
c. preoperational, sensorimotor, concrete operational, formal operational
d. preoperational, concrete operational, formal operational, sensorimotor

9. A child can be born a drug addict because:
a. drugs used by the mother will pass into the child's bloodstream.
b. addiction is an inherited personality trait.
c. drugs used by the mother create genetic defects in her chromosomes.
d. the fetus's blood has no resistance to drugs.

10. A child is shown two identical quantities of a liquid—one in a tall, thin tube, the other in a short, wide jar. The child is asked which container has the most liquid in order to determine if she has mastered the concept of:
a. deductive reasoning.
b. inductive reasoning.
c. sensorimotor logic.
d. conservation.

11. Which is the correct order of stages of prenatal development?
a. zygote, fetus, embryo
b. zygote, embryo, fetus
c. embryo, zygote, fetus
d. embryo, fetus, zygote

12. The term "critical period" refers to:
a. prenatal development.

b. the initial two hours after a child's birth.

c. the preoperational stage.

d. a restricted time for learning.

13. Which of the following was *not* found by Harlow in socially deprived monkeys?

a. The females were abusive mothers.

b. They had difficulty mating.

c. They showed extreme fear or aggression when first seeing other monkeys.

d. They showed abnormal physical development.

14. Children having secure attachment to their parents:

a. usually become permissive parents.

b. usually are more competent in social situations.

c. are often less achievement-oriented.

d. more often prefer to play with adults than with other children.

15. Between the ages of 7 and 12, children are in the:

a. sensorimotor stage.

b. preoperational stage.

c. concrete-operational stage.

d. formal-operational stage.

SAMPLE ESSAY QUESTIONS

1. Identify Piaget's stages of cognitive development. Discuss the ways in which thought processes change, and identify one major accomplishment of each stage.

2. Describe the course of physical development in the zygote, the embryo, and the fetus. Identify the effects of teratogens on prenatal development.

3. Discuss the effects of social deprivation on social and emotional development.

4. Discuss two major theoretical issues that pervade developmental psychology.

5. Contrast the effects of various parental styles on the development of the self-concept in children.

PROJECT:
CONSERVATION

One of the most important landmarks of the stage of concrete operations is the achievement of conservation. The child learns that a substance remains the same even when its appearance changes. A 5-year-old, preoperational child believes that a piece of clay changed in shape is also changed in amount.

Conservation is not an ability children either have or do not have at a specific age. It evolves over a period of time. Furthermore, the age at which conservation occurs has been shown to vary with the type of task and features of the test situation, such as the types of materials used and how questions are phrased.

Make arrangements to test several children between 2 and 7 years of age. If you don't have younger siblings, cousins, or friends with young children, see if your school has an early childhood program. If you must observe a child you do not know, be sure to get permission from the parent or guardian.

Conservation of Substance. Give the child two equal balls of clay. After the child has agreed that they are the same, flatten one ball into a pancake and ask: "Which has more clay?"

Conservation of Liquid. Fill two identical glasses with the same amount of water. While the child watches, pour the water from one glass into a third which is shorter but wider than the first glass. Ask the child: "Which glass has more water?"

Conservation of Number. Line up 5 pennies directly in front of the child and 5 more directly in front of you. Each set should be arranged so that the pennies are closely spaced, with adjacent ones touching. Ask the child: "Who has more pennies?" Do not allow the child to count the pennies before answering. Now, with the child watching, spread your pennies out (keeping them evenly spaced). Again ask: "Who has more pennies?"

Depending on the number tested, group the children into several age categories. Analyze your results by calculating, for each category, the percentage of children who demonstrated conservation on each task.

Questions to Consider

1. At about what age did conservation begin to occur?

2. Are the results the same for each type of task?

3. Do you think that the way in which the experiment was conducted could have influenced the results? Try phrasing conservation problems in different ways as you retest a preoperational child.

4. Based on your experience, do you believe that children could be taught conservation at a younger age? Try it!

Reference Goldschmid, M. L., and Bentler, P. M. (1968). The dimensions and measurement of conservation. *Child Development, 39,* 787–815.

WHERE TO LOOK FOR MORE INFORMATION

Several excellent journals contain research articles in developmental psychology. Visit your library and look through recent issues of *Child Development, Developmental Psychology, Merrill-Palmer Quarterly,* and *Human Development.*

Psychology and Children: Current research and practice. *American Psychologist, 34,* 1979.

This special issue is devoted entirely to research on cognitive, social, personality, and emotional development

Phillips, J. L. (1969). *The origins of intellect: Piaget's theory.* San Francisco: W. H. Freeman.

This excellent book is a very readable summary of Piaget's theory.

A number of recent articles summarize the incredible abilities of the newborn child. Here are some.

Pines, M. (1982, February). Baby, you're incredible. *Psychology Today.* 48–53.

Restak, R. M. (1982, January). Newborn knowledge. *Science 82,* 58–65.

ANSWERS

PROGRESS TEST 1

1. d (p. 69)	6. a (p. 72)	11. a (p. 75)
2. a (p. 81)	7. b (p. 67)	12. b (p. 77)
3. b (p. 80)	8. b (p. 74)	13. c (p. 64)
4. c (p. 83)	9. a (p. 71)	14. a (p. 65)
5. c (p. 66)	10. d (p. 64)	15. d (p. 68)

PROGRESS TEST 2

1. a (p. 71)	6. a (p. 64)	11. b (p. 65)
2. c (p. 78)	7. d (p. 83)	12. d (p. 73)
3. c (p. 71)	8. a (p. 70)	13. d (p. 74)
4. d (p. 72)	9. a (p. 66)	14. b (p. 79)
5. c (p. 73)	10. d (p. 81)	15. c (p. 81)

CHAPTER 4

Adolescence, Adulthood, and Later Life

CHAPTER OVERVIEW

The overriding assumption of modern developmental psychology is that development is lifelong. Chapter 4 explores a wide range of behaviors, including physical, cognitive, and social development during adolescence, adulthood, and later life. The final section of the chapter is a reconsideration of two major developmental issues: the importance of genes and experience in development, and whether development is best described as a continuous process or as a sequence of stages.

Your major challenge in this chapter is to become familiar with several important stage theories of development. These include Kohlberg's theory of moral development, Erikson's stages of psychosocial development, Levinson's stages of adulthood, and Piaget's theory of cognitive development.

GUIDED STUDY

The text chapter should be studied one section at a time. Before you read, preview each section by skimming it, noting headings and boldface items. Then read the appropriate section objectives from the following outline. Keep these objectives in mind, and as you read the chapter section, search for the informa-

tion that will complete each one. You may wish to write out answers for each objective as soon as you finish reading that section of the chapter.

Adolescence (pp. 89–97)

1. Describe the major physical changes that occur in males and females at puberty, including primary sex characteristics, secondary sex characteristics, and menarche.

2. Contrast the effects of early physical maturation on social development in boys and girls.

3. Explain how formal-operational thinking differs from preadolescent thinking.

4. Contrast preconventional, conventional, and postconventional moral reasoning.

5. State two major criticisms of Kohlberg's theory of moral development.

6. Identify several factors that influence identity formation during adolescence.

Adulthood (pp. 98–104)

7. Describe the major physical changes that take place during adulthood, including menopause, and changes in muscular strength and reaction time.

8. Describe how learning and memory abilities change during adulthood.

9. Describe Levinson's stage theory of adult social development.

10. Give several reasons that stage theories of adult development are controversial.

11. Discuss the significance of family and work for adult social development.

Later Life (pp. 104–110)

12. State the major physical and cognitive changes associated with aging.

13. Contrast cross-sectional and longitudinal studies and explain why they may yield conflicting findings concerning intellectual changes associated with aging.

CHAPTER REVIEW

When you have finished reading the chapter, complete the sentences that follow. Using your hand or a strip of paper, cover the correct answers in the margin and fill in each blank. Verify your answer by uncovering the correct one. As you proceed, evaluate your performance for each chapter section. *Do not continue with the next section until you understand why each margin term is the correct answer.* If you need to, review or re-read the appropriate chapter section in the text before continuing.

14. Discuss how changes in crystallized intelligence and fluid intelligence produce a stable IQ throughout the life-span.

15. Identify and describe the five stages of adjustment to dying proposed by Kübler-Ross.

Reflections on the Developmental Issues (pp. 110–115)

16. Describe the results of twin and adoption studies of the heritability of personal and social traits.

17. State the evidence for the heritability of temperament.

18. Discuss evidence for the stability of personality over the life-span.

Adolescence (pp. 89–97)

1. Adolescence begins with the time of developing sexual maturity known as _____.

puberty

2. A two-year growth spurt begins in girls at about the age of _____, and in boys at age _____.

11; 13

3. During this growth spurt, the development of the reproductive organs, or _____ sex characteristics, occurs.

primary

4. The nonreproductive sexual traits such as enlarging breasts, pubic hair, and male voice change are called _____ sex characteristics.

secondary

5. The first menstrual period, called _____, occurs at about age _____. In boys, the first ejaculation occurs at about age _____.

menarche

13

14

6. Studies by Jones have shown that early-maturing boys tend to be _____ (more/less) popular than boys who mature late. For girls, early maturation is often _____ (more/less) advantageous.

more

less

7. Piaget's final stage of cognitive development is the stage of _____ _____. The adolescent in this stage is capable of thinking logically by using _____ rather than concrete propositions.

8. Some critics of Piaget believe that formal logic may begin _____ (earlier/later) than Piaget believed.

9. The theorist who proposed that children progress through six moral stages is _____.

10. These stages are divided into three basic levels: _____, _____, and _____.

11. The preconventional stage of morality is believed to occur in children before the age of _____.

12. During this stage, children obey rules in order to avoid _____ or gain _____.

13. Conventional reasoning ability begins during early _____.

14. Postconventional morality generally begins after age _____.

15. During this stage a person follows what his or her conscience perceives as ethical principles that are _____.

16. Kohlberg's theory has been criticized on two grounds. The first is that moral reasoning does not always predict a person's _____.

17. The second criticism suggests that the theory suffers from _____ bias, with the postconventional stages reflecting the moral beliefs of educated, _____-class people in countries such as the United States, Britain, and Israel.

18. Carol Gilligan has suggested that Kohlberg's theory may also be biased toward the perspective of _____ (males/females).

19. According to Erikson, the task of adolescence is to develop a clear sense of self, or _____.

20. Between the ages of 13 and 23, self-esteem gradually _____.

formal operations

abstract

earlier

Kohlberg

preconventional
conventional
postconventional

9

punishment; rewards

adolescence

20

universal

actions

cultural
middle

males

identity

increases

21. Gilligan has suggested that, while males are more individualistic and concerned with forming an identity, females are more concerned with forming intimate _____.

relationships

22. Adolescence is typically a time of increasing influence from one's _____ and decreasing influence from _____.

peers

parents

23. Contrary to popular belief, studies have shown that the _____ gap between adolescents and parents is actually quite small.

generation

Adulthood (pp. 98–104)

24. Early adulthood extends from about age _____ to age _____.

20

40

25. During adulthood, age _____ (is/is not) a very good predictor of a person's traits.

is not

26. The cessation of the menstrual cycle, known as _____, occurs at about age _____. This biological change results from lowered levels of the hormone _____. Whether a woman's experience during this time is unhappy, or otherwise, depends largely on her _____.

menopause; 50

estrogen

attitude

27. Studies of developmental changes in learning and memory show that during early and middle adulthood, there is a decline in the ability to _____ new information. There is little decline in the ability to _____ new information, however.

recall

recognize

28. According to Erikson, the challenge during young adulthood is to achieve _____ with others. In middle age the challenge, in which one becomes less self-absorbed and more caring for the world, is called _____.

intimacy

generativity

29. Levinson has proposed a stage theory of adulthood in which there are early adult, midlife, and late adult _____, each of which is stressful but is then generally followed by a period of stability.

transitions

30. Contrary to popular opinion, job and marital dissatisfaction do not surge during the forties, thus suggesting that a midlife _____ need not occur.

crisis

31. The term used to refer to the culturally preferred timing for

leaving home, getting a job, marrying, and so on is the
_____ _____ .

social clock

32. According to Freud, the healthy adult is one who can
_____ and _____ .

love; work

33. The "traditional family" of father, mother, and children now encompasses only about _____ percent of American households.

30

34. For most couples, the children's leaving home produces a feeling of freedom and satisfaction with their relationship. Some, however, become distressed and sense a loss of purpose. This is called the _____ _____ syndrome.

empty nest

Later Life (pp. 104–110)

35. Although the elderly are _____ (more/less) subject to long-term ailments such as arthritis, they suffer short-term ailments such as flu _____ (more/less) often.

more

less

36. At birth, the average person has a life expectancy of _____ years. People who reach age 65 can expect to reach at least age _____ .

74

80

37. The disease that causes progressive senility is _____ disease. This disease has been linked to an insufficient supply of the neurotransmitter _____ .

Alzheimer's

acetylcholine

38. A research study in which people of various ages are tested at the same time is called a _____-_____ study.

cross-sectional

39. A research study in which the same people are retested over a period of years is called a _____ study.

longitudinal

40. The accumulation of stored information that comes with education and experience is called _____ intelligence. This ability tends to _____ with age.

crystallized

increase

41. The ability to reason abstractly is referred to as _____ intelligence. This capability tends to _____ with age.

fluid

decrease

42. Contrary to society's stereotype, during the retirement years satisfaction with life is generally _____ (high/low).

high

43. According to Erikson, the final task of adulthood is achieving a sense of _____ .

integrity

44. The theorist who proposed that dying patients experience an adjustment sequence of five stages is _____-_____. In her specified order, these stages are _____, _____, _____, _____, and _____.

Kübler-Ross

denial; anger
bargaining; depression
acceptance

Reflections on the Developmental Issues
(pp. 110–115)

45. Two factors known to influence development are _____ and _____.

genes; experience

46. The term that refers to the early personality or emotional excitability of a child is _____. Several studies have indicated that this characteristic may largely be determined by _____.

temperament

heredity

47. Three major theories considered in this chapter are the theory of cognitive development proposed by _____, the theory of moral development proposed by _____, and the theory of psychosocial development proposed by _____.

Piaget

Kohlberg

Erikson

48. Research on the consistency of personality shows that some traits, such as those that are related to _____ and _____, are more stable than others, such as social attitudes.

intelligence
temperament

FOCUS ON PSYCHOLOGY:
PASSAGES

Gail Sheehy has identified a number of life patterns that appear common. Among men, the most typical are:

Wunderkind. This male has an extremely high achievement motivation and often is a workaholic. He usually attains career success early in life. Career success may be combined with marriage, although the Wunderkind typically marries not for love, but for practical or status reasons.

Locked-in. This male makes both career and marriage commitments early, but does so without much self-examination. The locked-in male typically goes through life feeling comfortable and safe, but also held back and stifled.

Transient. This is the male who seems to avoid the usual social commitments of early adulthood, perhaps from a desire to avoid losing his youth.

Integrator. This pattern is, according to Sheehy, less common. It represents men who combine their career ambitions with genuine family commitment, including taking care of children.

In women, the following patterns are typical:

Caregiver. According to Sheehy, most women elect to be caregivers. Their focus in life is on human relations. Any personal ambitions are worked out through support of a close relation (typically a husband).

Integrator. This woman attempts to start a career, a marriage, and have children all at the same time. Sheehy reports that, while a significant number are able to do so successfully in their thirties, few are able to do so in their twenties.

Nurturer. This woman has career objectives in her twenties, but postpones achieving them in order to enter marriage and start a family.

Achiever. This woman defers starting a family until her career is well established.

Think about these life patterns. Why, as young adults, are there fewer male than female integrators? Why more female than male caregivers? Might these patterns reflect gender differences in how children are socialized? Which patterns best describe your mother and father? Which of these patterns do you presently feel best predicts *your* future?

PROGRESS TEST 1

Circle your answers to the following questions and check them with the answer key at the end of this chapter. Be sure to consult the appropriate pages of the text to understand the correct answer for any missed question.

1. According to Erikson, the central psychological challenges of adolescence, young adulthood, and middle age are:
a. identity formation; intimacy; generativity.
b. intimacy; identity formation; generativity.
c. generativity; intimacy; identity formation.
d. intimacy; generativity; identity formation.

2. Which theorist is most frequently associated with the study of stages of adult development?
a. Erikson
b. Levinson
c. Kohlberg
d. Gilligan

3. In Kübler-Ross's theory, which of the following is the correct sequence of stages?
a. denial; anger; bargaining; depression; acceptance

b. anger; denial; bargaining; depression; acceptance
c. depression; anger; denial; bargaining; acceptance
d. bargaining; anger; depression; denial; acceptance

4. In preconventional morality:
a. one obeys out of a sense of social duty.
b. one conforms to the rules of a higher social order.
c. one obeys to avoid punishment or to gain rewards.
d. one has internalized the fundamental human rights of a democracy.

5. Which of the following is correct?
a. There is no relationship between age of maturation and social development.
b. Early-maturing girls are more popular and self-assured than girls who mature late.
c. Early maturation places both boys and girls at a social disadvantage.
d. Early-maturing boys are more popular and self-assured than boys who mature late.

6. A person's general ability to think abstractly is called _____ intelligence. This ability generally _____ with age.
a. fluid; does not decrease
b. fluid; decreases
c. crystallized; decreases
d. crystallized; does not decrease

7. An elderly person who can look back on life with satisfaction and reminisce with a sense of completion is experiencing Erikson's stage of:
a. generativity.
b. intimacy.
c. integrity.
d. fulfillment.

8. According to Piaget, the abstract thinking required for the use of formal logic is indicative of the stage of:
a. preoperational thought.
b. concrete operations.
c. formal operations.
d. preconceptual thought.

9. Adolescence is marked by the onset of:
a. an identity crisis.
b. parent-child conflict.
c. the concrete operations stage.
d. puberty.

10. Memory tests have shown that the ability to _____ new information _____ during early and middle adulthood.
a. recall; declines
b. rehearse; declines
c. recognize; declines
d. learn; declines

11. Which of the following statements concerning the effects of aging is true?
a. Most elderly people eventually become senile.
b. Elderly people suffer more short-term ailments such as flu than do younger adults.
c. Among the elderly, there are 30 percent more widows than widowers.
d. Adults who remain active in their later years have more stamina than sedentary people.

12. The disorder that causes progressive senility in 5 to 10 percent of elderly people is:
a. Hodgkin's disease.
b. senility.
c. Alzheimer's disease.
d. neurogravia.

13. Administering a test to the same group of individuals at different ages is called a _____ study.
a. double blind
b. cross-sectional
c. longitudinal
d. retrospective

14. In Levinson's theory, during the mid-thirties depression and reassessment of life are common. This is referred to as the:
a. midlife crisis.
b. identity crisis.
c. menopause.
d. generativity crisis.

15. The stage of life during which menstruation stops is called:
a. menarche
b. menopause
c. the midlife crisis
d. early adulthood

FOCUS ON PSYCHOLOGY:
AND YOU'RE STILL SINGLE?

Most theories of adult development are based on the assumption that everyone will eventually get married. This obviously is not the case. Increasingly, psychologists are studying single adults and comparing them to those who are married, widowed, and divorced. Here are some of their findings:

1. The number of single adults has increased dramatically in the past 30 years. In the 1950s about 96 percent of adults eventually married; today psychologists estimate that only about 90 percent will.

2. More single adults are male than female. This difference holds until about age 65, after which, because of longer life expectancy, females outnumber males.

3. Single adults, particularly males, tend to have significantly more emotional problems than married adults.

4. Single women tend to be better educated and have higher IQs and better jobs than married women *and single men.*

5. Single men generally had much poorer family relationships than single women. (Single women do, however, often report having had difficult relationships with their mothers.)

Overall, among single adults, females fare better than males. Among married adults, however, men seem to be happier and mentally healthier than females. Several explanations have been proposed for these differences. One suggests that in males being single is less likely to be a voluntary state than it is in females. What other explanations can you think of for these differences? If this trend toward single adulthood continues, what impact do you predict it will have on society?

Source: Bee, H. L., and Mitchell, S. K. (1984). *The developing person: A life span approach* (2nd ed.). New York: Harper & Row.

PROGRESS TEST 2

Progress Test 2 should be completed during a final chapter review. Do so after you thoroughly understand the correct answers for the Chapter Review and Progress Test 1.

1. In Kübler-Ross's theory, the first stage in dealing with one's dying is:
a. anger.
b. denial.
c. depression.
d. acceptance.

2. The research method in which different groups of people are tested at a given period of time is called a _____ study.
a. cross-sectional
b. longitudinal
c. psychosocial
d. retrospective

3. The "social clock" refers to:
a. the distribution of work and leisure time.
b. adulthood responsibilities.
c. age norms for starting a career, marrying, etc.
d. age-related changes in one's circle of friends.

4. The term that refers to the rudiments of an individual's personality is:
a. ego.
b. identity.
c. temperament.
d. integrity.

5. In Erikson's theory, the crisis of integrity versus despair occurs during:
a. adolescence.
b. young adulthood.
c. middle adulthood.
d. late adulthood.

6. Which of the following is characteristic of the stage of formal operations?
a. It usually begins at about age 8.
b. It is attained by everyone sooner or later.
c. It is followed by the stage of concrete operations.
d. It includes an ability to think abstractly.

7. A sense of morality that affirms the existence of fundamental human rights characterizes which of Kohlberg's stages?

a. preconventional morality
b. conventional morality
c. postconventional morality
d. generative morality

8. In Erikson's theory, males normally form _____ during adolescence and then become concerned with developing _____ during young adulthood.
a. identity; intimacy
b. intimacy; identity
c. trust; identity
d. identity; trust

9. Which of the following is *not* a secondary sex characteristic?
a. breast development
b. pubic hair
c. a voice change
d. menstruation

10. After menopause, most women:
a. experience extreme anxiety and a sense of worthlessness.
b. lose their sexual interest.
c. show a bodily response in which the hormone estrogen is abnormally high.
d. feel a new sense of freedom.

11. Retention of which of the following types of material would show the greatest decline with aging?
a. the names of famous people
b. the names of places
c. nonsense syllables
d. the words to a new song

12. A person's accumulation of stored information, called _____ intelligence, generally _____ with age.
a. fluid; declines
b. fluid; increases
c. crystallized; declines
d. crystallized; increases

13. Skeptics of the theory that personality is determined solely by heredity point out that similarities between identical twins:
a. may merely be coincidences.
b. are not often found.

c. are found, but only for unimportant traits such as height and weight.

d. may result from recessive rather than dominant genes.

14. The mid-twenties are usually the peak years for all but which of the following?

a. physical strength

b. reaction time

c. recall memory

d. professional achievements

15. Moral development is associated most closely with which of the following?

a. perceptual development

b. physical development

c. emotional dependence

d. cognitive development

SAMPLE ESSAY QUESTIONS

1. Describe each of the stages of moral reasoning proposed by Kohlberg.

2. Describe the eight psychosocial crises proposed by Erikson.

3. Discuss why the idealistic attitudes typical of adolescence might reflect cognitive development during this stage.

4. Contrast longitudinal and cross-sectional studies. From the results of such studies, which traits remain stable, and which change with age?

5. State the major criticisms of the theories proposed by Piaget, Kohlberg, and Levinson.

PROJECT:
HOW LONG WILL YOU LIVE?

Psychologist Richard Schulz has developed a test for calculating how long you can expect to live. It is important to note that this is merely a rough guide; the contribution of each of biological, social, and psychological variables to life-span is *relative* rather than absolute.

Start with a basic life expectancy of 67 years if you are male and 75 years if you are female. If you are presently in your fifties or sixties, add 10 years. If you are over and still active, add 2 more years.

Family History

1. Add 5 years if two or more of your grandparents lived to 80 or beyond.

2. Subtract 4 years if any parent, grandparent, sister, or brother died of heart attack or stroke before 50.

3. Subtract 2 years if anyone died from these diseases before 60.

4. Subtract 3 years for each case of diabetes, thyroid disorders, breast cancer, cancer of the digestive system, asthma, or chronic bronchitis among parents or grandparents.

Marital Status

5. If you are married, add 4 years.

6. If you are over 25 and not married, subtract 1 year for every unwedded decade.

Economic Status

7. Subtract 2 years if your family income is over $40,000 per year.

8. Subtract 3 years if you have been poor for the greater part of life.

Physique

9. Subtract 1 year for every 10 pounds you are overweight.

10. For each inch your girth measurement exceeds your chest measurement, deduct 2 years.

11. Add 3 years if you are over 40 and are not overweight.

Exercise

12. Regular and moderate (jogging 3 times a week), add 3 years.

13. Regular and vigorous (long-distance running 3 times a week), add 5 years.

14. Subtract 3 years if your job is sedentary.

15. Add 3 years if your job is active.

Alcohol

16. Add 2 years if you are a light drinker (1–3 drinks a day).

17. Subtract 5 to 10 years if you are a heavy drinker (more than 4 drinks per day).

18. Subtract 1 year if you are a teetotaler.

Smoking

19. Two or more packs of cigarettes per day, subtract 8 years.

20. One to two packs per day, subtract 4 years.

21. Less than one pack, subtract 2 years.

22. Subtract 2 years if you regularly smoke a pipe or cigars.

Disposition

23. Add 2 years if you are a reasoned, practical person.

24. Subtract 2 years if you are aggressive, intense, and competitive.

25. Add 1–5 years if you are basically happy and content with life.

26. Subtract 1–5 years if you are often unhappy, worried, and often feel guilty.

Education

27. Less than high school, subtract 2 years.

28. Four years of school beyond high school, add 1 year.

29. Five or more years beyond high school, add 3 years.

Environment

30. If you have lived most of your life in a rural environment, add 4 years.

31. Subtract 2 years if you have lived most of your life in an urban environment.

Sleep

32. More than 9 hours a day, subtract 5 years.

Temperature

33. Add 2 years if your home's thermostat is set at no more than 68 degrees F.

Health Care

34. Regular medical checkups and regular dental care, add 3 years.

35. Frequently ill, subtract 2 years.

Source: From *The psychology of death, dying, and bereavement* by Richard Schulz. Copyright © 1978 by Richard Schulz. Reprinted by permission of Random House, Inc.

WHERE TO LOOK FOR MORE INFORMATION

Schulz, Richard (1978). *The psychology of death, dying, and bereavement*. Reading, Mass.: Addison-Wesley.

Schulz provides a clearly written critical analysis of current research on death and dying. Also presented is an explanation of the longevity test presented here.

Munn, Norman L. (1983). More on chance encounters and life paths. *American Psychologist, 38,* 351–352.

A psychologist reflects on the importance of a chance encounter in his own life.

Sheehy, Gail (1976). *Passages: Predictable crises of adult life.* New York: Dutton.

Sheehy describes the life patterns that typify the many men and women she interviewed.

ANSWERS

PROGRESS TEST 1

1. a (pp. 97, 100, 108)
2. b (p. 100)
3. a (p. 109)
4. c (p. 94)
5. d (p. 91)

6. b (p. 108)
7. c (p. 109)
8. c (p. 92)
9. d (p. 90)
10. a (p. 99)

11. d (p. 105)
12. c (p. 106)
13. c (p. 107)
14. a (p. 101)
15. b (p. 99)

PROGRESS TEST 2

1. b (p. 109)
2. a (p. 106)
3. c (p. 101)
4. c (p. 112)
5. d (p. 109)

6. d (p. 92)
7. c (p. 96)
8. a (p. 97)
9. d (p. 90)
10. d (p. 99)

11. c (p. 106)
12. d (p. 108)
13. a (p. 111)
14. d (p. 100)
15. d (p. 102)

CHAPTER 5

Gender

CHAPTER OVERVIEW

Few aspects of our lives are more central to our existence than our being born male or female. Chapter 5 explores how men and women differ, and the degree to which these differences are the result of biological, cultural, and social factors. The chapter also examines gender roles. Are they converging, can they converge, or should they be eliminated?

Although the chapter has relatively few terms to master, it presents a number of important discussion topics. Carefully writing out answers to the Study Guide objectives in the Guided Study section and sample essay questions should be particularly helpful to you in mastering the material in this chapter.

GUIDED STUDY

The text chapter should be studied one section at a time. Before you read, preview each section by skimming it, noting headings and boldface items. Then read the appropriate section objectives from the following outline. Keep these objectives in mind, and as you read the chapter section, search for the information that will complete each one. You may wish to write out answers for each objective as soon as you finish reading that section of the chapter.

Gender Differences (pp. 120–125)

1. Define gender identity and explain why gender differences, rather than similarities, are most often reported.

2. Identify the reported differences between the genders in each of the following.

a. aggression

b. social power

c. empathy

d. verbal and spatial abilities

3. Discuss how gender differences in these behaviors tend to increase and decrease over the life-span.

Why Do the Genders Differ? (pp. 125–134)

4. Explain how sociobiologists attempt to account for the evolution of gender differences.

5. State evidence that hormonal differences, such as in the production of testosterone, may account for male–female differences.

6. Describe gender differences in hemispheric specialization and explain several theories of their origin.

7. Discuss evidence for the social roots of gender

differences provided by cultural variations and cases of gender assignment.

8. Identify the central idea behind each of the following theories of gender typing.

  a. identification theory

  b. cognitive-developmental theory

  c. social learning theory

  d. gender schema theory

9. Define gender role and explain how gender role expectations influence behavior.

10. Define androgyny and discuss evidence that traditional gender role differences are weakening.

CHAPTER REVIEW

When you have finished reading the chapter, complete the sentences that follow. Using your hand or a strip of paper, cover the correct answers in the margin and fill in each blank. Verify your answer by uncovering the correct one. As you proceed, evaluate your performance for each chapter section. *Do not continue with the next section until you understand why each margin term is the correct answer.* If you need to, go back and review or re-read the appropriate chapter section in the text before continuing.

1. The individual's sense of being male or female is called _____ _____ .

gender identity

Gender Differences (pp. 120–125)

2. For many traits, variation _____ (between/within) gender(s) is greater than variation _____ (between/within) gender(s).

within

between

3. Several lines of research suggest that the more aggressive gender is _____ .

masculine

4. Salary differences and political elections demonstrate that greater social power is held by the _____ gender.

masculine

5. The ability to understand and feel another person's feelings is called _____ .

empathy

6. When surveyed, women are more likely than men to describe themselves as empathic. In the laboratory, the difference in empathy is _____ (larger/smaller).

smaller

7. On tests of verbal abilities, women tend to score _____ than men.

higher

8. Speech defects such as stuttering occur mostly in _____ .

boys or men

9. On tasks requiring spatial abilities, the performance of _____ tends to be superior.

males

10. Boys and girls begin to prefer different types of games and toys during _____ .

infancy

11. Gender differences in aggression and social power appear by about age _____ .

social concern

12. Psychologist Carol Gilligan believes that the tendency for girls to be more cooperative and sharing than boys at play reflects the rudiments of a greater _____ _____ among adult women.

13. The superior verbal abilities of females become apparent during _____ .

adolescence

14. Personality differences between men and women peak in early _____ .

adulthood

15. Women often become more assertive, and men more emotionally expressive and less domineering, during _____ _____ .

middle age

16. The theory that people develop previously repressed characteristics of the opposite gender during the second half of life was proposed by _____ .

Jung

Why Do the Genders Differ? (pp. 125–134)

17. Sociobiologists argue that gender differences in aggressiveness, spatial abilities, and social power reflect _____ predispositions.

genetic

18. Sociobiology has been criticized for providing a rationalization of traditional gender differences and for offering _____ _____ explanations.

after-the-fact

19. In most mammals, the greatest amount of parental care is performed by the _____ .

female

20. As one moves up the evolutionary scale, fatherly involvement in parental care becomes _____ (more/less) variable.

more

21. The principal male sex hormone is _____ .

testosterone

22. Without sufficient testosterone, the embryo continues to develop as a _____ .

female

23. Genetic females who are prenatally exposed to overdoses of testosterone tend to exhibit more _____ behavior.

masculine

24. Violent criminals have been found to have levels of testosterone that are _____ than normal.

higher

25. One researcher has suggested that the tendency of mathematical "whiz kids" to be left-handed, nearsighted, and to suffer from allergies

2 or 3

or asthma may be linked with excess male _____ during prenatal development.

hormone

26. Researchers have found that male and female animal brains are noticeably different in the regions involved in _____, _____, and _____ behavior.

sexual
maternal; aggressive

27. The left hemisphere's specialization for language is _____ (more/less) pronounced in women than in men.

less

28. One theory proposes that the male's asymmetrical brain might be due to his slower _____ maturation.

physical

29. Studies of gender reassignment demonstrate that gender identity is primarily a _____ fact.

social

30. The extent to which the individual displays traditionally defined gender-role behavior is called _____-_____.

gender-typing

31. Freud referred to a child's unconscious adoption of the characteristics of the same-sex parent as _____.

identification

32. Freud's theory has been disputed, in part because children become gender-typed well before age _____.

5 or 6

33. Children typically _____ (do/do not) become gender-typed when the same-sex parent is not present.

do

34. The theory that children acquire gender-typed behaviors by observing others, and through rewards and punishments, is the _____ _____ theory.

social learning

35. In recognition of the child's active participation in the gender-typing process, Kohlberg proposed a _____-_____ theory.

cognitive-developmental

36. Kohlberg's theory suggests that a child's concept of gender matures along with his or her _____ ability.

cognitive

37. Bem has combined the social learning and cognitive-developmental theories into the _____ _____ theory.

gender schema

38. Bem believes that principles of cognitive development best explain the _____ of gender-typing, while the social learning approach best explains the _____ of gender typing.

process
content

39. The set of expected sex-related behaviors is referred to as a person's _____ _____ .

gender role

40. An examination of different societies points out that there are many _____ variations in gender roles.

cultural

41. The possession of both masculine and feminine qualities is called _____ .

androgyny

42. Research has shown that, in both men and women, positive self-esteem is linked to _____ traits.

masculine

43. Studies have indicated that marital satisfaction is higher in couples when one or both partners possesses _____ traits.

feminine

FOCUS ON PSYCHOLOGY:
SEXISM IN THE MASS MEDIA

Several studies have shown that males and females are often portrayed differently by the media, a situation that tends to perpetuate sexist stereotypes. In one study, Archer, Kimes, and Barrios (1978) evaluated 1750 photographs of individuals appearing in the advertisements and articles of various national magazines. With striking consistency, the results indicated that publications tended to emphasize the faces of men and the bodies of women: Less than half the average photograph of a woman was devoted to her face; about two-thirds of a man's photograph was devoted to his face. The authors found that this "face-ism" effect also occurred in college students asked to draw pictures capturing the "character of a real person." Both male and female students emphasized the man's face, drawing it about twice as large and in greater detail than the woman's. The authors suggest that these results reflect a disturbing tendency to view women more in terms of their physical characteristics, and men in terms of their personalities and intellects. Other studies have demonstrated that sexist stereotyping is also prevalent in television programs and even occurs in elementary school textbooks. Look for examples of sexist stereotyping in the media. Do you feel that such stereotyping is becoming more or less prevalent?

PROGRESS TEST 1

Circle your answers to the following questions and check them with the answer key at the end of this chapter. Be sure to consult the appropriate pages of the text to understand the correct answer for any missed question.

1. An individual's personal sense of being male or female is called:
a. gender type.
b. gender role.
c. gender identity.
d. gender.

2. In one experiment, people judged an infant's reaction to a jack-in-the-box. Those who were told the infant was a girl perceived the infant's reaction as fear; those told the infant was a boy perceived the reaction as anger. Which of the following conclusions may be drawn from this study?
a. Gender differences in emotionality are biologically based.
b. There are no gender differences in emotionality.
c. Girls are naturally more fearful than boys.
d. Just knowing a person's gender often elicits certain perceptions.

3. Which of the following is correct?
a. The belief that males tend to be more aggressive than females is not validated in laboratory experiments.
b. Throughout the world, hunting, fighting, and making war are primarily men's activities.
c. Cross-culturally there is no gender difference in aggressiveness.

d. Men commit more crimes than women, but not necessarily more violent crimes.

4. An example of androgyny would be:

a. parents for whom gender is irrelevant in performing household chores.

b. the woman who prides herself on her femininity.

c. the woman who demands to be treated as a man.

d. the "macho man."

5. As compared with girls, boys generally excel on tasks involving:

a. verbal skills.

b. social skills.

c. spatial skills.

d. musical skills.

6. In the Jacklin-Maccoby study, preschool girls who played with a boy partner:

a. tended to dominate play, due to their superior size.

b. tended to dominate play, due to their superior verbal skills.

c. reacted no differently from those who played with a girl.

d. tended to retreat or quietly watch the boy play with the toys.

7. Which statement best describes the relationship between gender differences and the life-span?

a. Gender differences first increase, then decrease.

b. Gender differences increase throughout the life-span.

c. Gender differences remain constant.

d. There is no consistent relationship between the two.

8. According to the theory of sociobiology, gender differences:

a. reflect the transmission of culture from generation to generation.

b. are biologically based and reflect the processes of natural selection and evolution.

c. are rather small in lower animals, but increase as one ascends the evolutionary scale.

d. decrease as one moves from the lower animals to humans.

9. Genetically, female animals given testosterone before birth:

a. continue to develop as normal females in all respects.

b. develop a masculine appearance, but retain female behavior patterns.

c. retain a feminine appearance, but develop masculine behavior patterns.

d. develop both masculine appearance and behavior patterns.

10. Which of the following is *not* true?

a. Violent criminals tend to have higher than normal levels of testosterone.

b. Aggressiveness can be manipulated by administering testosterone.

c. The relationship between testosterone and aggression occurs in a variety of cultures.

d. The relationship between testosterone and aggression is not found in animals.

11. Which of the following would result in the greatest impairment in verbal intelligence?

a. a right hemisphere injury in a male

b. a right hemisphere injury in a female

c. a left hemisphere injury in a male

d. a left hemisphere injury in a female

12. Which of the following is true concerning brain differences in men and women?

a. In all respects, male brains function more symmetrically than female brains.

b. In all respects, female brains function more symmetrically than male brains.

c. In some respects, female brains function more symmetrically than male brains.

d. None of the above is true.

13. The theory that children become gender-typed through identification with the same-sex parent was proposed by:

a. Bem.

b. Skinner.

c. Jung.

d. Freud.

14. Which theory proposes that children acquire gender roles through reinforcement, observation, and imitation?

a. identification

b. social learning

c. cognitive-developmental

d. gender schema

15. According to Bem, in order to raise a gender-aschematic child, a parent should:

a. make gender irrelevant to job assignments at home.

b. completely reverse the traditional gender roles at home.

c. raise the child with one domineering parent.

d. encourage and reward strongly gender-typed behaviors.

FOCUS ON PSYCHOLOGY:
MALE-ORIENTED PSYCHOLOGY

Psychological research on sex differences in behavior may in fact reflect nothing more than the bias of the experimenters themselves. During the early part of this century, for example, a major controversy centered about the relative intelligence of men and women. One research method involved measuring the size of the brain regions believed to be related to intelligence. The sizes in men and women would be compared, and the larger region would provide proof of that gender's intellectual superiority. As Mary Brown Parlee notes: "Most of the research studies had severe methodological problems. Researchers conducting autopsies, for example, often knew whether the brain they were examining came from a man or a woman *before* they measured it; the information could clearly have affected their judgment." The extent of this bias in interpretation is illustrated by the fact that estimates of the relative sizes of different brain regions in men and women shifted as opinion regarding the seat of the intellect in the brain changed. When the parietal lobes were considered most important, these regions were found to be larger in males. When other regions became the focal points of researchers' interests, they were discovered to be larger in males.

Zick Rubin (1981) provides other examples of historical sex bias in psychology. In personality and social psychology research, males are used as subjects about twice as often as females. Despite this selectivity, the results are generalized to both males and females, leading to the tendency to establish "male" behavior as the norm for all people. In addition,

males and females are selected for study on the basis of traditional gender stereotypes. Men are far more likely than women to be involved in studies of aggression; for studies of interpersonal attraction, the reverse is true. As Rubin notes: "As long as researchers' stereotypes affect their procedures in such ways, it is likely that the results of research will simply perpetuate the stereotypes." How widespread do you believe such biases are? What procedures should researchers follow in order to guard against such methodological errors?

PROGRESS TEST 2

Progress Test 2 should be completed during a final chapter review. Do this after you thoroughly understand the correct answers for the Chapter Review and Progress Test 1.

1. A flaw in the identification theory is that children may become gender-typed:

a. even in the absence of a same-sex parent.

b. well before the age of 10.

c. well after the age proposed by Freud.

d. at different ages, depending on the culture.

2. Kohlberg's theory that a child's concept of gender changes as the child matures is called the _____ theory.

a. identification

b. social learning

c. cognitive-developmental

d. gender schema

3. Androgyny refers to:

a. an individual who exhibits strongly gender-typed behaviors.

b. the behavior of genetic females who received higher than normal doses of testosterone prenatally.

c. an individual who engages in gender role reversal.

d. an individual's possession of both masculine and feminine qualities.

4. Research has shown that positive self-esteem tends to be linked to the possession of:

a. feminine traits.

b. masculine traits.

c. androgyny.

d. strongly gender-typed traits.

5. Which of the following is true?

a. In both self-report and laboratory studies, women show more empathy than men.

b. Men are more empathic than women.

c. In self-reports, but less consistently in the laboratory, women are more empathic than men.

d. In self-reports, but less consistently in the laboratory, men are more empathic than women.

6. On the scholastic aptitude test (SAT):

a. males have higher average scores than females overall.

b. males have higher average scores than females on the verbal portion.

c. males have higher average scores than females on the mathematical portion.

d. females have higher average scores on the mathematical portion.

7. The game and toy choices of infants:

a. do not yet show gender differences.

b. are already beginning to show gender differences.

c. are predictable by age but not by gender.

d. are not at all predictable.

8. Children who have had their gender reassigned:

a. tend not to accept their new identity.

b. only with great difficulty accept their new identity.

c. accept their new identity with relative ease.

d. tend to develop a gender confusion which persists throughout their lives.

9. Bem has found that people with the strongest gender schemas tend to:

a. be androgynous.

b. be strongly gender-typed.

c. experience gender identity confusion.

d. be oblivious to gender.

10. The set of expected behaviors for males and females is called:

a. gender assignment.

b. gender.

c. gender identity.

d. gender role.

11. Antill found that, among married couples:

a. marital satisfaction was highest in strongly gender-typed couples.

b. marital satisfaction was highest when the female possessed some masculine traits.

c. marital satisfaction was highest when the female was extremely feminine.

d. marital satisfaction was highest when either or both spouses possessed some feminine traits.

12. A person's gender is:

a. a biological fact.

b. a social fact.

c. a cultural fact.

d. all of the above.

13. In her gender schema theory, Bem proposes that:

a. gender identity has biological roots.

b. children become gender-typed despite their environments.

c. children form a concept of gender and evaluate themselves against it.

d. androgynous individuals were probably raised in a single-parent home.

14. Which of the following statements concerning gender differences is true?

a. For most traits, individual differences greatly exceed gender differences.

b. Most gender differences do not become obvious until adulthood.

c. Gender differences peak in late adulthood.

d. No consistent evidence has been found for a gender-based difference in any ability.

15. Which of the following best describes the current trend in traditional gender roles?

a. No change in attitudes or behavior has taken place.

b. Attitude but not behavioral change has occurred.

c. Gender roles have, if anything, diverged even more.

d. Gender roles have been changing, but have not been eliminated.

SAMPLE ESSAY QUESTIONS

1. Discuss whether traditional gender roles are changing.

2. Describe gender differences in brain functioning and explain several theories of their origin.

3. Contrast the identification, social learning, cognitive-developmental, and gender schema theories of gender-typing.

4. Identify how males and females differ in aggressiveness, verbal and spatial abilities, and empathy.

5. In what ways do gender differences appear to be related to an individual's age? Why do you think this is so?

PROJECT:
GENDER DIFFERENCES

Answer Yes or No to each of the following questions.

_____ **1.** Are females more "social" than males?

_____ **2.** Are females more susceptible to persuasion than males?

_____ **3.** Are males more aggressive than females?

_____ **4.** Do females have greater verbal ability than males?

_____ **5.** Are females better than males at simple repetitive tasks?

_____ **6.** Do males have greater analytical ability than females?

_____ **7.** Do males have greater mathematical ability than females?

_____ **8.** Do males have higher self-esteem than females?

_____ **9.** Do females have a lower motivation to achieve than males?

_____ **10.** Are males better than females on high-level tasks?

List five adjectives you would normally use to describe men and five you would use for women.

Men   *Women*

_____   _____

_____   _____

_____   _____

_____   _____

After reviewing several thousand books and journal articles on gender differences in behavior, Maccoby and Jacklin concluded that the correct answers to these questions are: (1) no; (2) no; (3) yes; (4) yes; (5) no; (6) no; (7) yes; (8) no; (9) no; (10) no.

How many of the questions did you answer correctly? If you missed any, do you think your errors might reflect traditional stereotypes of your own or of the opposite gender? Verbally administer this questionnaire to five male and five female friends who are not in your psychology class. Tabulate the results separately for males and females. Is there a gender difference in the number of questions missed? Are there consistencies in which questions males and females answer incorrectly? Do these reflect traditional gender stereotypes?

Review each of the adjectives you and your respondents assigned for men and women. Are there consistencies that reflect gender stereotypes? How do you think your behavior toward men and women is affected by these stereotypes?

Source: Maccoby, E. E., and Jacklin, C. N. (1974). *The psychology of sex differences*. Stanford, Calif.: Stanford University Press.

WHERE TO LOOK FOR MORE INFORMATION

Archer, D., Limes, D., and Barrios, M. (1978, September). Face-ism. *Psychology Today.*
This article discusses differences in how men and women are represented in the mass media.

Maccoby, E. E., and Jacklin, C. N. (1974, December). What we know and don't know about sex differences. *Psychology Today.*

Parlee, M. (1978, November). The sexes under scrutiny: From old biases to new theories. *Psychology Today.*

Rubin, Z., and McNeil, E. (1981). *The psychology of being human.* New York: Harper & Row.
Rubin discusses sex bias in psychological research.

ANSWERS

PROGRESS TEST 1

1. c (p. 121)
2. d (p. 121)
3. b (p. 121)
4. a (p. 133)
5. c (p. 123)

6. d (p. 124)
7. a (pp. 124–125)
8. b (p. 126)
9. d (pp. 126–127)
10. d (p. 127)

11. c (p. 127)
12. c (p. 127)
13. d (p. 129)
14. b (pp. 129–130)
15. a (p. 133)

PROGRESS TEST 2

1. a (p. 129)
2. c (pp. 129–130)
3. d (p. 133)
4. b (p. 133)
5. c (p. 122)

6. c (p. 123)
7. b (p. 124)
8. c (p. 128)
9. b (pp. 130–131)
10. d (p. 131)

11. d (p. 133)
12. d (p. 120)
13. c (p. 130)
14. a (pp. 120–121)
15. d (p. 132)

PART THREE

EXPERIENCING THE WORLD

CHAPTER 6

Sensation

CHAPTER OVERVIEW

Sensation refers to the process by which stimuli are detected and experienced. This chapter describes the sensations of vision, hearing, taste, touch, smell, kinesthesis, and equilibrium. It also presents research findings from studies of sensory restriction and subliminal perception.

There are many terms to learn and several theories you must understand. Many of the terms are related to the structure of the eye, ear, and other sensory receptors. Doing the chapter review several times, labeling the diagrams, and frequent rehearsal will help you to memorize these structures and their functions. The theories discussed include signal detection, the Young-Helmholtz and opponent-process theories of color vision, and two theories of pitch (frequency and place theories). As you study these theories, concentrate on trying to understand the strengths and weaknesses (if any) of each.

GUIDED STUDY

The text chapter should be studied one section at a time. Before you read, preview each section by skimming it, noting headings and boldface items. Then read the appropriate section objectives from the following outline. Keep these objectives in mind, and as you read the chapter section, search for the informa-

tion that will complete each one. You may wish to write out answers for each objective as soon as you finish reading that section of the chapter.

Sensing the World: Some Basic Principles
(pp. 140–144)

1. Define and distinguish the processes of sensation and perception.

2. Compare and contrast absolute and difference thresholds.

3. Discuss whether sensory information can be processed without conscious awareness.

4. Explain Weber's law and how difference thresholds are used to compare the sensitivities of different sensory modalities.

5. Define sensory adaptation.

Seeing (pp. 144–152)

6. Define and distinguish the following physical characteristics of light.

  a. wavelength

  b. hue

  c. intensity

  d. brightness

  e. complexity

  f. saturation

7. Describe the location of and state the function performed by each of the following parts of the eye.

a. pupil

b. iris

c. lens

d. retina

e. rods and cones

f. optic nerve

8. Explain the similarities between the eye and a camera.

9. Describe the function of feature detectors in visual perception.

10. Explain the causes of nearsightedness, farsightedness, and the decrease in visual acuity associated with aging.

11. State the differences in the visual sensitivity of rods and cones and explain how the eye adapts to darkness.

12. Describe the following theories of color vision:

a. Young-Helmholtz three-color theory

b. opponent-process theory

Hearing (pp. 152–155)

13. Define and distinguish the following physical characteristics of sound.

a. frequency

b. amplitude

c. complexity

14. State the function performed by each of the following parts of the ear.

a. outer ear

b. eardrum

c. middle ear

d. cochlea

15. Compare and contrast the place and frequency theories of pitch perception.

16. Explain how sounds are localized and why some sounds are more difficult to locate than others.

17. Distinguish conduction deafness from nerve deafness.

18. Discuss the psychological effects of noise.

The Other Senses (pp. 155–159)

19. List the primary sensations of touch and taste and explain the phenomenon of sensory interaction.

20. Contrast the senses of kinesthesis and equilibrium.

Sensory Restriction (pp. 159–160)

21. Discuss the psychological effects of restricted sensory input.

CHAPTER REVIEW

When you have finished reading the chapter, complete the sentences that follow. Using your hand or a strip of paper, cover the correct answers in the margin and fill in each blank. Verify your answer by uncovering the correct one. As you proceed, evaluate your performance for each chapter section. *Do not continue with the next section until you understand why each margin term is the correct answer.* If you need to, go back and review or re-read the appropriate chapter section in the text before continuing.

Sensing the World: Some Basic Principles (pp. 140–144)

1. The process by which a stimulus is detected and coded is _____. The mental process by which sensations are organized and interpreted is _____.

sensation

perception

2. The absolute _____ refers to the minimum amount of stimulation necessary for a sensation to be detected _____ percent of the time.

threshold

50

3. The theory that absolute thresholds depend not only on the signal but also on a person's psychological state is the _____ _____ theory.

signal detection

4. Some people claim to have experienced "below threshold," or _____, perception; but their claims are probably unwarranted.

subliminal

5. Although stimuli may be too weak to cross our threshold for conscious awareness, they may be strong enough to elicit a response in our _____ cells.

receptor

6. The minimum difference required to distinguish two stimuli 50 percent of the time is called the _____ _____.

difference threshold

7. Another term for this value is the _____ _____ _____.

just noticeable difference

8. The principle that the difference threshold is not a constant amount but a constant percentage is known as _____ _____.

Weber's law

9. After constant exposure to a stimulus, the receptor cells of our senses begin to fire less vigorously; this phenomenon is called _____ _____.

sensory adaptation

Seeing (pp. 144–152)

10. In the process of transduction, stimulus energy is converted into _____ activity.

neural

11. The visible spectrum of light is a small portion of the larger spectrum of _____ waves.

electromagnetic

12. The distance from one light wave peak to the next is called _____. This value determines the wave's color, or _____.

wavelength

hue

13. The amount of energy, or _____, determines the _____ of a light.

intensity

brightness

14. The mixture of wavelengths, or _____, determines a light's colorfulness, or _____.

complexity

saturation

In the following diagram, label each numbered part of the eye.

15. _____   pupil

16. _____   iris

17. _____   lens

18. _____   retina

19. _____   blind spot

20. _____   fovea

21. _____   optic nerve

22. Light enters the eye through a small opening called the _____; the size of this opening is controlled by the colored _____.   pupil

iris

23. By changing its curvature, the _____ can focus the image of an object onto the _____, lying at the back of the eyeball.   lens

retina

24. The process by which the lens changes shape to focus light is called _____.   accommodation

25. The retina's receptor cells are the _____ and _____.   rods

cones

26. From the rods and cones, the neural signals pass to the neighboring _____ cells, then to a network of _____ cells.   bipolar

ganglion

27. The ganglion cells converge to form the _____ _____, which carries the visual information to the _____.   optic nerve

brain

28. Where this nerve leaves the eye, there are no receptors; thus the area is called the _____ _____.   blind spot

29. There are approximately _____ million cones.   6

30. Most cones are clustered around the point of central focus, called the _____, whereas the rods are concentrated in the _____ region of the retina.   fovea

outer

31. Most cones have their own individual _____ cell to communicate with the visual cortex.   bipolar

32. Hubel and Wiesel discovered that neurons in the _____ of the brain respond only to specific features   cortex

of what is viewed. They called these neurons _____ _____ .
feature detectors

33. Clarity or sharpness of vision is called _____ .
acuity

34. If you have blurred vision for distant objects, then you are _____ and your eyeball is _____ than normal.
nearsighted; longer

35. If you have blurred vision for close objects, then you are _____ and your eyeball is _____ than normal.
farsighted; shorter

36. As we age, the lens _____ , and the eye tends to become _____ .
hardens
farsighted

37. In addition, as we age, the retina receives less light, due to a reduction in the diameter of the _____ .
pupil

38. Unlike cones, in dim light the rods are _____ (sensitive/insensitive).
sensitive

39. Adapting to a darkened room will take the retina approximately _____ minutes.
20

40. A visual image fixated on the same retinal spot will soon _____ .
disappear

41. According to the Young-Helmholtz theory, the eyes have three color receptors: one that reacts most strongly to _____ , one to _____ , and one to _____ .
red; green
blue

42. After staring at a green square for a while, you will see the color _____ , its _____ color.
red; opponent

43. Hering's theory of color vision is called the _____-_____ theory.
opponent-process

44. According to this theory, after visual information leaves the receptors, it is analyzed in terms of pairs of opponent colors: _____ versus _____ , and _____ versus _____ .
red; green
yellow; blue

Hearing (pp. 152–155)

45. Sound energy consists of _____- _____ waves.
air-pressure

46. The pitch of a sound is derived from the _____ of its wave.
frequency

47. The amplitude of a sound wave corresponds to the sound's _____.

loudness

48. The complexity of a sound wave corresponds to its purity, or _____.

timbre

49. The ear is divided into three parts: the _____ ear, the _____ ear, and the _____ ear.

outer
middle; inner

50. The outer ear channels air-pressure changes toward the _____, a membrane that vibrates with sound waves.

eardrum

51. The middle ear amplifies the sound via the vibrations of three small bones: the _____, _____, and _____.

hammer; anvil
stirrup

52. In the inner ear, a coiled tube called the _____ contains the receptor cells for hearing.

cochlea

53. One theory of pitch perception proposes that different pitches activate different places on the cochlea's membrane; this is the _____ theory.

place

54. This theory has difficulty accounting for how we hear _____-pitched sounds, which do not have such localized effects.

low

55. A second theory proposes that neural impulses, sent to the brain at the same frequency as the sound wave, allow the perception of different pitches. This is the _____ theory.

frequency

56. This theory fails to account for the perception of _____-pitched sounds, because individual neurons cannot fire faster than _____ times per second.

high
1000

57. For the higher pitches, cells may alternate their firing to match the sound's frequency, according to the _____ principle.

volley

58. Sound travels at approximately _____ miles per hour.

750

59. Sounds that come from directly ahead, behind, overhead, or beneath our ears are difficult to _____, because they strike the two ears simultaneously.

localize

60. Conduction deafness refers to problems in mechanical conduction in the _____ ear.

middle

61. Problems in the cochlea or the auditory nerve can cause _____ deafness.

nerve

62. This type of hearing loss is greatest in the _____ frequency ranges.

higher

63. Studies have shown that noise may affect not only our hearing, but our behavior as well. Studies by Glass and Singer have shown that _____ noise is the most upsetting.

unpredictable

The Other Senses (pp. 155–159)

64. The sense of touch is actually a mixture of four senses: _____, _____, _____, and _____.

pressure; warmth
cold; pain

65. The four basic taste sensations are: _____, _____, _____, and _____.

sweet
sour; salty
bitter

66. Taste receptors are concentrated in different areas. Sweet and salty spots are at the _____ of the tongue; bitter at the _____ of the tongue.

tip
back

67. When the sense of smell is blocked, as when we have a cold, foods do not taste the same; this illustrates _____ at work.

sensory interaction

68. Like taste, smell is a _____ sense.

chemical

69. The system for sensing the position and movement of body parts is called _____.

kinesthesis

70. The sense that monitors the movement of the whole body is _____.

equilibrium

71. The receptors for kinesthesis are located all over the body in _____, _____, and _____.

muscles; tendons
joints

72. The receptors for equilibrium are located in the _____ canals of the _____ ear.

semicircular; inner

73. Some psychologists have found that people attempting to control their smoking or eating may benefit from sessions of _____ restriction.

sensory

FOCUS ON PSYCHOLOGY:
HEALTH BENEFITS OF LIGHT

Scientists in the field of photobiology (the study of the effects of light on plants and animals) have begun to believe that light may be important not only for vision, but for mental and physical health as well. Some believe that the winter depression experienced by many people may result from a lack of exposure to sunlight during the shorter daylight hours of winter. In one instance, a patient's depression was alleviated after artificial light was used for several days to lengthen the patient's winter day. Although the effects of light on mood are far from conclusive, light is being used to treat various blood and skin diseases, and to control seasonal behavior in animals. Farmers, for example, have long known that egg production can be increased through the use of artificial light, which simulates the longer days of spring and triggers hormonal responses in chickens. The control system for this light-behavior circuit is the pineal gland of the brain; in some animals, this gland varies its production of the hormone melatonin in direct response to the amount of daylight. Research has shown that the hormonal system of humans also responds to light—a fact that is intriguing to psychologists studying seasonal variations in such behaviors as depression and suicide.

Researchers are also investigating the effects of fluorescent lighting on office workers. Overexposure to it is believed by some to contribute to the demineralization of bones. Unlike natural light, fluorescent bulbs emit light deficient in the ultraviolet and blue-green wavelengths, the wavelengths that help the body absorb calcium. In addition, several studies suggest that ultraviolet light may contribute to skin cancer. Further research into the effects of various wavelengths of light is clearly needed before findings can be considered conclusive. While these issues remain controversial, scientists are speculating that light may prove useful in the prevention of certain diseases and in the treatment of jet lag, sleep disorders, and other emotional disturbances.

PROGRESS TEST 1

Circle your answers to the following questions and check them with the answer key at the end of this chapter. Be sure to consult the appropriate pages of the text to understand the correct answer for any missed question.

Multiple-Choice Questions

1. Which of the following is true?
   a. The absolute threshold in any sensory modality is a constant.
   b. The absolute threshold in any sensory modality varies somewhat.
   c. The absolute threshold is defined as the minimum amount of stimulation necessary for a sensation to be detected 75 percent of the time.
   d. The absolute threshold is defined as the minimum amount of stimulation necessary for a sensation to be detected 60 percent of the time.

2. Stimuli that are too weak to cross the threshold for conscious awareness:
   a. may trigger a small response in sense receptors.
   b. will be processed fully by the unconscious.
   c. will not be processed at all.
   d. do none of the above.

3. If you can just notice the difference between 10- and 11-pound weights, which of the following could you differentiate from a 100-pound weight?
   a. 101 lb
   b. 105 lb
   c. 110 lb
   d. There is no basis for prediction.

4. A decrease in sensory responsiveness accompanying an unchanging stimulus is called:
   a. sensory fatigue.
   b. potentiation.
   c. sensitization.
   d. sensory adaptation.

5. The size of the pupil is controlled by the:
   a. lens.
   b. retina.
   c. cornea.
   d. iris.

6. The process by which the lens changes its curvature is:

a. accommodation.
b. assimilation.
c. focusing.
d. transduction.

7. The receptor of the eye that functions best in dim light is the:
a. fovea.
b. rod.
c. cone.
d. bipolar cell.

8. The Young-Helmholtz theory proposes that:
a. there are three different types of color-sensitive cones.
b. retinal cells are excited by one color and inhibited by its complementary color.
c. there are four different types of cones.
d. rod, not cone, vision accounts for the greatest acuity.

9. Frequency is to pitch as _____ is to _____.
a. wavelength; loudness
b. amplitude; loudness
c. wavelength; volume
d. amplitude; volume

10. The receptors for hearing are located:
a. in the outer ear.
b. in the middle ear.
c. in the inner ear.
d. throughout the ear.

11. The place theory of pitch perception does not account for how we hear:
a. low-pitched sounds.
b. middle-pitched sounds.
c. high-pitched sounds.
d. chords (two pitches simultaneously).

12. The hearing losses that occur with age are especially pronounced for:
a. low-pitched sounds.
b. middle-pitched sounds.
c. high-pitched sounds.
d. chords.

Matching Items

Match each of the structures with its function.

_____ 1. lens
_____ 2. iris
_____ 3. pupil
_____ 4. rods
_____ 5. cones
_____ 6. middle ear
_____ 7. inner ear
_____ 8. tip of tongue
_____ 9. back of tongue
_____ 10. semicircular canals
_____ 11. sensors in joints

a. amplifies sound
b. sweet receptors
c. equilibrium sense
d. controls pupil
e. accommodation
f. kinesthesis
g. bitter receptors
h. admits light
i. color vision
j. vision in dim light
k. transduction of sound

FOCUS ON PSYCHOLOGY:
BIONIC SENSES

The retina of the eye is responsible for changing light energy into nerve impulses, but the occipital region of the brain is where the sensations of vision occur. Vision can therefore occur without stimulation of the eye by light. For example, if you close your eyes and gently press on them, you will see spots of light called phosphenes. The pressure is converted into nerve impulses which stimulate the brain, simulating a visual experience. Similarly, a blow to the back region of the head will cause one to "see stars," again as a result of stimulation of the visual areas of the occipital lobe. These phenomena suggest that, even though a person may be blind as a result of an eye injury or a damaged optic nerve, as long as the occipital region is intact, it should be possible to elicit visual sensations through direct stimulation of the brain. In one study, an array of 64 electrodes was implanted in the occipital region of a man blinded for several decades by a damaged retina. With a television camera connected, the video image was converted into a pattern of electrical impulses. When the electrodes were activated, the subject reported seeing spots of light in his visual field. Although such systems are only in the earliest stages of development, some have enabled individuals to discriminate letters and simple shapes. The drawing below illustrates a prototype of a system in which a tiny camera and computer are mounted in a glass eye and eyeglass frame, allowing the person to detect shapes and thus giving him or her much greater freedom of movement (Dobell, 1977).

A similar system is being produced for those who have lost their hearing because disease has destroyed the cochlea of the inner ear. Normally, the cochlea converts sound energy into nerve impulses, which pass through the auditory nerve to the brain. The Ineraid system consists of eight tiny wires implanted in the skull. A small microphone in the ear connects to a miniature computer the person wears on a belt. Sound picked up by the microphone is converted into electrical impulses by the computer, which are then fed into the auditory nerve. Using this system, some deaf persons have regained as much as 70 percent of their hearing.

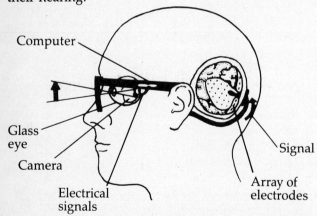

Computer

Glass
eye

Camera

Electrical
signals

Signal

Array of
electrodes

Source: Dobelle, William H. (1977). "Current status of research on providing sight to the blind by electrical stimulation of the brain," *Journal of Visual Impairment and Blindness, 71*(7), pp. 290–297. Reprinted by permission of the American Foundation for the Blind.

PROGRESS TEST 2

Progress Test 2 should be completed during a final chapter review. Do this after you thoroughly under-

stand the correct answers for the Chapter Review and Progress Test 1.

Multiple-Choice Questions

1. Glass and Singer found that noise was most stressful:
   a. when it was repetitive and predictable.
   b. when it was unpredictable.
   c. when it was high in frequency.
   d. when it was a rhythmic, low-frequency sound.

2. Of the four distinct skin senses:
   a. only warmth has a definable receptor.
   b. only cold has a definable receptor.
   c. only pressure has a definable receptor.
   d. only pain has a definable receptor.

3. The process by which sensory information is converted into neural energy is:
   a. adaptation.
   b. feature detection.
   c. spiking.
   d. transduction.

4. The receptors for taste are located in the:
   a. taste buds.
   b. cochlea.
   c. fovea.
   d. cortex.

5. The receptors for the sense of equilibrium are located in the:
   a. muscles.
   b. tendons.
   c. joints.
   d. inner ear.

6. According to the opponent-process theory:
   a. there are three types of color-sensitive cones.
   b. color vision begins in the cortex.
   c. color receptors respond to one color's wavelength and its complementary color in an opposing fashion.
   d. all of the above are true.

7. Nerve deafness is caused by:
   a. wax buildup in the outer ear.
   b. damage to the eardrum.
   c. blockage in the middle ear due to infection.
   d. damage to the cochlea.

8. Which sense enables you to feel yourself wiggling your toes even with your eyes closed?
a. equilibrium
b. kinesthesis
c. the skin senses
d. the tactile senses

9. The frequency theory of hearing best explains our sensation of:
a. the lowest pitches.
b. pitches of intermediate range.
c. the highest pitches.
d. all of the above.

10. Hubel and Wiesel discovered feature detectors in the _____ of a monkey's visual system.
a. fovea
b. optic nerve
c. iris
d. cortex

11. Weber's law states:
a. The absolute threshold for any sensory modality is a constant.
b. The jnd for any sensory modality is a constant.
c. The absolute threshold for any sensory modality is a constant percentage.
d. The jnd for any sensory modality is a constant percentage.

12. Nearsightedness refers to the condition in which:
a. the lens has become thickened and inflexible.
b. the lens is too thin.
c. the eyeball is longer than normal.
d. the eyeball is shorter than normal.

Matching Items

Label the parts of the eye.

1. _____
2. _____
3. _____
4. _____
5. _____
6. _____
7. _____

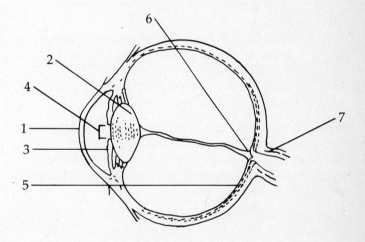

Label the parts of the ear.

1. _____
2. _____
3. _____
4. _____
5. _____
6. _____
7. _____
8. _____

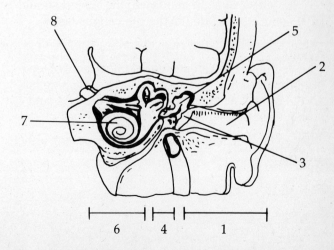

SAMPLE ESSAY QUESTIONS

1. Discuss the evidence for subliminal perception.

2. How does sensory restriction affect behavior?

3. Contrast the processing of information in the retina and in the visual cortex.

4. How do rods and cones differ?

5. Explain how the ear differentially codes sounds of different frequencies.

PROJECT:
SENSORY INTERACTIONS

Even the simplest behaviors typically require the coordinated interaction of several senses. The following demonstration illustrates the importance of sensory interactions in taste and balance sensitivity.

Taste

You will need one volunteer for this experiment, four or five foods with different tastes, a blindfold, several cotton balls, and a glass of water. For your tastes, try mashing several of the following into separate pastes: apples, potatoes, carrots, pears, plums.

Blindfold your subject and ask him or her to sample and identify each taste. Give the subject a sip of water in between tastes. Assuming that you have selected tastes that are not too exotic, the subject should have no trouble identifying them.

Have your volunteer put a piece of cotton in each nostril. Have the subject repeat the taste test. Without the senses of sight and smell, the subject should have some trouble identifying the various tastes.

Balance

This demonstration illustrates the importance of feedback from vision and equilibrium in maintaining balance. You will need one volunteer, a blindfold, and a swivel chair.

Have a volunteer balance on one foot for as long as he or she is able. Keep track of the time.

Now blindfold the subject and again have him or her balance on one leg. Record how long the subject is able to maintain balance. With visual feedback absent, the subject should experience greater difficulty in maintaining balance.

As a final demonstration, spin the subject rapidly in the chair several times in order to bias his or her equilibrium. The blindfolded subject should then again attempt to balance on one foot. Again record his or her time.

Questions

1. What do these results demonstrate about taste and balance?

2. What long-term effects do you think blindness would have on taste and balance?

3. For what other abilities can you predict that sensory interactions would be important?

WHERE TO LOOK FOR MORE INFORMATION

Hellman, H. (1982, April). Guiding light. *Psychology Today*.

This article summarizes research in the field of photobiology, including the effects of light on cancer, depression, and other human conditions.

Coren, S., Porac, C., and Ward, L. M. (1979). *Sensation and perception*. New York: Academic Press.

This book is an excellent general reference for the field of sensation and also suggests a number of fascinating demonstrations of sensory phenomena.

Dobelle, W. H. (1977). Current status of research on providing sight to the blind by electrical stimulation of the brain. *Journal of Visual Impairment and Blindness, 71*, 290–297.

Success for the "bionic ear." (1984, March 12). *Time*.

These articles describe remarkable achievements in restoring vision and hearing with prosthetic devices that directly stimulate the brain.

ANSWERS

PROGRESS TEST 1

Multiple-Choice Questions

1. b (p. 140)
2. a (p. 142)
3. c (p. 143)
4. d (p. 143)

5. d (p. 145)
6. a (p. 145)
7. b (p. 147)
8. a (p. 151)

9. b (p. 152)
10. c (p. 153)
11. a (p. 154)
12. c (p. 155)

Matching Items

1. e (p. 145)
2. d (p. 145)
3. h (p. 145)
4. j (p. 145)

5. i (p. 145)
6. a (p. 153)
7. k (p. 153)
8. b (p. 157)

9. g (p. 157)
10. c (p. 159)
11. f (p. 158)

PROGRESS TEST 2

Multiple-Choice Questions

1. b (p. 156)
2. c (p. 157)
3. d (p. 144)
4. a (p. 157)

5. d (p. 159)
6. c (pp. 151–152)
7. d (p. 155)
8. b (p. 158)

9. a (p. 154)
10. d (p. 147)
11. d (p. 143)
12. c (p. 149)

Matching Items

Parts of Eye

1. cornea
2. lens
3. iris

4. pupil
5. retina
6. blind spot

7. optic nerve

Parts of Ear

1. outer ear
2. auditory canal
3. eardrum

4. middle ear
5. auditory bones
6. inner ear

7. cochlea
8. auditory nerve

CHAPTER 7

Perception

CHAPTER OVERVIEW

Chapter 7 explores a variety of issues concerning how we organize and interpret our sensations as meaningful perceptions. These include the relative importance of heredity and experience, how we perceive depth, perceptual constancies, and the phenomena of perceptual set, sensory restriction, and ESP.

In addition to the terms covered in the Basic Issues and Perceptual Organization sections, this chapter deals with two important issues. The first has to do with the role of experience in perception. Make sure you understand the results of studies of recovery from blindness, early sensory restriction, adaptation to distorted environments, and perceptual set. A second issue you should be able to discuss concerns the criticism and defense of ESP. For mastery of this material, make sure you formulate and write answers to the appropriate chapter objectives and essay questions.

GUIDED STUDY

Before you read, preview each section by skimming it, noting headings and boldface items. Then read the appropriate section objectives from the following outline. Keep these objectives in mind, and as you read the chapter section, search for the information that will complete each one. You may wish to write out answers for each objective as soon as you finish reading that section of the chapter.

Basic Issues in Perception (pp. 165–167)

1. Distinguish between the empiricist and nativist theories of perception.

Perceptual Organization (pp. 167–175)

2. Define Gestalt.

3. Explain each of the following principles of perceptual organization.

a. figure-ground

b. proximity

c. similarity

d. closure

e. continuation

4. Describe the following cues to depth perception and indicate in each case whether binocular or monocular vision is required.

a. relative size

b. overlap

c. retinal disparity

d. aerial perspective

e. convergence

f. texture

g. relative height

h. relative motion

5. Describe each of the following perceptual constancies.

a. size constancy

b. shape constancy

c. brightness constancy

d. color constancy

6. Describe the following visual illusions and how the size-distance relationship helps explain each.

a. Müller-Lyer illusion

b. moon illusion

Interpretation: Do We Learn to Perceive?
(pp. 175–181)

7. State the effects of early sensory restriction on visual perception.

8. Explain how the results of experiments on perceptual adaptation and recovery from blindness support the empiricist viewpoint.

9. Explain the phenomenon of perceptual set and give an example of how it can influence perception.

10. Discuss the cocktail party effect and whether we are ever affected by stimuli that we are unaware of.

Is There Perception Without Sensation?
(pp. 181–184)

11. Describe each of the following forms of extrasensory perception:

a. telepathy

b. clairvoyance

c. precognition

d. psychokinesis

12. Discuss several reasons that most research psychologists are skeptical about the existence of extrasensory perception.

CHAPTER REVIEW

When you have finished reading the chapter, complete the sentences that follow. Using your hand or a strip of paper, cover the correct answers in the margin and fill in each blank. Verify your answer by uncovering the correct one. As you proceed, evaluate your performance for each chapter section. *Do not continue with the next section until you understand why each margin term is the correct answer.* If you need to, go back and review or re-read the appropriate chapter section in the text before continuing.

1. Perception refers to how we _____ and _____ sensations as meaningful phenomena.

    organize

    interpret

Basic Issues in Perception (pp. 165–167)

2. The belief that we learn to perceive the world by experiencing it was proposed by the philosophical school called _____.

    empiricism

3. One philosopher of this school was _____ _____.

    John Locke

4. He believed that at birth the mind is _____.

    blank

5. On the other side were philosophers who maintained that knowledge comes from innate ways of organizing sensory experiences. These philosophers were the _____.

    nativists

6. One philosopher of this school was _____ _____.

    Immanuel Kant

7. Your text suggests that the nativist approach describes many of the ways we _____ sensations, while how we _____ sensations may best be described by the empiricist approach.

organize
interpret

Perceptual Organization (pp. 167–175)

8. The German word for "form" or "whole" is _____ .

Gestalt

9. As the Gestalt psychologists have often said: "The whole is different from the _____ _____ _____ _____ ."

sum of its parts

10. When we view a scene, we see the central object, or _____ , as distinct from surrounding stimuli, or the _____ .

figure
ground

11. Proximity, similarity, closure, and continuation are examples of Gestalt principles of _____ _____ .

perceptual organization

12. The principle that we organize stimuli into smooth, continuous patterns is called _____ .

continuation

13. The principle that items are grouped to create a complete, whole object is _____ .

closure

14. The grouping of items closest to each other is the principle of _____ .

proximity

15. The principle that items that look alike are grouped is called _____ .

similarity

16. Although the images that fall on our retinas are _____ -dimensional, our perception is _____ -dimensional.

two
three

17. Gibson and Walk developed the _____ _____ to test depth perception in infants.

visual cliff

18. Their research has shown that this ability is probably _____ .

innate

For questions 19 through 26, identify the depth perception cue that is defined.

19. Any cue that requires both eyes: _____ _____

binocular cue

20. Any cue that requires only one eye: _____ _____

monocular cue

21. Each eye receives a different image of an object: _____ _____

retinal disparity

22. Our eyes focus inward when we view near objects: _____

convergence

23. An object partially covered by another is seen as farther away: _____

overlap

24. As we move, objects at different distances appear to move at different rates: _____ _____

relative motion

25. Objects lower in the visual field are seen as nearer: _____ _____

relative height

26. Objects that appear hazy are seen as farther away: _____ _____

aerial perspective

27. Our tendency to see objects as unchanging in size, shape, and brightness is called _____ _____.

perceptual constancy

28. Several illusions, including the Müller-Lyer, are explained by the interplay between perceived _____ and perceived _____.

size
distance

29. The moon illusion refers to the fact that the moon seems _____ near the horizon than high in the sky.

larger
distance

30. This illusion occurs because _____ cues at the horizon make the moon seem farther away.

31. The illusion in which a horizontal line with receding wings appears shorter than one with outward-pointing wings is the _____-_____ illusion.

Müller-Lyer

32. People who have been raised in environments without a lot of straight lines _____ (do/do not) experience this illusion as strongly.

do not

33. Research has shown that size constancy is a _____ ability.

learned

34. The tendency to perceive an object as having a constant amount of whiteness even while its illumination varies is _____ _____.

whiteness constancy

35. When your view is restricted to only part of a familiar object, its color may seem to vary with the light that shines on it. This shows that _____ constancy depends on the _____ in which an object is viewed.

color

context

36. The tendency of vision to dominate the other senses is referred to as _____ _____ .

visual capture

Interpretation: Do We Learn to Perceive?
(pp. 175–181)

37. Concerning the nature-nurture issue, as we move up the animal scale, the importance of _____ in perception increases.

learning

38. Studies of cases in which vision has been restored show that, when *seeing* familiar objects for the first time, patients typically _____ (can/cannot) recognize them.

cannot

39. Studies of sensory restriction demonstrate that visual experiences during _____ are critical for perceptual development.

infancy

40. Blakemoor and Cooper discovered that the visual neurons of kittens raised in a vertical-stripe environment _____ (would/would not) later respond to horizontal stimuli.

would not

41. In contrast to lower animals, humans given glasses that shift or invert the visual field _____ (will/will not) adapt to the distorted perception.

will

42. What we see is greatly influenced by our assumptions and expectations, that is, by our _____ _____ .

perceptual set

43. The ability to attend selectively to one voice among many is referred to as the _____ _____ _____ .

cocktail party effect

44. Our perceptual schemas are largely acquired through _____ , as reflected in children's drawings at different ages.

learning

45. Even when we know that two interpretations of an object are possible, our attention is _____ : It is focused on a particular aspect of what we are experiencing.

selective

Is There Perception Without Sensation?
(pp. 181–184)

46. Perception outside the range of normal sensation is called

_____ _____ .

extrasensory perception

47. Psychologists who study ESP are called _____ .

parapsychologists

48. The form of ESP in which people claim to be capable of reading others' minds is called _____ .

telepathy

49. A person who "senses" that a friend is in danger might claim to have the ESP ability of _____ .

clairvoyance

50. An ability to "see" into the future is called

_____ .

precognition

51. A person who claims to be able to levitate and move objects is claiming the power of _____ .

psychokinesis

52. Critics point out that a major difficulty for parapsychology is that ESP phenomena are not consistently _____ .

reproducible

53. When the clairvoyance experiment conducted by Layton and Turnbull was repeated, the results of both experiments were nearly identical to what one would expect on the basis of

_____ .

chance

54. Skeptics also note that people believe in ESP as a result of a tendency to _____ experiences and to recall events that confirm their _____ .

misperceive

expectations

FOCUS ON PSYCHOLOGY:
PERCEPTUAL ILLUSIONS IN ANIMALS?

You are already familiar with the Müller-Lyer illusion, illustrated below. Shown these two line drawings, most people believe that the horizontal line in (a) is longer than the one in (b).

(a)   (b)

The illusion is due to the effect of perceived distance on perceived size. Since the horizontal line in (a) resembles the junction of ceiling, floor, and walls of the corner of a room, perceptually it appears closer and thus shorter. The horizontal line in (b) resembles the outside corner of a building, so it appears longer. Do animals experience the Müller-Lyer illusion? To answer this question, Mallott and Mallott (1970) first trained pigeons to peck at a picture like that shown below. The researchers used food as a reward.

After the birds had learned to peck at the picture, they were shown horizontal lines of various lengths. In each case, the vertical line segments were replaced by either inward- or outward-pointing arrows, as in the Müller-Lyer figure. Which line [(a) or (b) below] do you think the birds responded to? They chose (b). Although line segment (a) is the same length as the one the pigeon had learned to peck at, the Müller-Lyer effect makes it appear shorter. Line (b), although longer, appears more similar to the training stimulus than does (a). It appears that pigeons, which have excellent vision, are as sensitive as humans to the Müller-Lyer illusion.

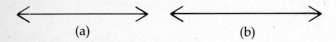

(a)   (b)

PROGRESS TEST 1

Circle your answers to the following questions and check them with the answer key at the end of the chapter. Be sure to consult the appropriate pages of the text to understand the correct answer for any missed question.

1. Which theory of perception holds that knowledge comes from innate ways of organizing our sensory experiences?
   a. behaviorist
   b. nativist
   c. empiricist
   d. Gestalt

2. The historical movement associated with the statement "The whole is different from the sum of its parts" is:
   a. structuralism.
   b. behaviorism.
   c. functionalism.
   d. Gestalt psychology.

3. The principle that items will be grouped together to create a complete, whole object is called:
   a. closure.
   b. similarity.
   c. continuation.
   d. proximity.

4. The figure-ground relationship demonstrates that:
   a. perception is largely innate.
   b. perception is simply a point-for-point representation of sensation.

   c. the same stimulus can trigger more than one perception.
   d. different people see different things when viewing a scene.

5. When we stare at an object, each of our eyes receives a slightly different image, providing a depth cue known as:
   a. convergence.
   b. linear perspective.
   c. relative motion.
   d. retinal disparity.

6. As we move, viewed objects cast changing shapes on our retinas, although we do not perceive the objects as changing. This is the phenomenon of:
   a. perceptual constancy.
   b. relative motion.
   c. linear perspective.
   d. retinal disparity.

7. When there is a conflict between visual information and that from the other senses, _____ seems to dominate. This is called:
   a. vision; visual eminence
   b. vision; visual capture
   c. kinesis; the balance principle
   d. equilibrium; the balance principle

8. The variety of ESP in which a person claims to be able to read another's mind is:
   a. psychokinesis.
   b. precognition.
   c. clairvoyance.
   d. telepathy.

9. Which of the following was *not* mentioned as a critique of parapsychology?
   a. ESP has not been consistently reproducible.
   b. Parapsychology has suffered from a number of frauds or hoaxes.
   c. The tendency to recall only events that confirm their expectations accounts for much of people's belief in ESP.
   d. There have been no controlled laboratory studies of ESP.

10. The cocktail party effect refers to:
   a. the effects of random noise on a person's perception of low pitches.

b. the effects of random noise on a person's mood.

—**c.** the ability to attend selectively to one stimulus.

d. the cumulative effect of multiple low-amplitude sounds on the inner ear.

11. Kittens reared seeing only horizontal lines appear to be blind to vertical lines later in life. This is due to the fact that:

a. brain neurons have atrophied.

b. retinal receptor cells have not developed.

c. many of the neurons in the visual cortex did not develop.

—**d.** neurons normally tuned to vertical lines become tuned to horizontal lines.

12. Congenitally blind adults who have had their vision restored:

a. are almost immediately able to recognize familiar objects.

b. typically fail to recognize familiar objects.

c. are unable to follow moving objects with their eyes.

d. have excellent eye-hand coordination.

13. Studies with the visual cliff have provided evidence that much of depth perception is:

—**a.** innate.

b. learned.

c. innate in lower animals, but learned in humans.

d. innate in humans, but learned in lower animals.

14. The insensitivity of Zulu Indians to the Müller-Lyer illusion is due to their:

a. poorer vision.

b. failure to understand the test itself.

—**c.** lack of experience with the straight lines of a "carpentered" world.

d. inexperience with figure-ground relationships.

15. The moon illusion is due to the fact that:

—**a.** distance cues at the horizon make the moon seem farther away and therefore larger.

b. distance cues at the horizon make the moon seem closer and therefore larger.

c. distance cues at the horizon make the moon seem farther away and therefore smaller.

d. distance cues at the horizon make the moon seem closer and therefore smaller.

FOCUS ON PSYCHOLOGY:
FIGURE-GROUND RELATIONSHIPS AND COGNITIVE STYLES

Look at the figures below. In each row, can you find the figure on the left embedded in one or more of those on the right? If you want to test yourself more accurately, consult the book listed at the end of this chapter.

From A. F. Grasha (1983). *Practical Applications of Psychology* (2nd ed.). Little, Brown, p. 50. Copyright © by Little, Brown and Co. Reprinted by permission of the publisher.

According to Witkin, Goodenough, and Oltman (1977), people who have little trouble finding embedded figures such as these possess *field-independence.* People who cannot as easily separate figure-ground relationships are said to be *field-dependent.* Neither type, say Witkin and his colleagues, is more intelligent or has better spatial abilities than the other. Rather, the field-independence/dependence dimension reflects different cognitive styles. For example, field-independent people prefer to work by themselves, enjoy theoretical or abstract problems, and are less susceptible to peer influence. Field-dependent people, on the other hand, prefer to work in groups, are good at solving interpersonal problems, and are more affected by extrinsic motivation.

In testing over a thousand students, Witkin and his colleagues found that cognitive style was generally predictive of students' college majors and future occupations. Field-dependent students had such majors as education, nursing, and speech therapy. Their eventual occupations included clinical psychology, social work, teaching, and law enforcement, all fields that emphasize working with others. Field-independent students tended to major in science and mathematics and later took jobs in areas that did not depend on interpersonal relations. Both types of students reported satisfaction with their majors. Students who appeared in fields that did not match their cognitive styles, however, had lower grades and felt less satisfaction with their careers.

PROGRESS TEST 2

Progress Test 2 should be completed during a final chapter review. Do so after you understand thoroughly the correct answers for the Chapter Review and Progress Test 1.

1. According to the _____ view, we learn to perceive the world.
   a. phenomenological
   b. nativist
   c. empiricist
   d. Gestalt

2. The tendency to organize stimuli into smooth, uninterrupted patterns is called:
   a. closure.
   b. continuation.
   c. similarity.
   d. proximity.

3. Which of the following is *not* a monocular depth cue?
   a. relative size
   b. convergence
   c. aerial perspective
   d. relative motion

4. A psychic who claims to be able to levitate objects is claiming to have the power of:
   a. psychokinesis.
   b. precognition.
   c. clairvoyance.
   d. telepathy.

5. Experiments with distorted visual environments demonstrate that:
   a. adaptation rarely takes place.
   b. animals adapt readily, but humans do not.

   c. humans adapt readily, but lower animals typically do not.
   d. perception is not affected.

6. The phenomenon that refers to how an individual's expectations influence perception is called:
   a. perceptual set.
   b. binocular disparity.
   c. convergence.
   d. visual capture.

7. The field of psychology known for the development of principles of perceptual organization is:
   a. empiricism.
   b. nativism.
   c. structuralism.
   d. Gestalt psychology.

8. The tendency to perceive hazy objects as being at a distance is known as _____. This is a _____ depth cue.
   a. linear perspective; binocular
   b. linear perspective; monocular
   c. aerial perspective; binocular
   d. aerial perspective; monocular

9. The phenomenon of size constancy is based upon the close connection between an object's perceived _____ and its perceived _____.
   a. size; shape
   b. size; distance
   c. size; brightness
   d. shape; distance

10. Which of the following statements best describes the effects of sensory restriction?
   a. It produces functional blindness when it is experienced for any length of time at any age.
   b. It has greater effects on humans than on animals.
   c. It has more damaging effects when experienced during infancy.
   d. It has greater effects on adults than on children.

11. Psychologists who study ESP are called:
   a. psychics.
   b. telepaths.

c. parapsychologists.

d. perceptualists.

12. The depth cue that occurs when we watch moving objects as we are moving is:

a. convergence.

b. overlap.

c. aerial perspective.

d. relative motion.

13. Which of the following is true concerning ESP?

a. Most ESP researchers are quacks.

b. There have been a large number of reliable demonstrations of ESP.

c. Most research psychologists are skeptical of the claims of defenders of ESP.

d. There have been reliable laboratory demonstrations of ESP, but the results are no different from those that would occur by chance.

14. Each time you see your car, it projects a different image on the retinas of your eyes, yet you do not perceive it as changing. This is due to:

a. perceptual set.

b. binocular disparity.

c. perceptual constancy.

d. convergence.

15. The term Gestalt means:

a. vision.

b. sensation.

c. perception.

d. whole.

SAMPLE ESSAY QUESTIONS

1. Describe the Gestalt principles of perceptual organization.

2. Discuss the nature-nurture issue as it applies to perception. Consider evidence from studies of recovery from blindness, perceptual adaptation, and sensory restriction.

3. Explain why research psychologists tend to be skeptical about the existence of ESP.

4. Describe the cues we typically use in perceiving depth.

5. Describe the various types of perceptual constancy.

PROJECT:
DEMONSTRATING PERCEPTUAL PHENOMENA

A number of interesting perceptual phenomena can be demonstrated quite easily, without a great deal of equipment. Try several of those listed below.

The Autokinetic Effect. This illusion occurs when a stationary spot of light appears to move about in random fashion. In a completely darkened room, place a small high-intensity lamp on a table. Bring in a volunteer and ask the person to report what he or she sees while staring at the lamp. After a few minutes, the light should appear to move. This effect has been attributed to involuntary eye movements that are not monitored by the visual system. These are then misattributed to the stationary spot of light.

The Phi Phenomenon. A second example of apparent motion is called the phi phenomenon. This illusion forms the basis of motion pictures or television programs. A television screen consists of a matrix of hundreds of tiny light-emitting spots, each of which can be illuminated independently. "Movement" on the screen actually consists of the consecutive and synchronized illumination of the appropriate spots, not the actual passage of one light across the screen. This phenomenon can easily be demonstrated. Hold one hand, with your index finger pointing straight up, about 12 inches in front of your eyes. Keep your hand steady in front of your face. Close your right eye, leaving the left open. Now close your left eye, while simultaneously opening your right eye. Quickly alternate opening your right and left eyes while looking at your hand. Your finger should appear to move back and forth.

Convergence and Retinal Disparity. One powerful binocular depth cue is the extent to which the eyes converge when looking at objects at various distances. Hold a pencil vertically in front of your face, at arm's length. Slowly bring the pencil closer, until it is touching your nose. As you hold it there, you will begin to feel an uncomfortable "cross-eyed" sensation. This muscular feedback provides the cue to the distance of the viewed object. As you moved the pencil toward your eyes, you may also have noticed that at one point, the image of the pencil split into two. These images correspond to the slightly different images received by each of your eyes, as a result of their being set several inches apart. As the text points out, retinal disparity is the basis for the depth perceived in 3-D movies, a phenomenon known as *stereoscopic vision*.

Afterimages and Bidwell's Ghost. After a flashbulb goes off in front of your face, you may see two after-images. The first, a positive afterimage, involves the persistence of the bright spot for only a moment. The negative afterimage consists of the light's complementary color—a dark spot which may linger for several seconds. Under certain conditions, the photoreceptors of the eyes may experience an afterimage which persists for a considerable length of time. This phenomenon is called *Bidwell's ghost*. To see it, you need a friend and a high-intensity lamp, or a very bright flashlight. You must first become completely dark-adapted. This will require sitting for about 20 minutes in the darkened room. When completely adapted, have your friend quickly flash the light in your eyes. The light should be kept on for only a fraction of a second. For the next few minutes, you should be able to see the "ghost" no matter where you look in the room.

WHERE TO LOOK FOR MORE INFORMATION

Coren, S., Porac, C., and Ward, L. M. (1979). *Sensation and perception*. New York: Academic Press.

This book is an excellent reference for topics and demonstrations in sensation and perception.

Eysenck, H. J., and Sargent, S. (1984). *Explaining the unexplained: Mysteries of the paranormal*. London: Weidenfeld & Nicolson.

This book is a lively treatment of parapsychology by respected British psychologists.

Grasha, Anthony F. (1983). *Practical applications of psychology* (2nd ed.). Boston: Little, Brown. Pp. 50–53.

Witkin, H. A., Goodenough, D. R., and Oltman, P. K. (1977). Role of field-dependent and field-independent cognitive styles in academic evolution: A longitudinal study. *Journal of Educational Psychology, 69*, 197–211.

The book and journal article provide detailed background and testing procedures for the phenomena of field-dependency and field-independency.

Mallott, R. W., and Mallott, M. K. (1970). Perception and stimulus generalization. In W. C. Stebbins (Ed.). *Animal psychophysics: The design and conduct of sensory experiments*. New York: Appleton-Century-Crofts.

This article explains the test procedure for determining the sensitivity of pigeons to the Müller-Lyer illusion. The other articles in the book illustrate how research into other sensory processes can be undertaken with animal subjects.

ANSWERS

PROGRESS TEST 1

1. b (p. 167)
2. d (p. 167)
3. a (p. 169)
4. c (p. 168)
5. d (p. 170)

6. a (p. 172)
7. b (p. 175)
8. d (p. 181)
9. d (pp. 182–184)
10. c (p. 178)

11. d (p. 176)
12. b (p. 176)
13. a (p. 170)
14. c (p. 174)
15. a (p. 173)

PROGRESS TEST 2

1. c (p. 167)
2. b (p. 169)
3. b (pp. 171–172)
4. a (p. 181)
5. c (p. 177)

6. a (p. 179)
7. d (p. 167)
8. d (p. 171)
9. b (p. 173)
10. c (pp. 175–176)

11. c (p. 181)
12. d (p. 172)
13. c (pp. 182–184)
14. c (p. 172)
15. d (p. 167)

CHAPTER 8

States of Consciousness

CHAPTER OVERVIEW

Consciousness can be experienced in various states, each involving a focused awareness of perception, thoughts, and feelings. Chapter 8 covers daydreaming, sleep and dreaming, hypnosis, drugs, and near-death experiences.

Most of the terminology in this chapter is introduced in two sections: Sleep and Dreaming, and Drugs and Consciousness. The remainder of the chapter is a discussion of two major theoretical issues: why we sleep, and whether hypnosis is a unique state of consciousness.

GUIDED STUDY

The text chapter should be studied one section at a time. Before you read, preview each section by skimming it, noting headings and boldface items. Then read the appropriate section objectives from the following outline. Keep these objectives in mind, and as you read the chapter section, search for the information that will complete each one. You may wish to write out answers for each objective as soon as you finish reading that section of the chapter.

Studying Consciousness (pp. 189–190)

1. Define consciousness and discuss its significance in the history of psychology.

Daydreaming (pp. 190–191)

2. Discuss daydreaming and its function in daily life.

Sleep and Dreams (pp. 191–194)

3. Define circadian rhythm.

4. List and describe the brain waves characterizing the waking state and the four stages of sleep.

5. Describe the cyclical nature of the four stages of sleep.

6. List the physiological changes that characterize REM sleep in males and females.

Why We Sleep (pp. 194–198)

7. Discuss the effects of sleep deprivation.

8. Describe each of the following sleep disorders.

a. insomnia

b. narcolepsy

c. sleep apnea

d. night terrors

9. Compare and contrast dreaming and daydreaming.

10. Explain Freud's theory of dreaming.

11. Describe the information processing theory of dreaming.

Hypnosis (pp. 198–205)

12. Describe the characteristics of those who are most responsive to hypnotic suggestion.

13. Discuss whether hypnosis allows a person to perform otherwise impossible feats.

14. Discuss whether hypnosis can produce:

a. posthypnotic amnesia

b. age regression

c. pain relief

15. Explain how meditation differs from hypnosis.

16. Describe the divided consciousness theory of hypnosis and explain the concept of the hidden observer.

Drugs and Consciousness (pp. 205–211)

17. Describe the physiological and psychological effects of each of the following drugs.

a. alcohol	**d.** placebo
b. heroin	**e.** LSD
c. amphetamine	**f.** marijuana

Near-Death Experiences (pp. 211–212)

18. Describe the phenomenon of the near-death experience and explain the theory that such experiences are best understood as hallucinatory activity.

19. Compare and contrast the positions of dualists and monists on the mind-body issue.

CHAPTER REVIEW

When you have finished reading the chapter, complete the sentences that follow. Using your hand or a strip of paper, cover the correct answers in the margin and fill in each blank. Verify your answer by uncovering the correct one. As you proceed, evaluate your performance for each chapter section. *Do not continue with the next section until you understand why each margin term is the correct answer.* If you need to, go back and review or re-read the appropriate chapter section in the text before continuing.

Studying Consciousness (pp. 189–190)

1. Although psychology began as the study of consciousness, the difficulty of defining such a concept led most psychologists to switch to direct _____ of behavior.

observation

2. This school of psychology is known as _____.

behaviorism

3. Consciousness is defined as "selective _____ to ongoing perceptions, thoughts, and feelings."

attention

4. Consciousness has a limited _____, is relatively slow, and processes things in succession, unlike _____ processes.

capacity

unconscious

Daydreaming (pp. 190–191)

5. Psychologists have discovered that most people _____ (do/do not) daydream each day.

do

6. Compared to older adults, young adults spend _____ (more/less) time daydreaming.

more

7. The fact that daydreams help us prepare for the future and provide relaxation suggests that daydreaming is not only pleasurable, but _____ .

adaptive

8. For children, daydreaming in the form of imaginative play is important to _____ and cognitive development.

social

Sleep and Dreams (pp. 191–194)

9. The daily sleep-waking cycle follows a 24-hour clock called the _____ _____ .

circadian rhythm

10. During the day, body _____ peaks, and then begins dropping as the person falls asleep.

temperature

11. When the circadian rhythm is interrupted, as when we are traveling, we may experience _____ _____ .

jet lag

12. The rhythm of sleep cycles was discovered when Aserinsky noticed that, at periodic intervals during the night, the _____ of sleeping infants would move rapidly.

eyes

13. The relatively slow brain waves of the awake, relaxed state are known as _____ waves.

alpha

14. Bursts of brain-wave activity are called _____ _____ . These bursts tend to occur during stage _____ of sleep.

sleep spindles

2

15. Unlike in stage 1, a person in this stage is clearly _____ .

asleep

16. Large, slow brain waves are called _____ waves. These predominate during stage _____ sleep. During this stage it is difficult to _____ a person.

delta

4

awaken

17. It is also during this stage that people may engage in sleep _____ and sleep _____ .

talking; walking

18. After about an hour of sleep, the brain waves become more _____ , like those of stage _____ sleep.

rapid; 1

19. During this period the body becomes aroused, breathing becomes more rapid, there is an increase in _____ , and penile arousal or vaginal congestion occurs.

heart rate

20. Also during this period, the _____ move rapidly, giving this sleep stage the name _____ sleep.

eyes

REM

21. Although the body appears to be aroused, the _____ of the body remain relaxed and motionless.

muscles

22. William Dement has found that approximately _____ percent of the people awakened during REM sleep report that they have been _____ .

80

dreaming

23. The mental activity that occurs during REM sleep is _____ (more/less) emotional, vivid, and storylike than it is during other sleep stages.

more

24. The sleep cycle repeats itself about every _____ minutes.

90

25. As the night progresses, stage _____ sleep becomes briefer and _____ periods become longer.

4

REM

26. Approximately _____ percent of a night's sleep is spent in REM.

20 to 25

Why We Sleep (pp. 194–198)

27. Studies of sleep deprivation show that the effects are generally _____ , and include irritability and occasional inattention.

mild

28. During sleep, a growth hormone is released by the _____ gland.

pituitary

29. Adults sleep _____ (more/less) than children, and so release _____ (more/less) growth hormone.

less

less

30. Studies have indicated that after strenuous exercise we tend to sleep for longer periods and to increase our stage _____ sleep.

4

31. Newborns spend about _____ of their time asleep; elderly people only about _____ .

two-thirds

one-fourth

32. Webb and Campbell found that sleep patterns between _____ twins were similar, suggesting a possible _____ basis for individual differences in sleep habits.

identical

genetic

33. A recurring difficulty in falling asleep defines _____ .

insomnia

34. This sleep disorder is experienced by approximately _____ percent of adults.

15

35. Sleeping pills and alcohol may make the problem worse, as they tend to _____ REM sleep.

reduce

36. The sleep disorder in which a person experiences uncontrollable sleep attacks is _____.

narcolepsy

37. When a sleep attack occurs, the person typically enters _____ sleep directly.

REM

38. Individuals suffering from _____ _____ stop breathing while sleeping.

sleep apnea

39. Some researchers believe that crib death, called the _____ _____ _____ syndrome, may be related to this disorder.

sudden infant death

40. The disorder in which a person experiences terrifying dreams is called _____ _____.

night terrors

41. Unlike nightmares, these dreams usually happen early in the night during stage _____ of sleep.

4

42. The genital arousal that typically occurs during REM sleep usually _____ (does/does not) reflect a sexual dream.

does not

43. There _____ (does/does not) seem to be a consistent gender difference in dream content.

does

44. Although females tend to dream equally often of males and females, males tend to dream more about _____.

males

45. Freud referred to the actual content of dream imagery as its _____ _____.

manifest content

46. Freud believed that this content is a censored version of the true meaning, or _____ _____, of the dream.

latent content

47. According to Freud, most of the dreams of adults reflect _____ wishes.

erotic

48. A second theory of dreams is that they serve an _____ processing function.

information

49. Support for this theory is provided by the fact that after stressful experiences, _____ sleep tends to increase.

REM

50. In addition, studies have shown that REM sleep facilitates _____.

memory

51. A third class of theories proposes that dreaming serves some _____ function.

physiological

52. One theory proposes that REM sleep provides stimulation to a developing infant's brain. Support for this is provided by the fact that newborns spend about _____ their sleep in REM.

half

53. Other theories propose that dreams are elicited by neural activity originating in the lower regions of the brain, such as the _____.

brainstem

54. After being deprived of REM sleep, a person spends more time in REM sleep; this is the _____ _____ effect.

REM rebound

55. REM sleep occurs in mammals, but not in fish and other animals whose behavior is less influenced by _____.

learning

Hypnosis (pp. 198–205)

56. The suggestion that a person forget certain things while under hypnosis may produce _____ _____.

posthypnotic amnesia

57. The discovery of hypnosis is attributed to _____, who claimed to have discovered the principle of body _____.

Mesmer
magnetism

58. At that time, hypnosis was referred to as _____.

mesmerism

59. To a certain degree, nearly everyone is hypnotically _____.

suggestible

60. People who are most responsive to hypnosis are those who can readily focus their attention on a task, and who are very _____.

creative

61. The weight of research evidence suggests that hypnosis _____ (does/does not) allow a person to perform feats which are impossible in the unhypnotized state.

does not

62. In an effort to help patients relive traumatic events in their childhood, Freud often used the hypnotic technique of _____ _____.

age regression

63. Studies by Orne show that the age-regressed memories of a person under hypnosis are _____ (more/no more) accurate than the memories of unhypnotized persons.

no more

64. Hypnosis has helped some people diet and quit smoking through the use of _____ suggestions.

posthypnotic

65. Approximately _____ percent of people can be hypnotized deeply enough to undergo surgery without anesthesia.

10

66. Hypnotic pain relief is not facilitated through the release of the neurotransmitters called _____.

endorphins

67. One theory is that hypnosis separates, or _____, the sensory and emotional aspects of pain.

dissociates

68. In meditation, attention may be focused on a word or phrase called a _____.

mantra

69. Unlike hypnosis, meditation tends to _____ metabolism and is characterized by a very relaxed state.

decrease

70. Hypnosis _____ (is/is not) a unique physiological state.

is not

71. One explanation of behavior under hypnosis is that the subject may merely be acting out a _____.

role

72. Hilgard has advanced the idea that during hypnosis there is a _____ between different levels of consciousness.

dissociation

73. The existence of a separate consciousness, which is aware of what takes place during hypnosis, is expressed in the concept of the _____ _____.

hidden observer

Drugs and Consciousness (pp. 205–211)

74. Drugs that alter moods and perceptions are called _____ drugs.

psychoactive

75. Drug users who require increasing doses to experience a drug's effects have developed _____.

tolerance

76. If a person experiences withdrawal symptoms after ceasing to use a drug, the person has developed a physical _____.

dependence

77. Regular use of a drug to relieve stress reflects _____ dependence.

psychological

78. The three broad categories of drugs discussed in the text are: _____, which tend to slow body functions; _____, which speed body functions; and _____, which alter perception.

depressants
stimulants
hallucinogens

79. These drugs all work within the body at the _____ of neurons, affecting the activity of the chemical _____.

synapses
neurotransmitters

80. Low doses of alcohol, which is classified as a _____, reduce arousal from the _____ nervous system.

depressant
sympathetic

81. Alcohol also affects memory by interfering with the process of transferring experiences into _____-_____ memory.

long-term

82. The psychological effects of alcohol are also influenced by the user's _____ state.

psychological

83. Opium, morphine, and heroin also _____ neural functioning. Together, these drugs are called the _____.

depress
opiates

84. When artificial opiates are present, the brain stops producing its own, the _____.

endorphins

85. The most widely used stimulants are _____, _____, _____, and _____.

caffeine
nicotine; amphetamines
cocaine

86. Amphetamines may act by causing the release of neurotransmitter substances such as _____.

norepinephrine

87. The importance of a user's expectations on the effect of a drug is indicated by the fact that, under experimental conditions, users often cannot distinguish actual drugs from chemically inert drugs called _____.

placebos

88. Hallucinogens are also referred to as _____.

psychedelics

89. LSD is chemically similar to the neurotransmitter _____.

serotonin

90. According to Siegel, the brain hallucinates in the same way when deprived of _____ experiences, when under the influence of _____, or from a lack of oxygen.

sensory
drugs

91. The active ingredient in marijuana is abbreviated as _____.

THC

92. Marijuana has been used therapeutically with those who suffer from _____ and cancer.

glaucoma

93. Like alcohol, marijuana impairs motor _____ and interferes with the formation of _____ memories.

coordination
permanent

Near-Death Experiences (pp. 211–212)

94. The reports of people who have had near-death experiences are very similar to the _____ reported by drug users.

hallucinations

95. That the mind and the body are distinct entities is the position of the _____ .   dualists

96. In contrast, the _____ believe that the mind and the body are one.   monists

FOCUS ON PSYCHOLOGY:
BIORHYTHMS ARE NOT BIOLOGICAL RHYTHMS

Many behaviors occur on a very regular schedule; these clocklike cycles are known as biological rhythms. Some, such as sleep, blood pressure, and body temperature, operate on a 24-hour cycle (*circadian rhythm*). Other behavioral cycles occur over much shorter intervals. An example of this type of *ultradian rhythm* is the 90-minute REM/NREM cycle that occurs during the larger circadian rhythm of sleep. Still other behavioral cycles occur over periods of time longer than one day. The menstrual cycle is one example of such an *infradian rhythm*. The relatively new field of *chronobiology* is the study of the mechanisms, or *biological clocks*, that regulate these rhythms and of the effect on individuals when a normal rhythm is disrupted by jet lag, stress, or a work shift change. In these cases of *dyschronism*, the person becomes irritable, has lapses of concentration, and often suffers from insomnia (Hilts, 1984).

Recently researchers have suggested that human behavior is affected by three other biorhythmic cycles: a 28-day emotional cycle, a 23-day physical cycle, and a 33-day intellectual cycle. Each is divided in half, into an initial positive phase and a second negative phase, during which a person might tend to be depressed or accident-prone, for example. To determine whether you are in the positive or the negative phase today, simply count the number of days since your birthdate and divide by the number of days in a given cycle.

You may have heard of the use of biorhythm charts by coaches to predict the performance of athletes, and by businesses to warn workers of days when they might be accident-prone. While some reports have shown that accident rates did decline when employees were warned of critical dates, systematic comparisons of biorhythm charts with individuals' *past* experiences provide no support for the existence of biorhythms. In one study (Wolcott et al., 1977), the dates of several hundred airline accidents were compared with the biorhythm charts of those individuals responsible for each accident. No significant correlation between the two was found.

PROGRESS TEST 1

Circle your answers to the following questions and check them against the answer key at the end of this chapter. Be sure to consult the appropriate pages of the text to understand the correct answer for any missed question.

Multiple-Choice Questions

1. As defined by the text, consciousness includes which of the following?
   a. daydreaming
   b. sleeping
   c. hypnosis
   d. all of the above

2. Which of the following groups tends to daydream the most?
   a. elderly men
   b. elderly women
   c. infants
   d. young adults

3. Jet lag is experienced when our _____ is disrupted.
   a. daydreaming
   b. REM sleep
   c. circadian rhythm
   d. stage 4 sleep

4. Sleep spindles predominate during which stage of sleep?
   a. stage 2
   b. stage 3
   c. stage 4
   d. REM

5. During which stage of sleep does the body experience arousal of heart rate, breathing, and the genitals?
a. stage 2
b. stage 3
c. stage 4
d. REM

6. The sleep cycle is approximately _____ minutes in duration.
a. 30
b. 50
c. 75
d. 90

7. Which of the following best describes the effects of sleep deprivation?
a. Emotional instability occurs.
b. Muscular coordination is disrupted.
c. Hallucinations and other abnormal cognitions typically occur.
d. It has little effect on highly motivating tasks.

8. One effect of sleeping pills is to:
a. depress REM sleep.
b. increase REM sleep.
c. depress stage 2 sleep.
d. increase stage 2 sleep.

9. A person who falls asleep in the midst of a heated argument probably suffers from:
a. sleep apnea.
b. narcolepsy.
c. night terrors.
d. insomnia.

10. Which of the following is classified as a depressant?
a. amphetamine
b. LSD
c. marijuana
d. alcohol

11. The discovery of modern hypnosis is generally attributed to:
a. Freud.
b. Mesmer.
c. Orne.
d. Hilgard.

12. Which of the following statements concerning hypnosis is true?
a. People will do anything under hypnosis.
b. Hypnosis is the same as sleeping.
c. Hypnosis is not associated with a distinct physiological state.
d. Hypnosis produces pain relief by triggering endorphin production.

Matching Items

_____ 1. surface meaning of dreams
_____ 2. deeper meaning of dreams
_____ 3. stage of sleep associated with delta waves
_____ 4. sleep stage associated with muscular relaxation
_____ 5. sleep disorder in which breathing stops
_____ 6. sleep disorder occurring in stage 4 sleep
_____ 7. opium
_____ 8. marijuana
_____ 9. cocaine
_____ 10. placebo
_____ 11. category of mood- and perception-altering drugs

a. hallucinogen
b. depressant
c. psychoactive
d. night terrors
e. manifest content
f. stimulant
g. inert drug
h. sleep apnea
i. stage 4 sleep
j. REM sleep
k. latent content

FOCUS ON PSYCHOLOGY:
MEDITATION AND RESTING

Many people use meditation for both physiological and psychological relaxation. In the United States, the most popular technique is TM, or transcendental meditation. Several studies have shown that during TM a variety of physiological changes associated with relaxation take place. Over the past 15 to 20 years, meditation has also been used to treat a number of disorders in which stress has been implicated. These include hypertension, asthma, drug abuse, insomnia, stuttering, and some psychiatric disorders.

Because of the widespread interest in meditation, psychologist David Holmes at the University of Kansas reviewed several dozen studies on the effects of meditation on physiological arousal, in particular on heart rate, respiration rate, blood pressure, skin temperature, oxygen consumption, and muscle tension. Surprisingly, he found no consistent physiological differences between meditating subjects and control subjects who were merely resting. Holmes points out that meditation may promote relaxation in subtle ways that do not show up in standard physiological measures. Holmes also notes that most of the studies involved the use of transcendental meditation, which can be learned in only a few sessions. It is possible that subjects who are more experienced or those using another technique might show more consistent physiological relaxation while meditating. On the other hand, Holmes argues that the case for unique physiological changes accompanying meditation has been overstated. Perhaps meditation is no different from resting.

PROGRESS TEST 2

Progress Test 2 should be completed during a final chapter review. Do so after you thoroughly understand the correct answers for the Chapter Review and Progress Test 1.

Multiple-Choice Questions

1. Which of the following statements regarding REM sleep is true?
a. Adults spend more time than infants in REM.
b. REM deprivation results in a REM rebound.
c. People deprived of REM sleep adapt easily.
d. After a stressful experience, REM sleep decreases.

2. Which theorists believe that the mind and the body are separate entities?
a. the behaviorists
b. the monists
c. the dualists
d. the Freudians

3. Alcohol has the most profound effect on:
a. the transfer of experience to long-term memory.
b. immediate memory.
c. previously established long-term memories.
d. all of the above.

4. A person's EEG shows a high proportion of alpha waves. This person is most likely:
a. dreaming.
b. in stage 4 sleep.
c. in stage 3 sleep.
d. awake and relaxed.

5. Circadian rhythms are the:
a. brain waves that occur during stage 3 sleep.
b. muscular tremors that occur during opiate withdrawal.
c. regular body rhythms that occur on a 24-hour schedule.
d. brain waves that are indicative of REM sleep.

6. A person who requires increasing amounts of a drug in order to feel any effect has developed:
a. tolerance.
b. physical dependency.
c. psychological dependency.
d. resistance.

7. Which of the following statements concerning near-death experiences is true?
a. Less than 1 percent of dying patients report them.
b. They typically consist of fantastic, mystical imagery.
c. They are more commonly experienced by females than by males.
d. They resemble drug-induced hallucinations.

8. Which of the following is *not* characteristic of REM sleep?
a. genital arousal
b. increased muscular tension

c. irregular heart rate
d. irregular breathing

9. Which of the following is *not* a stimulant?
a. amphetamine
b. caffeine
c. nicotine
d. alcohol

10. Which of the following statements reflects a difference between hypnosis and meditation?
a. Hypnosis produces a physiological state that is distinctly different from normal waking consciousness.
b. Brain waves of meditators indicate a highly aroused state.
c. Hypnosis produces larger changes in heart rate and blood pressure.

d. Metabolism slows during meditation.

11. According to Hilgard, hypnosis is:
a. no different from a state of heightened motivation.
b. a hoax perpetrated by frauds.
c. the same as dreaming.
d. a dissociation between different levels of consciousness.

12. Which of the following are *not* psychoactive drugs?
a. hallucinogens
b. depressants
c. stimulants
d. none of the above

Matching Items

_____ 1. early name for hypnosis
_____ 2. disorder in which sleep attacks occur
_____ 3. brain wave of awake, relaxed person
_____ 4. brain wave activity during stage 2 sleep
_____ 5. sleep stage associated with dreaming
_____ 6. sound used during meditation
_____ 7. natural painkiller produced by the brain
_____ 8. neurotransmitter that LSD resembles
_____ 9. neurotransmitter triggered by amphetamine use
_____ 10. theory that dreaming reflects erotic drives
_____ 11. theory that hypnosis is a split in consciousness

a. Freud's theory
b. serotonin
c. mesmerism
d. alpha
e. dissociation
f. narcolepsy
g. norepinephrine
h. sleep spindle
i. endorphin
j. REM
k. mantra

SAMPLE ESSAY QUESTIONS

1. Discuss the three theories of dreaming mentioned in the text.

2. Discuss whether hypnosis is a unique state of consciousness.

3. Describe a typical night's sleep.

4. Describe and contrast the effects of drugs in the following categories: stimulants, depressants, hallucinogens.

5. Describe the phenomenon of the near-death experience. What explanation of this phenomenon is offered by the text?

PROJECT:
A SLEEP AND DREAM DIARY

As the text indicates, the reasons for sleep and dreaming have not been pinpointed. Researchers are fairly certain, however, that the amount of sleep people need seems to increase when they are experiencing stress or some strenuous physical or mental activity. Dream content is a particularly fascinating topic. Too often, on awakening people are unable to remember much of the previous night's dreams. Typically, the only dreams they remember are the vivid ones. Some researchers believe that such dream recall indicates that dreams primarily reflect activity of the emotional, creative, right hemisphere of the brain. In laboratory studies, however, people often report dreaming about rather ordinary daily events.

Try collecting data on your own dreams for several weeks. Place a dimly lit lamp and a pad and pencil next to your bed. In the morning, write down anything you recall from the previous night's dreaming. With practice, you may be able to instruct yourself to take notes immediately after a REM episode, during the subsequent half-waking NREM stage. Each morning, note the total amount of time spent sleeping that night, the number of dreams you were able to recall, and a general description of your mood at the end of the previous day. You might also enlist a few friends to keep track of their sleep and dreaming behavior so that you will have more data to analyze. After several weeks, analyze your data by answering the following questions.

1. Was there a relationship between the amount of sleep and the mood of your subjects?

2. Did dream content or recall vary with sleep duration?

3. What effect, if any, did mood have on dream recall? On dream content?

4. Was there improvement in dream recall as the experiment progressed?

5. Based on your knowledge of hemispheric differences, what percentage of recalled dreams appears to reflect right-hemisphere activity?

WHERE TO LOOK FOR MORE INFORMATION

Bowers, K. S. (1976). *Hypnosis for the seriously curious.* Monterey, CA: Brooks/Cole.

A critical, objective discussion of hypnosis.

Holmes, D. S. (1984, January). Meditation and somatic arousal reduction: A review of the experimental evidence. *American Psychologist.*

The author reviews several dozen studies on the physiological effects of meditation.

Hilts, L. (1984, September). Clocks that make us run. *Omni.*

A review of current research on biological clocks.

Wallace, B., and Fisher, L. E. (1983). *Consciousness and behavior.* Boston: Allyn & Bacon.

This book presents a readable, authoritative review of research on hypnosis, dreaming, meditation, and other varieties of consciousness.

Wolcott, J. H., McMeekin, R. R., Burgin, R. E., and Yanowith, R. E. (1977). Correlation of general aviation accidents with the biorhythm theory. *Human Factors, 19,* 283–293.

An interesting study that fails to support the biorhythm theory.

ANSWERS

PROGRESS TEST 1

Multiple-Choice Questions

1. d (p. 190)
2. d (p. 190)
3. c (p. 191)
4. a (p. 192)

5. d (p. 193)
6. d (p. 193)
7. d (p. 194)
8. a (p. 195)

9. b (p. 195)
10. d (p. 207)
11. b (p. 199)
12. c (p. 203)

Matching Items

1. e (p. 196)
2. k (p. 196)
3. i (p. 193)
4. j (p. 193)

5. h (p. 195)
6. d (p. 195)
7. b (p. 207)
8. a (p. 207)

9. f (p. 207)
10. g (p. 207)
11. c (p. 207)

PROGRESS TEST 2

Multiple-Choice Questions

1. b (p. 198)
2. c (p. 212)
3. a (p. 208)
4. d (p. 192)

5. c (p. 191)
6. a (p. 206)
7. d (p. 211)
8. b (p. 193)

9. d (p. 207)
10. d (p. 204)
11. d (p. 205)
12. d (p. 207)

Matching Items

1. c (p. 199)
2. f (p. 195)
3. d (p. 192)
4. h (p. 192)

5. j (p. 193)
6. k (p. 204)
7. i (p. 209)
8. b (p. 209)

9. g (p. 209)
10. a (p. 196)
11. e (p. 205)

PART FOUR

LEARNING AND THINKING

CHAPTER 9

Learning

CHAPTER OVERVIEW

No topic is closer to the heart of psychology than *learning*, a change in an organism's behavior due to experience. Chapter 9 covers the basic principles of three forms of learning: classical conditioning, in which we learn to anticipate significant events; operant conditioning, in which the consequences of our behaviors determine their future likelihood; and observational learning, in which we learn by observing and imitating others.

The chapter also covers several important issues, including the generality of principles of learning, the role of cognitive processes in learning, and how learning is constrained by the biological predispositions of different species.

GUIDED STUDY

The text chapter should be studied one section at a time. Before you read, preview each section by skimming it, noting headings and boldface items. Then read the appropriate section objectives from the following outline. Keep these objectives in mind, and as you read the chapter section, search for the information that will complete each one. You may wish to write out answers for each objective as soon as you finish reading that section of the chapter.

1. Define and differentiate the following.
a. learning
b. classical conditioning
c. operant conditioning
d. observational learning

Classical Conditioning (pp. 220–227)

2. Explain why classical conditioning confirms the doctrine of learning by association.

3. Describe the basic procedure of classical conditioning and define each of the following.
a. conditioned stimulus
b. unconditioned stimulus
c. conditioned reinforcer
d. unconditioned reinforcer

4. Describe extinction and spontaneous recovery; explain how they relate to classical conditioning.

5. Define and contrast the phenomena of generalization and discrimination as they relate to classical conditioning.

6. Discuss the role of cognitive processes in classical conditioning.

7. Explain why learning may be constrained by biological predispositions, using research on taste aversion to support your claim.

Operant Conditioning (pp. 227–237)

8. Contrast respondent and operant behavior as they apply to classical and operant conditioning.

9. Describe the procedure of behavior shaping.

10. Define and contrast the following types of reinforcers.

 a. positive reinforcer

 b. negative reinforcer

 c. primary reinforcer

 d. secondary reinforcer

11. Compare the effects of immediate and delayed reinforcement.

12. Describe the following schedules of reinforcement and give an example of each.

 a. fixed-interval

 b. fixed-ratio

 c. variable-interval

 d. variable-ratio

13. Define punishment and identify its undesirable side effects.

14. Give examples of escape learning and avoidance learning.

15. Describe how principles of operant conditioning have been applied in each of the following areas.

 a. computer-assisted instruction

 b. economics

 c. self-control

16. Explain how latent learning and the overjustification effect point to the importance of cognitive processes in learning.

Learning by Observation (pp. 237–238)

17. Describe observational learning and give examples of its everyday occurrence in children.

CHAPTER REVIEW

When you have finished reading the chapter, complete the sentences that follow. Using your hand or a strip of paper, cover the correct answers in the margin and fill in each blank. Verify your answer by uncovering the correct one. As you proceed, evaluate your performance for each chapter section. *Do not continue with the next section until you understand why each margin term is the correct answer.* If you need to, review or re-read the appropriate chapter section in the text before continuing.

1. A change in an organism's behavior due to experience is called

_____ .   learning

2. Even simple animals such as the sea snail _____   aplysia

can learn simple _____ between stimuli.   associations

3. The type of learning in which the organism learns to anticipate

significant events is called _____ conditioning.   classical

4. The tendency of organisms to repeat acts that produce favorable

outcomes forms the basis of _____ conditioning.   operant

5. Learning by watching others is called _____   observational learning

_____ .

Classical Conditioning (pp. 220–227)

6. During the seventeenth century, philosophers such as John Locke

argued that an important factor in learning is the

_____ of events occurring in a sequence.   association

7. Classical conditioning was developed by the Russian physiologist _____ _____ .

Ivan Pavlov

8. While studying digestion in dogs, Pavlov discovered that the dogs would begin salivating at the mere sight of food. He referred to this behavior as _____ secretions.

psychic

9. In Pavlov's classic experiment, a bell, or _____ _____ , is sounded just before food, the _____ _____ , is placed in the animal's mouth.

conditioned stimulus

unconditioned stimulus

10. The animal will salivate in response to food. This salivation is called the _____ _____ .

unconditioned response

11. The interval between the CS and UCS that is optimal for conditioning is about _____ second.

one-half

12. If the UCS is an aversive stimulus such as an electric shock, then the conditioned response will be _____ .

fear

13. Classical conditioning is adaptive, since it helps organisms _____ for events that are about to occur.

prepare

14. When the UCS is presented prior to the CS, conditioning _____ (does/does not) occur.

does not

15. If a CS is repeatedly presented without the UCS, the phenomenon of _____ occurs.

extinction

16. The phenomenon in which an extinguished CR reappears following a rest is called _____ _____ .

spontaneous recovery

17. Subjects often respond to a similar stimulus as they would to the original CS. This phenomenon is called _____ .

generalization

18. With training, however, animals can learn not to respond to irrelevant stimuli. This ability is called _____ .

discrimination

19. Pavlov's work was also influential because it gave the new science of psychology an example of how phenomena could be studied _____ , without relying upon subjective techniques such as introspection.

objectively (or experimentally)

20. Pavlov's work gave momentum to the emerging American school of _____ .

behaviorism

21. A chief proponent of behaviorism was the American psychologist _____ .

Watson

22. In their famous experiment, Watson and Raynor used _____ conditioning to train an infant to fear a rat.

classical

23. Increasingly, behaviorists are becoming aware that _____ processes have a place in the science of psychology.

cognitive

24. Simple _____-response learning seems to be the most accurate way to describe the abilities of animals with relatively small amounts of cortex.

stimulus

25. On occasion, when a well-learned route in a maze was blocked, rats chose an alternative route, acting as if they were consulting a _____ map.

cognitive

26. Experiments by Rescorla and Wagner demonstrate that when a CS and a UCS are randomly paired, conditioning _____ (does/does not) take place.

does not

27. This demonstrates that a CS must reliably _____ the UCS for an association to develop.

predict

28. The importance of cognitive processes in human conditioning is demonstrated by the failure of classical conditioning as a treatment for _____.

alcoholism

29. Garcia found that rats would associate electric shock with visual and auditory stimuli, but not with _____.

taste

30. He also discovered that rats would associate _____ with taste, but not with other stimuli.

sickness

31. Garcia found that taste aversion conditioning would occur even when the delay between the CS and the UCS was more than one _____ in duration.

hour

32. Results such as these demonstrate that the principles of learning are constrained by the _____ _____ of each animal species.

biological predispositions

Operant Conditioning (pp. 227–237)

33. Classical conditioning involves simple, _____ responses.

involuntary

34. For more complex, _____ responses, _____ conditioning is more relevant.

voluntary
operant

35. Skinner has referred to the automatic responses of classical conditioning as _____ behavior.

respondent

36. In contrast, he labels behavior that is more spontaneous and that is influenced by its consequences as _____ _____ .

operant behavior

37. Skinner designed an apparatus, called the _____ _____ , to investigate learning in animals.

Skinner box

38. The procedure in which a person teaches an animal to perform an intricate behavior by building up to it in small steps is called behavior _____ .

shaping

39. This method involves reinforcing _____ approximations of the desired behavior.

successive

40. A stimulus that strengthens the behavior that leads to its presentation is a _____ _____ .

positive reinforcer

41. A stimulus such as shock that reinforces the behavior that leads to its termination is a _____ _____ .

negative reinforcer

42. Reinforcers such as food and shock that do not rely on learning are called _____ _____ .

primary reinforcers

43. Reinforcers that derive their power through association with primary reinforcers are called _____ _____ .

secondary reinforcers

44. Immediate reinforcement _____ (is/is not) more effective than _____ reinforcement.

is
delayed

45. The procedure involving reinforcement of each and every response is called _____ _____ .

continuous reinforcement

46. Under these conditions, learning is _____ . When this type of reinforcement is discontinued, however, _____ is rapid.

rapid

extinction

47. Situations in which responses are only intermittently reinforced involve _____ reinforcement.

partial

48. Under these conditions, learning is generally _____ (faster/slower) than it is with continuous reinforcement.

slower

49. The learned behavior is, however, very resistant to _____ .

extinction

50. Reinforcement of the first response after a set interval of time defines the _____-_____ schedule.

fixed-interval

51. On such a schedule, responding generally _____ as the end of the interval approaches.

increases

52. When behavior is reinforced after a set number of responses, a _____-_____ schedule is in effect.

fixed-ratio

53. On this schedule, the animal typically will _____ after receiving a reinforcement.

pause

54. Unpredictable pop quizzes are an example of a _____-_____ schedule of reinforcement.

variable-interval

55. When reinforcement occurs after an unpredictable number of responses, a _____-_____ schedule is being used.

variable-ratio

56. An aversive consequence that decreases the likelihood of the behavior that preceded it is called _____.

punishment

57. Punished behavior is not forgotten, it is _____ and may reappear later.

suppressed

58. One side effect of the use of punishment is that the subject may come to _____ the conditioning situation.

fear

59. The procedure in which a subject learns to make a response in order to terminate an aversive stimulus is called _____ learning.

escape

60. If the subject can learn to *prevent* the aversive stimulus, the procedure involves _____ learning.

avoidance

61. Because punishment arouses hostility, it promotes _____.

aggression

62. The use of teaching machines and programmed textbooks was an early application of the operant conditioning principle of _____ to education.

shaping

63. More recently, the availability of computers has led to the use of _____-_____ instruction techniques.

computer-assisted

64. Operant conditioning principles have also been applied in the field of business and in books offering advice on _____-_____.

self-control

65. Animals may learn from experience, even without reinforcement. When the learning is not apparent until reinforcement has been provided, _____ _____ is said to have occurred.

latent learning

66. When people are rewarded for doing what they already enjoy, their intrinsic motivation may be undermined; this is the

_____ _____ .

overjustification effect

67. Research indicates that both classical and operant conditioning are constrained by each species' _____ predispositions.

biological

Learning by Observation (pp. 237–238)

68. Learning by imitation is called observational learning, or

_____ .

modeling

69. The psychologist best known for research on observational learning is _____ .

Bandura

70. In one experiment, the child who viewed an adult punch an inflatable doll played _____ (more/less) aggressively than the child who had not observed aggressive behavior.

more

71. Children will also model positive or _____ behaviors.

prosocial

FOCUS ON PSYCHOLOGY:
BEHAVIOR PRINCIPLES IN ACTION

Reinforcement and Extinction of Fads

Fads come and go. Stated another way, a new behavior or clothing style spreads in popularity as the people who try the fad receive attention, a powerful social reinforcer; it then fades as attention declines and boredom sets in. A few years ago, for example, lightbulb eating became a fad on many campuses (Baldwin and Baldwin, 1981). Those brave enough to try discovered the secret was to chew the bulb into extremely fine pieces before swallowing. The attention of other students provided such powerful positive reinforcement that others began to imitate the behavior, and the fad caught on. The fad spread until its novelty wore off. After seeing several people eat lightbulbs, most people lost interest. Without the social reinforcement, the bulb eaters were placed on extinction and the fad died out. Some fads, such as clothing styles, follow cycles of reinforcement and extinction that are longer but no less predictable.

The Congressional Skinner Box

Miller (1980) reports that the rate at which Congress passes bills varies with the length of time it has been in session. At the beginning of a congressional session, few bills are passed. As the session continues, the rate of passage increases gradually, peaking just prior to adjournment. The graph below illustrates the

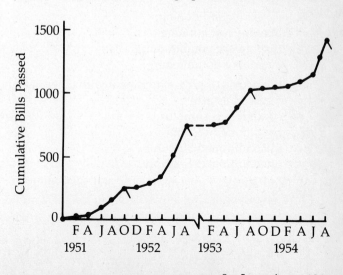

cumulative rate at which bills were passed over a four-year period. The diagonal slashes indicate the dates of adjournment. Miller suggests that adjournment represents a powerful reinforcer for the completion of legislative business. These dates create a fixed-interval schedule of reinforcement and result in the familiar scalloped response pattern typical of this schedule. Can you identify schedules of reinforcement that operate in your life? Does your behavior fit the predicted patterns of responding?

PROGRESS TEST 1

Circle your answers to the following questions and check them with the answer key at the end of this chapter. Be sure to consult the appropriate pages of the text to understand the correct answer for any missed question.

Multiple-Choice Questions

1. Learning is best defined as:
   a. any behavior emitted rather than elicited by an organism.
   b. a change in the behavior of an organism.
   c. a change in the behavior of an organism due to experience.
   d. behavior based on operant rather than respondent conditioning.

2. The type of learning associated with B. F. Skinner is:
   a. classical conditioning.
   b. operant conditioning.
   c. respondent conditioning.
   d. avoidance conditioning.

3. In Pavlov's original experiment with dogs, the meat served as a(n):
   a. conditioned stimulus.
   b. conditioned response.
   c. unconditioned stimulus.
   d. unconditioned response.

4. You always rattle the box of dog biscuits before giving your dog a treat. As you do so, your dog salivates. Rattling the box thus is a(n) _____; your dog's salivation is a(n) _____.

a. conditioned stimulus; conditioned response
b. conditioned stimulus; unconditioned response
c. unconditioned stimulus; conditioned response
d. unconditioned stimulus; unconditioned response

5. In order to obtain a reward, a monkey learns to press a lever when a 1000-Hz tone is on, but not when a 1200-Hz tone is on. What kind of training is this?
   a. extinction
   b. generalization
   c. discrimination
   d. classical

6. Which of the following statements concerning reinforcement is correct?
   a. Learning is most rapid with partial reinforcement.
   b. Learning is most rapid with continuous reinforcement, but partial reinforcement produces the greatest resistance to extinction.
   c. Learning is fastest and resistance to extinction is greatest following continuous reinforcement.
   d. Learning is fastest and resistance to extinction is greatest following partial reinforcement.

7. You are expecting an important letter in the mail. As the regular delivery time approaches, you glance more and more frequently out the window, searching for the letter carrier. Your behavior in this situation is being reinforced by which schedule?
   a. fixed-ratio
   b. variable-ratio
   c. fixed-interval
   d. variable-interval

8. Which of the following schedules of reinforcement produces the highest, most consistent rate of response?
   a. fixed-ratio
   b. variable-ratio
   c. fixed-interval
   d. variable-interval

9. Jack finally takes out the garbage in order to

get his father to stop pestering him. Jack's behavior is being influenced by:
  a. positive reinforcement.
— b. negative reinforcement.
  c. primary reinforcement.
  d. punishment.

10. When a conditioned stimulus is presented without an accompanying unconditioned stimulus, _____ will soon take place.
  a. generalization
  b. discrimination
— c. extinction
  d. aversion

11. One difference between classical and operant conditioning is that:

  a. in classical conditioning the responses are voluntary.
  b. in operant conditioning the responses are triggered by preceding stimuli.
— c. in classical conditioning the responses are involuntary.
  d. in operant conditioning the responses are involuntary.

12. In Garcia's studies of taste aversion learning, rats learned to associate:
  a. taste with electric shock.
  b. sights and sounds with sickness.
— c. taste with sickness.
  d. taste and sounds with electric shock.

Matching Items

_____ 1. learning to prevent an aversive stimulus
_____ 2. tendency for similar stimuli to evoke a CR
_____ 3. terminating an aversive stimulus
_____ 4. an innately reinforcing stimulus
_____ 5. an acquired reinforcer
_____ 6. responses are reinforced after an unpredictable amount of time
_____ 7. each and every response is reinforced
_____ 8. reinforcing closer and closer approximations of a behavior
_____ 9. the reappearance of an extinguished CR
_____ 10. presenting an aversive stimulus
_____ 11. learning that becomes apparent only after reinforcement is provided

  a. shaping
  b. punishment
  c. spontaneous recovery
  d. latent learning
  e. avoidance learning
  f. negative reinforcement
  g. primary reinforcement
  h. generalization
  i. secondary reinforcement
  j. continuous reinforcement
  k. variable-interval schedule

FOCUS ON PSYCHOLOGY:
PHOBIAS

As the text indicates, many human emotions are probably acquired through classical conditioning. Phobias, or irrational fears, may be acquired when a neutral stimulus becomes associated with a fear-producing unconditioned stimulus. An individual may have acquired a phobia for dogs, for example, if as a child he or she became frightened while petting one. The fear may become associated with dogs (or any similar stimulus) even though it may have been the parents' fright, not the dog, that elicited the child's fear. Phobias, then, are irrational conditioned responses of fear. In this example, can you identify the CS? the CR? the UCS? the UCR? Do you have any strong fears for which you have no rational explanation? Can you imagine how you might have acquired them?

One widely used technique for eliminating phobias is *systematic desensitization*, which will be discussed in detail in Chapter 17. In this approach, the phobic CS is paired with a new, nonaversive UCS. The phobic person first constructs a *hierarchy of fears*. This is a ranking of five to ten situations associated with the CS, from most to least feared. In the case of a phobia for dogs, the hierarchy might appear as below:

(Most feared) **1.** Allowing a dog to lick my face
                 2. Holding my hand out to greet a dog
                 3. Holding a dog on a leash
                 4. Passing by a person with a dog on a leash
(Least feared) **5.** Sitting across a room from a dog

Next the person is taught deep relaxation using biofeedback, meditation, or some other technique. While relaxed, the person envisions each situation in the hierarchy. Desensitization proceeds until the person can imagine and/or actually engage in each of the behaviors in the hierarchy. When successful, desensitization changes each situation from a fear-arousing CS to a relaxation-promoting CS. Desensitization has proved most successful in the treatment of phobias for specific objects or situations. When a person is experiencing anxiety that is not specifically attached to a stimulus, other techniques may be more effective.

PROGRESS TEST 2

Progress Test 2 should be completed during a final chapter review. Do so after you thoroughly understand the correct answers for the Chapter Review and Progress Test 1.

Multiple-Choice Questions

For questions 1 to 4, use the following information.

As a child, you were playing in the yard one day when a neighbor's cat wandered over. Your mother (who has a terrible fear of animals) screamed and snatched you into her arms. Her behavior caused you to cry. You now have a fear of cats.

1. Identify the CS:
a. your mother's behavior
b. your crying
c. the cat
d. your fear today

2. Identify the US:
a. your mother's behavior
b. your crying
c. the cat
d. your fear today

3. Identify the CR:
a. your mother's behavior
b. your crying
c. the cat
d. your fear today

4. Identify the UR:
a. your mother's behavior
b. your crying
c. the cat
d. your fear today

5. A possible reason for long-suppressed fears to resurface suddenly is that they:
a. were acquired through operant conditioning.
b. were acquired through modeling.
c. may show spontaneous recovery.
d. may generalize to new situations.

6. Rats finding a well-traveled route blocked will choose an alternative route to their goal. It is as though they have a(n) _____ of the maze.
a. cognitive map
b. mental map
c. generalized stimulus picture
d. mental picture

7. In distinguishing between negative reinforcers and punishment, we note that:
a. punishment, but not negative reinforcement, involves use of an aversive stimulus.
b. with negative reinforcement, the likelihood of a response is decreased by the presentation of an aversive stimulus.
c. with negative reinforcement, the likelihood of a response is increased by the presentation of an aversive stimulus.
d. with negative reinforcement, the likelihood of a response is increased by the termination of an aversive stimulus.

8. The piecework, or commission, method of payment is an example of which reinforcement schedule?
a. fixed-interval
b. variable-interval
c. fixed-ratio
d. variable-ratio

9. Learning to put on your coat *before* going outside is an example of which type of learning?
a. discrimination learning
b. punishment
c. escape learning
d. avoidance learning

10. When people are paid for performing tasks they enjoy, their self-motivation may actually decrease. This is called:
a. latent learning.
b. the overjustification effect.
c. secondary reinforcement.
d. vicarious conditioning.

11. You teach your dog to fetch the paper by giving him a cookie each time he does so. This is an example of:
a. operant conditioning.
b. classical conditioning.
c. secondary reinforcement.
d. partial reinforcement.

12. Bill once had a blue car that was in the repair shop more than it was out. He now will not even consider owning blue or green cars. His aversion to green is an example of:
a. discrimination.
b. generalization.
c. latent learning.
d. the overjustification effect.

True–False Items

_____ **1.** Operant conditioning involves behavior that is primarily involuntary.

_____ **2.** The optimal interval between CS and UCS is about 15 seconds.

_____ **3.** Negative reinforcement decreases the likelihood that a response will recur.

_____ **4.** The learning of a new behavior proceeds most rapidly with continuous reinforcement.

_____ **5.** As a rule, variable schedules of reinforcement produce more consistent rates of responding than fixed schedules do.

_____ **6.** Cognitive processes are of relatively little importance in learning.

_____ **7.** Although punishment may be effective in suppressing behavior, it can have several undesirable side effects.

_____ **8.** All animals, including rats and birds, are biologically predisposed to associate taste cues with sickness.

_____ **9.** Whether the CS or UCS is presented first seems not to matter in terms of the ease of classical conditioning.

_____ **10.** Spontaneous recovery refers to the tendency of extinguished behaviors to reappear suddenly.

SAMPLE ESSAY QUESTIONS

1. In what ways are punishment and reinforcement alike? How are they different? What are the side effects of punishment?

2. Discuss the history of the concept of cognition in learning. What evidence supports its importance?

3. What is meant by the phrase "learning is constrained by biological predispositions"?

4. Compare and contrast classical with operant conditioning.

5. Describe the four major types of reinforcement schedules.

PROJECT:
CLASSICAL AND OPERANT CONDITIONING
OF RESPONSES

Classical Conditioning

It is easy to demonstrate the development of a classically conditioned response. In this experiment, we will condition an eyeblink to a specific sound. You will need a volunteer, a straw, and some sort of noisemaker (a "cricket," or clicker, is ideal). Have the volunteer sit down. Explain that you will periodically make a sound and blow a puff of air into the subject's eye. Demonstrate both the clicker and the air puff. Before you begin conditioning trials, determine if the clicker is a neutral stimulus. Click the cricket several times without blowing into the subject's eye. Do this until the subject no longer blinks when the clicker is sounded. Now begin conditioning. Sound the clicker and then immediately blow a puff of air into the subject's eye. Do this 25 times, waiting 10 seconds between each time. After the conditioning trials, test for a conditioned response by sounding the clicker alone. Did the subject blink? Continue with these extinction trials (spaced 10 seconds apart) until the subject fails to blink on 5 consecutive trials. How long did it take for extinction to occur? If possible, bring the subject back a day or two later and test for spontaneous recovery by again sounding the clicker. Finally, recondition the subject with 10 or 15 clicker-air puff trials, and test for generalization to other sounds such as finger snapping or tapping a pencil.

Operant Conditioning

Following the procedure outlined in Chapter 9 of the text, you should be able to use shaping to teach a dog or cat a new skill. Decide on a specific response the pet is to learn. Rolling over or sitting up are good choices for dogs. You will also need to find an effective reinforcer. Some sort of biscuit or dog treat is favored by animal trainers. This primary reinforcement should be accompanied by effusive praise (secondary reinforcement) whenever the dog makes a successful response. Finally, decide on a vocal command and/or hand signal that will cue the dog. This signal is called a *discriminative stimulus.* Your task is to reinforce successive approximations of the final behavior. Begin by reinforcing a simple approximation that is already in the dog's repertoire. For rolling over, it might simply be having the dog lie down on your command. Reinforce this behavior several times. Next, say ''Roll over,'' and withhold reinforcement until the dog (usually out of frustration) makes a closer approximation (such as rotating slightly in one direction). Now, consistently reinforce turning in this direction. Gradually shape the animal, moving to closer and closer approximations of the desired behavior. With practice (and a great deal of patience), you should be able to teach the dog a variety of new tricks.

WHERE TO LOOK FOR MORE INFORMATION

Baldwin, J. D., and Baldwin, J. I. (1981). *Behavior principles in everyday life*. Englewood Cliffs, NJ: Prentice-Hall.

Miller, L. K. (1980). *Principles of everyday behavior analysis* (2nd ed.). Monterey, CA: Brooks/Cole.

Two very readable books that illustrate the widespread influence of classical and operant conditioning in our lives.

The *Journal of Applied Behavior Analysis* publishes research in which operant procedures have been applied to human behaviors. Although technical, these articles are generally very readable and interesting.

ANSWERS

PROGRESS TEST 1

Multiple-Choice Questions

1. c (p. 219)
2. b (p. 227)
3. c (p. 221)
4. a (p. 221)

5. c (p. 223)
6. b (p. 229)
7. c (p. 230)
8. a (p. 230)

9. b (p. 229)
10. c (p. 223)
11. c (p. 227)
12. c (p. 226)

Matching Items

1. e (p. 231)
2. h (p. 223)
3. f (p. 229)
4. g (p. 229)

5. i (p. 229)
6. k (p. 230)
7. j (p. 229)
8. a (p. 228)

9. c (p. 223)
10. b (p. 231)
11. d (p. 236)

PROGRESS TEST 2

Multiple-Choice Questions

1. c (p. 221)
2. a (p. 221)
3. d (p. 221)
4. b (p. 221)

5. c (p. 223)
6. a (p. 235)
7. d (p. 229, 231)
8. c (p. 230)

9. d (p. 231)
10. b (p. 236)
11. a (p. 227)
12. b (p. 223)

True–False Items

1. False (p. 227)
2. False (p. 222)
3. False (p. 229)
4. True (p. 229)

5. True (p. 230)
6. False (p. 235)
7. True (p. 231)
8. False (p. 226)

9. False (p. 222)
10. True (p. 223)

CHAPTER 10

Memory

CHAPTER OVERVIEW

Chapter 10 explores human memory as a system that processes information in three steps. *Encoding* is the process of putting information into the memory system. *Storage* is the passive mechanism by which information is maintained in memory. *Retrieval* is the process by which information is accessed from memory through recall or recognition.

The chapter also discusses the importance of organization and imagery in encoding new memories, how memory is represented physically in the brain, and how forgetting may reflect failure to encode, store, or find appropriate retrieval cues. As you study this chapter, try applying some of the memory and study tips discussed in the text.

GUIDED STUDY

The text chapter should be studied one section at a time. Before you read, preview each section by skimming it, noting headings and boldface items. Then read the appropriate section objectives from the following outline. Keep these objectives in mind, and as you read the chapter section, search for the information that will complete each one. You may wish to write out answers for each objective as soon as you finish reading that section of the chapter.

Forming Memories (pp. 244–259)

1. Explain the similarities between human memory and the computer as information-processing systems.

2. Describe Sperling's experiment and why its results support the concept of iconic memory.

3. Explain the process of encoding; give examples of visual, acoustic, and semantic encoding.

4. Contrast automatic and effortful processing; give examples of the type of information we usually process in each way.

5. Describe how Ebbinghaus studied memory and explain the relationship between retention and the amount of time spent learning.

6. Give an example of the serial position effect.

7. Discuss the importance of meaning and imagery in encoding and give examples of each.

8. Define and give several examples of mnemonic devices.

9. Describe the process of chunking and how it aids memory.

10. Explain the differences between short- and long-term memory.

11. Describe the research implicating each of the following in the physical basis of memory.

a. electrical activity

b. RNA

c. serotonin

12. Describe each of the following methods of measuring memory.

a. recall

b. recognition

c. relearning

13. Describe and give several examples of state-dependent memory.

14. Explain the process of memory construction and its implications for eyewitness testimony and hypnotically refreshed memories.

CHAPTER REVIEW

When you have finished reading the chapter, complete the sentences that follow. Using your hand or a strip of paper, cover the correct answers in the margin and fill in each blank. Verify your answer by un-

Forgetting (pp. 259–264)

15. Explain the relationship of each of the following to forgetting.

a. encoding failure

b. decay

c. proactive interference

d. retroactive interference

e. retrieval failure

Improving Memory (pp. 264–265)

16. Explain the SQ3R study technique.

covering the correct one. As you proceed, evaluate your performance for each chapter section. *Do not continue with the next section until you understand why each margin term is the correct answer.* If you need to, review or re-read the appropriate chapter section in the text before continuing.

Forming Memories (pp. 244–259)

1. Both human memory and computers can be viewed as _____-processing systems.

information

2. Each system faces three tasks: _____, _____, and _____.

encoding

storage; retrieval

3. George Sperling found that when people were briefly shown three rows of letters, they could recall only about _____ of them.

half

4. When Sperling sounded a tone immediately after a row of letters was flashed to indicate which letters were to be recalled, the subjects were much _____ (more/less) accurate.

more

5. This suggests that people have a brief photographic, or _____, memory.

iconic

6. This type of memory lasts only briefly, for if Sperling's tone was delayed by as little as one _____, the memory was gone.

second

7. Sensory memory for sounds is called _____ memory.

echoic

8. This memory, which lasts about _____ seconds, fades _____ (more/less) rapidly than iconic memory.

3 or 4; less

9. Encoding the meaning of words is referred to as _____ encoding; encoding by sound is called _____ encoding; encoding the image of words is _____ encoding.

semantic
acoustic
visual

10. Asked to repeat letters immediately after seeing a list of them, people tend to make acoustic errors _____ (more of-ten/less often) than visual errors. One hour later, errors tend to be _____ .

more often

semantic

11. For many years, psychologists believed that these errors reflected the operation of two types of memory: _____-_____ storage for sound and _____-_____ memory for mean-ing.

short-term

long-term

12. More recent evidence suggests that memory for meaning _____ (can/cannot) be encoded immediately.

can

13. A different distinction has now been made between memory that is _____ and that which is _____ .

automatic; effortful

14. Encoding of some attributes is automatic and unlearned, such as encoding of _____, _____, and _____ .

space; time
frequency

15. The automatic processing of word meaning, however, is _____ .

learned

16. In the Hasher and Zacks experiment, subjects told that they would later be asked to estimate a word's frequency in a list _____ (did/did not) improve their performance as compared with that of an uncued group.

did not

17. Peterson and Peterson found that, when _____ was prevented by asking subjects to count backward, memory for a syllable was gone almost completely after approximately _____ seconds.

rehearsal

18

18. A pioneering researcher of verbal memory was _____ .

Ebbinghaus

19. In order to study memory with uncontaminated verbal material, he created lists of _____ syllables.

nonsense

20. Ebbinghaus found that the longer he studied a list of nonsense syllables, the _____ (fewer/greater) the number of repetitions he required to relearn it later.

fewer

21. After material has been learned, additional repetition, or over-learning, usually _____ (will/will not) increase retention.

will

22. The tendency to remember the first and last items in a list best is called the _____ _____

_____ .

serial position effect

23. When a delay is imposed before the test of recall, the _____ items tend to be recalled.

first

24. Craik and Watkins found that merely repeating information _____ (was/was not) sufficient for a person to form a permanent memory.

was not

25. Craik and Tulving gave subjects a list of words to remember. Of three types of encoding strategies (visual, acoustic, and semantic), _____ encoding resulted in the greatest retention.

semantic

26. Visual encoding is also called _____ .

imagery

27. Your earliest memories are generally of events that occurred when you were _____ years old.

3 or 4

28. Concrete, high-imagery words tend to be remembered _____ (better/worse) than abstract, low-imagery words.

better

29. Memory aids are known as _____ devices.

mnemonic

30. Many of these aids rely on the use of _____ imagery.

visual

31. Using a jingle, such as the one that begins "One is a bun," is an example of the _____-_____ system.

peg-word

32. Memory may be aided by grouping information into familiar units called _____ .

chunks

33. One mnemonic device involves forming words from the first letters of words to be remembered; the resulting word is called an

_____ .

acronym

34. In addition to chunks, material may also be processed into

_____ .

hierarchies

35. If you are able to retrieve something from memory, you must have engaged in the passive process of _____ .

storage

36. Our short-term memory capacity is approximately
_____ items.

7

37. Adults _____ (do/do not) have a greater memory span than children.

do

38. In contrast, our permanent memory capacity is_____.

unlimited

39. Recall by people under hypnosis _____ (is/is not) reliable.

is not

40. Lashley attempted to locate memory by cutting out pieces of rats' _____ after they had learned a maze.

cortexes

41. He found that, no matter where he cut, the memory _____ (was/was not) interfered with.

was not

42. Gerard found that a hamster's memory remained even after its body temperature had been lowered to a point where the brain's _____ activity stopped.

electrical

43. Earlier studies of memory had suggested that memory might reside in the chemical molecules of _____.

RNA

44. More recent studies indicate that memory begins as _____ activity, but experiences a structural change as it becomes permanent.

electrical

45. Researchers believe that the structural change that occurs in memory takes place at the _____ between neurons.

synapses

46. This theory seems potentially correct, due to evidence that certain disorders, such as _____ disease, disrupt memory through the loss of brain tissues that secrete important neurotransmitters.

Alzheimer's

47. Researchers Kandel and Schwartz have found that when learning occurs, the neurotransmitter _____ is released in greater amounts, making synapses more efficient.

serotonin

48. Alcohol and other drugs classified as _____ impede memory formation.

depressants

49. Hormones released under stress may actually _____ learning and memory.

boost (or improve)

50. The ability to retrieve information that is not present is called _____.

recall

51. Bahrick found that, twenty-five years after graduation, people could not remember the names of their classmates, but they could _____ their yearbook pictures.

recognize

52. If you have learned something and then forgotten it, you will probably be able to _____ it _____ (more/less) quickly than you did originally.

relearn; more

53. Studies have shown that retention is best when learning and testing are done in the same _____ .

context

54. The type of memory in which emotions serve as retrieval cues is called _____-_____ memory.

state-dependent

55. Research has shown that events are often recalled on the basis of past experience, rather than the actual event being recalled. This illustrates the process of memory _____ .

construction

56. In one study, students given tests that helped them to evaluate their knowledge learned _____ (as well as/more slowly than) students who were repeatedly shown factual statements.

as well as

Forgetting (pp. 259–264)

57. Most memory failures reflect a failure to _____ the material properly.

encode

58. Studies by Ebbinghaus and Bahrick indicate that most forgetting occurs _____ after learning.

soon (or quickly)

59. Research suggests that memories are lost not only because they _____ with time, but also as a result of interference.

decay

60. Jenkins and Dallenbach found that if subjects went to sleep after learning, their memory for a list of nonsense syllables was _____ (better/worse) than it was had they stayed awake.

better

61. The interference of previous learning with current learning is called _____ _____ .

proactive interference

62. The interfering effect of learning new material on efforts to recall material previously learned is called _____ _____ .

retroactive interference

63. When information that is stored in memory temporarily cannot be found, _____ _____ has occurred.

retrieval failure

64. Freud proposed that motivated forgetting, or _____ , may protect a person from painful memories.

repression

Improving Memory (pp. 264–265)

65. The SQ3R study technique stands for the following stages:

_____, _____,

_____, _____,

_____.

survey; question

read; recite

review

FOCUS ON PSYCHOLOGY:
INFANTILE AMNESIA

What is your earliest memory? If you are like most people, it is of an event that occurred when you were about 3 years old. Why is it that the experiences of our earlier years are forgotten? Freud suggested that, at about age 7, memories of the earlier oral, anal, and phallic stages of development are *repressed* in memory, protecting the child from dealing with this anxiety-laden material. Since most of us remember events from earlier years, Freud's theory is obviously flawed. Why then do we all have *infantile amnesia?* Several contemporary explanations have been proposed. According to the *encoding specificity hypothesis,* memory is improved when retrieval occurs in the same context as encoding. In one study, for example, researchers had scuba divers learn lists of words on land or under water. Later, during a test of recall, memory was best when testing occurred in the same context as had learning. This phenomenon may explain why, when visiting your old school or neighborhood, memories come rushing back.

A second explanation of infantile amnesia is that adults and children organize their experiences in conceptually different ways. As Piaget put it, the cognitive *schemes* of children differ at each age. Just as the child cannot understand adult logic, adults are unable to retrieve memories encoded by the mind of a child. This theory is similar to the phenomenon of *state-dependent memory*—information encoded in one psychological or physiological state is best retrieved in that same state. In one study, Bower (1981) put groups of students into sad or happy moods and then asked them to retrieve childhood memories. Happy subjects tended to recall happy incidents; sad subjects remembered sad incidents. Bower also points out that the nervous system is not completely formed at birth. During early childhood, the brain continues to mature, at least until about age 4. While the extent

of its influence is not known, brain immaturity may play a role in infantile amnesia.

A third proposed explanation of infantile amnesia is based on the *linguistic determinism hypothesis.* Adult memories are typically based on semantic encoding and retrieval. Infantile amnesia may simply be a result of the child's lack of language. This would explain why the earliest memories appear at the age when language acquisition is well under way. On the basis of this discussion, what advice would you offer a friend who was attempting to retrieve his or her memories of early childhood experiences?

PROGRESS TEST 1

Circle your answers to the following questions and check them with the answer key at the end of the chapter. Be sure to consult the appropriate pages of the text in order to understand the correct answer for any missed question.

Multiple-Choice Questions

1. The three steps in memory information processing are:
a. input, processing, output.
b. input, storage, output.
c. input, storage, retrieval.
d. encoding, storage, retrieval.

2. Visual sensory memory is referred to as:
a. iconic memory.
b. echoic memory.
c. photomemory.
d. semantic memory.

3. Memories fade from our sensory memories after approximately:
a. 1 hour.
b. 1 minute.
c. 1 second.
d. 1/16 second.

4. Which of the following is *not* a measure of retention?

a. recall   **c.** relearning
b. recognition   **d.** retrieval

5. Our immediate memory span is approximately _____ items.

a. 2   **c.** 7
b. 5   **d.** 15

6. Techniques that aid memory are called:
a. consolidation techniques.
b. imagery techniques.
c. encoding strategies.
d. mnemonic devices.

7. One way to increase the amount of information in memory is to group it into larger familiar units. This process is referred to as:
a. consolidating.
b. chunking.
c. memory construction.
d. encoding.

8. Kandel and Schwartz have found that when learning occurs, more of the neurotransmitter _____ is released into synapses.

a. ACh   **c.** serotonin
b. dopamine   **d.** noradrenaline

9. Resear
that:
a. memo
ence.
b. memo
sumpt
c. memo
from
d. long-t
about

10. Conte
one study
or under
with the
a. learne

Matching Items

_____ **1.** the type of sensory memory that decays more slowly than visual sensory memory
_____ **2.** the process by which information gets into the memory system
_____ **3.** mental pictures that aid memory
_____ **4.** the blocking of painful memories
_____ **5.** the phenomenon in which one's mood can influence retrieval
_____ **6.** memory for a list of words is affected by word order
_____ **7.** "one is a bun, two is a shoe" mnemonic system
_____ **8.** "the magical number seven, plus or minus two"
_____ **9.** new learning interferes with previous knowledge

image onto the second dot pattern. If they are able to do so, the combination of dots produces a recognizable group of letters or numbers. If you think that you might be an eidetiker, consult Stromeyer's article (see Where to Look for More Information) for information on scoring this test. Before you become envious of the abilities of eidetikers, be aware that some find photographic memory annoying. Imagine having random images of pages from books or from study notes coming to consciousness uncontrollably, years after first seeing them!

PROGRESS TEST 2

Progress Test 2 should be completed during a final chapter review. Do so after you thoroughly understand the correct answers for the Chapter Review and Progress Test 1.

Multiple-Choice Questions

1. Which of the following best describes the typical forgetting curve?
a. a steady, slow decline in retention over time
b. a steady, rapid decline in retention over time
c. a rapid initial decline in retention, becoming stable thereafter
d. no decline in retention with time

2. In Sperling's memory experiment, subjects were shown three rows of letters, followed at different times by a low-, medium-, or high-pitched tone. The subjects were able to report:
a. all three rows with perfect accuracy.
b. only the top row of letters.
c. only the middle row of letters.
d. any one of the three rows of letters.

3. Which of the following measures of retention is the least sensitive?
a. recall
b. recognition
c. relearning
d. savings

4. Subjects are shown a list of letters and asked to repeat them. Their errors in retrieval are typically:
a. semantic errors.
b. visual errors.

tructor at Har-
ine a picture or
literal mental
ears. This phe-
photographic
mply reflect su-
tructor's ability
as if she had a
ing a poem (in
able to write it
. She can copy
is able to copy

Psychology

y used test of
of this discus-
pattern of dots
age of it. They
project the first

c. acoustic errors.

d. based on spatial characteristics of the letters.

5. According to the serial position effect, when recalling a list of words you should have the greatest difficulty with those:

a. at the beginning of the list.

b. in the middle of the list.

c. at the end of the list.

d. at the end and in the middle of the list.

6. Craik and Watkins gave subjects a list of words to be recalled. When they were tested *after a delay*, the items that were best recalled were:

a. at the beginning of the list.

b. in the middle of the list.

c. at the end of the list.

d. in the middle and at the end of the list.

7. Craik and Tulving instructed subjects to process lists of words visually, acoustically, or semantically. In a subsequent recall test, which type of processing resulted in the greatest retention?

a. visual

b. acoustic

c. semantic

d. acoustic and semantic equally beneficial

8. Lashley's studies, in which rats learned a maze and then had various parts of their brains surgically removed, showed that:

a. the memory was disrupted when higher brain areas were removed.

b. the memory was disrupted when lower brain areas were removed.

c. the memory was disrupted when any region of the brain was removed.

d. the memory remained no matter which area of the brain was tampered with.

9. The importance of neurotransmitters in the formation of new memories is confirmed by _____ disease, which disrupts memory through the loss of brain tissue.

a. Munsinger's

b. Alzheimer's

c. Lou Gehrig's

d. Wertheimer's

10. Which type of drug tends to disrupt memory formation?

a. stimulants

b. stress hormones

c. depressants

d. opiates

11. The sober person who is unable to find a housekey that he or she hid while drunk is demonstrating the phenomenon of:

a. confabulation.

b. drug-induced forgetting.

c. state-dependent memory.

d. retroactive interference.

12. Studies by Loftus and Palmer, in which subjects were quizzed about a film of an accident, indicate that:

a. when quizzed immediately, subjects can recall very little, due to the stress of witnessing an accident.

b. when questioned as little as one day later, their memory was very inaccurate.

c. most subjects had very accurate memories up to 6 months later.

d. eyewitness testimony may be affected by misleading information, such as how questions are phrased.

True–False Items

_____ 1. Studying that is distributed over time produces better retention than cramming.

_____ 2. Most psychologists accept the distinction between two different types of memory: short-term and long-term.

_____ 3. Generally speaking, memory for pictures is better than memory for words.

_____ 4. Studies of age regression through hypnosis indicate that memory is permanent, due to the reliability of such reports.

_____ 5. Studies in which researchers attempted chemically to transfer memory from one organism to another have not been reliably duplicated.

_____ 6. Studies by Ebbinghaus show that most forgetting takes place soon after learning.

_____ 7. Decay, rather than interference, seems to best describe why forgetting occurs.

_____ 8. Recall of newly acquired knowledge is no better after sleeping than after being awake for the same period of time.

_____ 9. Time spent in imaging, chunking, and associating material with what you already know is more effective than repeating information again and again.

_____ 10. The final step in the SQ3R technique is "recite."

SAMPLE ESSAY QUESTIONS

1. Describe the three components of the information processing model of memory.

2. Compare and contrast the decay and interference theories of forgetting. Explain the several varieties of interference.

3. Discuss the various ways information may be encoded.

4. Describe the research that has led to theories of how memory is represented physically.

5. Discuss several important factors in the retrieval of memories.

PROJECT:
MEMORY SPAN AND CHUNKING

The text explains that our immediate memory span seems to be limited to about 7 units of information. Grouping items into larger units, or chunks, may increase the amount of information we are able to hold in memory. For this demonstration, you will need several volunteers with pencil and paper. Explain to them that you will read several sets of digits. They are to listen carefully *until you finish with a set*, and then write down the digits in the order of presentation. Read each set in Test A at a slow, even pace. After you have presented all the sets, read them again, allowing the subjects to check which numbers they recalled correctly in each set.

Test A

1-3-8-7-2
4-9-0-1-3-8
2-8-7-4-6-5-9
8-0-1-3-5-2-7-4
0-2-8-3-4-1-9-6-5
2-8-7-9-0-1-3-4-5-6
3-7-1-2-8-4-0-5-6-9-0
9-2-1-8-7-0-5-3-4-2-6-8

Using the graph at the end of this section, plot the percentage of subjects who correctly recalled all the digits of each set. Draw a curve using a solid line. What is the average memory span?

Now, ask your subjects to again listen to sets of digits and write them down. Use Test B. Read each chunk quickly, pausing briefly between chunks. For example, the first set would be read: "four, twenty-three" (pause) "nineteen." When all sets have been presented, check the results and plot them on the graph, using a dashed line to connect the points. What effect did chunking have on retention?

Test B

423-19
267-198
390-675-2
573-291-43
721-354-456
245-619-832-2
141-384-515-89
201-315-426-762

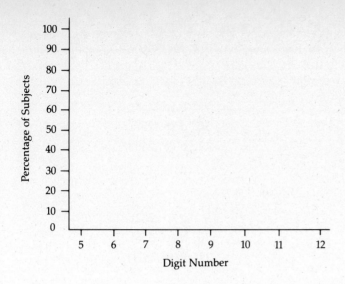

WHERE TO LOOK FOR MORE INFORMATION

Bower, G. H. (1985, June). Mood and memory. *Psychology Today*.

A renowned memory researcher discusses state-dependent memory.

Stromeyer, C. F. (1970, November). Eidetikers. *Psychology Today*.

A description of the remarkable abilities of people with photographic memory.

ANSWERS

PROGRESS TEST 1

Multiple-Choice Questions

1. d (p. 245)
2. a (p. 246)
3. c (p. 246)
4. d (p. 256)

5. c (p. 253)
6. d (p. 251)
7. b (p. 252)
8. c (p. 255)

9. b (p. 258)
10. d (p. 257)
11. b (p. 260)

Matching Items

1. k (p. 246)
2. h (pp. 246–247)
3. i (pp. 250–251)
4. a (p. 264)

5. j (p. 257)
6. c (p. 249)
7. d (p. 251)
8. e (p. 253)

9. g (p. 262)
10. b (p. 256)
11. f (p. 262)

PROGRESS TEST 2

Multiple-Choice Questions

1. c (p. 260)
2. d (p. 246)
3. a (p. 256)
4. c (p. 250)

5. b (p. 249)
6. a (p. 249)
7. c (p. 250)
8. d (p. 254)

9. b (p. 255)
10. c (p. 255)
11. c (p. 257)
12. d (p. 258)

True–False Items

1. True (p. 264)
2. False (p. 247)
3. True (p. 250)
4. False (p. 254)

5. True (pp. 254–255)
6. True (p. 248)
7. False (p. 261)
8. False (p. 262)

9. True (pp. 251–252)
10. False (p. 265)

CHAPTER 11

Thinking and Language

CHAPTER OVERVIEW

Most of Chapter 11 deals with thinking, with emphasis on how people logically—and at times illogically—use deductive and inductive reasoning when making decisions and attempting to solve problems. The rest of the chapter is concerned with language, including its structure, development in children, and relationship to thinking. Two theories of language acquisition are evaluated: Skinner's theory that language acquisition is based entirely on learning, and Chomsky's theory that humans have a biological predisposition to acquire language.

GUIDED STUDY

The text chapter should be studied one section at a time. Before you read, preview each section by skimming it, noting headings and boldface items. Then read the appropriate section objectives from the following outline. Keep these objectives in mind, and as you read the chapter section, search for the information that will complete each one. You may wish to write out answers for each objective as soon as you finish reading that section of the chapter.

Thinking (pp. 270–286)

1. Explain what *prototypes* are and how they are used to form concepts.

2. Define and contrast the following strategies for solving problems.

a. trial and error

b. hypothesis testing

c. algorithms

d. heuristics

3. Explain the phenomenon of confirmation bias.

4. Describe each of the following obstacles to problem solving.

a. fixation

b. mental set

c. functional fixedness

5. Give examples of the following heuristics.

a. representativeness heuristic

b. availability heuristic

6. Describe the overconfidence phenomenon.

7. Describe how a person's judgments may be affected by the way in which questions are framed.

8. Contrast deductive and inductive reasoning.

9. Explain the belief perseverance phenomenon.

10. Identify the ways in which human thought and computer programs are alike and different.

Language (pp. 287–294)

11. Define each of the following elements of language structure.

a. phonemes

b. morphemes

c. grammar

d. semantics

e. syntax

12. Describe language acquisition in children, noting the achievements in each of the following stages.

a. babbling stage

b. one-word stage

c. two-word stage

13. Discuss the theories of language development proposed by Chomsky and Skinner.

14. Describe the research on language acquisition that has been done with animals.

Thinking and Language (pp. 294–296)

15. Explain and evaluate the linguistic relativity hypothesis.

CHAPTER REVIEW

When you have finished reading the chapter, fill in the sentences that follow. Using your hand or a strip of paper, cover the correct answers in the margin and fill in each blank. Verify your answer by uncovering the correct one. As you proceed, evaluate your performance for each chapter section. *Do not continue with the next section until you understand why each margin term is the correct answer.* If you need to, go back and review or re-read the appropriate chapter section in the text before continuing.

Thinking (pp. 270–286)

1. People tend to organize specific items into general categories by forming _____.

concepts

2. Concepts are generally further organized into _____.

hierarchies

3. Collins and Quillian verified the hierarchical structure of concepts by measuring the _____ times of a person answering questions.

response

4. Concepts are typically formed through the development of a best example, or _____, of a category.

prototype

5. Although humans may not always think logically, we are especially capable of using our reasoning powers for _____ solving.

problem

6. Finding the solution to a problem by trying each possibility is called _____ _____ _____.

trial and error

7. Tentative assumptions about how to deal with a problem are called _____.

hypotheses

8. Logical, methodical, step-by-step procedures for solving problems are called _____.

algorithms

9. These strategies _____ (do/do not) guarantee that a solution to the problem will be found.

do

10. Rules of thumb, mental shortcuts, and intuition are problem-solving strategies called _____.

heuristics

11. The tendency to look for information that verifies our preconceptions is called the _____ _____.

confirmation bias

12. Not being able to take a new perspective when attempting to solve a problem is called _____.

fixation

13. One example of this obstacle to problem solving is the tendency to repeat solutions that have worked previously; this phenomenon is known as the development of a _____ _____.

mental set

14. When a person is unable to envision using an object in an unusual way, _____ _____ is operating.

functional fixedness

15. When you suddenly realize what the solution to a problem is, _____ has occurred.

insight

16. Animals _____ (have/have not) been shown to be capable of insight.

have

17. Wheeler and Janis have developed five stages for sound decision making. List these below.

a. _____

b. _____

c. _____

d. _____

e. _____

a. accept the challenge

b. search for alternatives

c. evaluate the alternatives

d. make a commitment

e. adhere to the decision

18. People judge how well something matches a particular prototype or concept; this is the _____ _____.

representativeness heuristic

19. When we judge the likelihood of something occurring in terms of how readily it comes to mind, we are using the _____ _____.

availability heuristic

20. The tendency of people to overestimate the accuracy of their knowledge is called the _____ phenomenon.

overconfidence

21. Research has shown that when subjects are given feedback on the accuracy of their judgments, their accuracy _____ (does/does not) increase.

does

22. Studies have shown that the phrasing, or _____, of questions greatly affects decision making.

framing

23. Logical thinking in which one derives conclusions, given certain assumptions, is called _____ _____ .

deductive reasoning

24. Inferring general principles from specific examples defines _____ _____ .

inductive reasoning

25. Research has shown that once we form a belief or a concept, it may take more convincing evidence for us to change the concept than it did to create it; this is called the _____ _____ phenomenon.

belief perseverance

26. The argument in which two statements, called _____ , lead to a conclusion is called the _____ .

premises
syllogism

27. A common error in human reasoning is our tendency to accept as logical conclusions that agree with our _____ .

opinions

28. The science of the development of computers and programs to simulate human thinking is called _____ _____ .

artificial intelligence

29. Unlike the computer, which must process information serially, humans can process many bits of information _____ .

simultaneously

Language (pp. 287–294)

30. The basic sound units of a language are its _____ . English has approximately _____ of these units.

phonemes
40

31. Phonemes are grouped into units of meaning called _____ .

morphemes

32. The system of rules that enables us to use our language to speak to and understand others is called _____ .

grammar

33. The system by which meaning is derived from words is the _____ of the language.

semantics

34. The system of rules we use to combine words into sentences is called _____ .

syntax

35. The first stage of language development, in which children spontaneously utter different sounds, is the _____ stage.

babbling

36. This stage typically begins at about _____ months of age.

3 or 4

37. The sounds children make during this stage are _____ (alike/different) for all languages.

alike

38. During the second stage of development, children convey complete thoughts using _____ _____.

single words

39. This stage begins at about _____ year(s) of age.

1

40. During the two-word stage, children speak in sentences containing mostly nouns and verbs. This type of speech is called _____ speech.

telegraphic

41. B. F. Skinner believes that language development follows the general principles of _____.

learning or association

42. Other theorists believe that humans are _____ prepared to learn language.

biologically

43. One such theorist is _____ _____.

Noam Chomsky

44. The dance language of the honeybee was discovered by the biologist _____.

von Frisch

45. Attempts to teach chimpanzees to *talk* _____ (have/have not) succeeded.

have not

46. The Gardners attempted to communicate with the chimpanzee Washoe by teaching her _____ _____.

sign language

47. Skeptics of the claims of chimp researchers have argued that much of what the chimps do when using sign language is simple _____ of their trainer's gestures.

imitation

48. A second limitation of chimpanzees is that, although they may acquire a rather large vocabulary of individual signs, their ability to put words together with correct _____ is very limited.

syntax

Thinking and Language (pp. 294–296)

49. Language shapes our thinking according to the
_____ _____ hypothesis.

linguistic relativity

50. One linguist who has proposed this hypothesis is
_____.

Whorf

51. In separate studies, Hyde and Martyna found that using the pronoun "he" (instead of "he or she") _____ (does/does not) influence people's thoughts concerning gender.

does

52. There is evidence that thinking _____ (can/cannot) occur without the use of language.

can

FOCUS ON PSYCHOLOGY:
BIRD SONG

Ethologists have long been intrigued with the beautiful and complicated songs that many birds acquire. Some develop repertoires of over 100 distinctive songs, each of which conveys a different message. In addition, some birds develop regional dialects or accents of the species' song, just as humans living in different regions of a country do. Are songs instinctive, or are they the result of learning? To answer this question, Peter Marler bred and raised birds in his laboratory, where he was able to control their experiences and monitor song development. He found that the role of learning in song development varied with the species being studied. The song of the white-crowned sparrow, for example, is largely learned. Those sparrows prevented from hearing their species' song as a result of being isolated or deafened at hatching failed to develop the normal song.

In contrast to the sparrow, the European cuckoo does not need to learn its song. Deafening or isolation from the species' song does not disrupt song development. Why this difference in the sparrow and the cuckoo? The answer may lie in the fact that cuckoos are *brood parasites*—they lay their eggs in the nests of birds of another species, which are duped into raising their young. If song development in the cuckoo were dependent upon learning, the young would probably acquire the host species' song. This would be disastrous to the cuckoo when it became an adult, because it would be unable to establish a territory or attract a mate. Song development that depends only on maturation is resistant to this possibility.

Some researchers have proposed that there is a critical period in the development of language in children. In order for language acquisition to proceed normally, the child must be exposed to language during this period. Some birds also have critical periods in song development. Princeton biologist James Gould has found that the white-crowned sparrow must hear its species' song between the 10th and 50th days after hatching, even though its song will not "crystallize" until much later, when it is a mature adult. Exposure to the song before or after this time frame has no effect on song development.

PROGRESS TEST 1

Circle your answers to the following questions and check them with the answer key at the end of this chapter. Be sure to consult the appropriate pages of the text to understand the correct answer for any missed question.

Multiple-Choice Questions

1. If all politicians are clever and Susan is a politician, then Susan must be clever. This statement is an example of:
a. confirmation bias.
b. inductive reasoning.
c. an acronym.
d. a syllogism.

2. The formation of a concept, which defines a variety of individual items, is an example of:
a. deductive reasoning.
b. inductive reasoning.
c. syllogistic reasoning.
d. conceptual bias.

3. When forming a concept, people often develop a best example, or _____, of a category.
a. denoter   **c.** prototype
b. standard   **d.** mental set

4. Confirmation bias refers to the tendency to:
a. avoid accepting logical arguments on the basis of deductive reasoning.
b. avoid accepting logical arguments on the basis of inductive reasoning.
c. search randomly through alternative solutions when problem solving.
d. look for information that is consistent with one's beliefs.

5. The English language has approximately _____ phonemes.
a. 25   **c.** 40
b. 35   **d.** 50

6. Which of the following is *not* true of the babbling stage?
a. It is imitation of adult speech.
b. It is the same in all cultures.
c. Deaf children also babble.
d. Babbling increasingly comes to resemble a particular language.

7. The child who says "Milk gone" is using:
a. babbling.
b. telegraphic speech.
c. holophrastic speech.
d. reflexive speech.

8. The chimpanzee Washoe was taught:
a. to speak about one dozen English words.
b. to talk by pushing buttons on a computer.
c. to use sign language.
d. to communicate with plastic tokens.

9. The linguistic relativity hypothesis states that:
a. language is primarily a learned ability.
b. language is largely an innate ability.
c. the size of a person's vocabulary reflects his or her intelligence.
d. our language shapes our thinking.

10. Which of the following best describes Chomsky's view of language development?
a. Language is an entirely learned ability.
b. Language is an innate ability.

c. Humans have a biological predisposition to acquire language.
d. There are no cultural influences on the development of language.

11. Failing to solve a problem that requires using an object in an unusual way illustrates the phenomenon of:
a. mental set.
b. functional fixedness.
c. fixation.
d. belief perseverance.

12. Which of the following is an example of the use of heuristics?
a. trying every possible letter order when unscrambling a word
b. considering each possible move when playing chess
c. looking at every angle when solving a problem
d. using rules of thumb and intuition based on past experience to solve a problem

Matching Items

_____ 1. reasoning in which one moves from specific examples to general principles

_____ 2. reasoning in which one derives specific conclusions from given assumptions

_____ 3. rules for combining words into sentences

_____ 4. the system by which meaning is derived from sentences

_____ 5. presuming that something is likely if it comes readily to mind

_____ 6. the tendency to overestimate the accuracy of one's judgments

_____ 7. being unable to see a new angle to a problem

_____ 8. problem solving by searching every possible solution

_____ 9. the sudden realization of the solution to a problem

_____ 10. tendency to repeat problem-solving techniques that worked in the past

_____ 11. the basic units of meaning in a language

a. syntax
b. morphemes
c. mental set
d. trial and error
e. availability heuristic
f. inductive reasoning
g. semantics
h. insight
i. deductive reasoning
j. overconfidence phenomenon
k. fixation

FOCUS ON PSYCHOLOGY:
COMPUTER THERAPY

Just how "smart" are computers? Remember, computers are only as smart as the humans who write the programs that run them. In 1965, MIT computer scientist Joseph Weizenbaum wrote a program called ELIZA as a means of exploring artificial intelligence. Weizenbaum was attempting to create a program that could engage in a "conversation" with a person. ELIZA was modeled after a nondirective Rogerian psychotherapist. "She" made no suggestions or interpretive comments. Instead, "she" responded to particular cue words, such as *crazy*, *mother*, and *anger*. When a cue word was encountered, ELIZA responded with a stock phrase. To other responses, ELIZA merely rephrased the person's remark or asked the person to elaborate on what he or she said. The original ELIZA has now been rewritten for home computers. Listed below is a transcript from a sample conversation between a person and ELIZA. ELIZA's remarks are in capital letters.

I'm afraid I may be going crazy.
IS IT BECAUSE YOU ARE AFRAID YOU MAY BE GOING CRAZY THAT YOU CAME TO ME?

I just haven't been myself lately.
CAN YOU ELABORATE ON THAT?

I'm always irritable, and I cry all the time.
CAN YOU THINK OF A SPECIFIC EXAMPLE?

This morning I cried because I couldn't find my keys.
YOUR KEYS—THAT'S INTERESTING.

Whenever anything goes wrong, I just blow up.
DO YOU SAY YOU BLOW UP FOR SOME SPECIAL REASON?

I never used to get so mad.
THAT'S QUITE INTERESTING.

It's like I'm losing control of myself.
HOW LONG HAVE YOU BEEN LOSING CONTROL OF YOURSELF?

I guess it started about the time my father died.
TELL ME MORE ABOUT YOUR FAMILY.

Since my father died, I haven't been the same.
LET'S TALK ABOUT YOUR FATHER.

I felt I always let him down.
WHAT INCIDENT ARE YOU THINKING OF?

How do you feel about the computer as a therapist? Do you think this type of interaction could have any therapeutic benefit? To get a better sense of how ELIZA works, you might try the PsychSim program, if your instructor has ordered it.

Source: Adapted from S. Williams, Disk therapy. *Science 84 magazine* (April). American Association for the Advancement of Science.

PROGRESS TEST 2

Progress Test 2 should be completed during a final chapter review. Do so after you thoroughly understand the correct answers for the Chapter Review and Progress Test 1.

Multiple-Choice Questions

1. Syllogisms illustrate our illogical tendency to:
   a. accept as logical those conclusions that agree with our own opinions.
   b. accept as logical those conclusions that disagree with our own opinions.
   c. underestimate the accuracy of our knowledge.
   d. refuse to accept any new information once our opinions are formed.

2. Phonemes are the basic units of _____ in language.
   a. sound
   b. meaning
   c. grammar
   d. syntax

3. Syntax refers to:
   a. the sounds in a word.
   b. how words are grouped into sentences.
   c. the system of deriving meaning from sentences.
   d. the meaning of different parts of speech.

4. Skinner and other learning theorists argue that language development is due to:
   a. imitation.
   b. reinforcement.

c. association.

d. all of the above.

5. Many psychologists are skeptical of claims that chimpanzees can acquire language, because the chimps have not shown the ability to:

a. use symbols meaningfully.

b. acquire speech.

c. develop even a small vocabulary using sign language or any other system.

d. order words together using proper syntax.

6. Representativeness and availability are examples of:

a. mental sets.

b. heuristics.

c. algorithms.

d. fixation.

7. The child who says "We goed to the store" is _____ a grammatical rule.

a. overgeneralizing

b. telegraphing

c. overextending

d. regularizing

8. The science that explores the computer's capability to simulate human behavior is called:

a. cryonics.

b. ethology.

c. artificial intelligence.

d. psychocybernetics.

9. Which of the following illustrates the availability heuristic?

a. using whatever tools and techniques are available to solve a problem

b. searching through potential solutions to a problem in some arbitrary sequence (e.g., alphabetically)

c. accepting as truthful the first solution mentioned by another person

d. giving more weight to evidence from first-hand sources than from statistically summarized evaluations of a greater number of cases

10. Which of the following illustrates the belief perseverance phenomenon?

a. Your belief remains intact even in the face of evidence to the contrary.

b. You refuse even to listen to arguments counter to your beliefs.

c. You tend to become flustered and angered when your beliefs are refuted.

d. You tend to search for information that supports your beliefs.

11. The syllogism is one form of:

a. mental set.

b. functional fixedness.

c. inductive reasoning.

d. deductive reasoning.

12. Which of the following is *not* cited by Chomsky as evidence that language acquisition cannot be explained by learning alone?

a. Children master the complicated rules of grammar with ease.

b. Children create sentences they have never heard.

c. Children make mistakes which suggest they are attempting to apply rules of grammar.

d. Children raised in isolation from language spontaneously begin speaking words.

True–False Items

_____ 1. In deductive reasoning, we begin with specifics.

_____ 2. According to the confirmation bias, people often interpret ambiguous evidence as support for their beliefs.

_____ 3. Most human problem solving involves the use of heuristics rather than reasoning that systematically considers every possible solution.

_____ 4. When asked, most people underestimate the accuracy of their judgments.

_____ 5. Studies have shown that in certain instances even animals may have insight reactions.

_____ 6. Mental set is an example of a fixation that occurs when we attempt to solve a problem.

_____ 7. Although the morphemes differ, the phonemes are the same for all languages.

_____ 8. Children of all cultures babble using the same phonemes.

_____ 9. Thinking without using language is not possible.

_____ 10. Unlike computers, which are limited to processing information serially, humans can process many different bits of information simultaneously.

SAMPLE ESSAY QUESTIONS

1. Describe the development of language in children.

2. Contrast the theories of language acquisition proposed by Chomsky and by Skinner.

3. Describe several obstacles to problem solving.

4. Explain the differences in inductive and deductive reasoning and give examples of how human reasoning is not always logical.

5. Discuss whether language acquisition has been demonstrated in chimpanzees.

PROJECT:
BRAINSTORMING

Brainstorming is a group problem-solving technique which originated in the field of advertising. Its purpose is to generate as many solutions to a problem as possible. As Adams (1974) has noted, brainstorming groups usually consist of five to ten people and follow four rules: (1) As ideas are generated by group members, no judgments or evaluations of any kind are permitted. (2) Any idea, no matter how wild, is to be encouraged. (3) The group should strive for a large quantity of possible solutions. (4) Group members should build upon or modify ideas submitted by others.

Adams feels that one of the major obstacles to creativity and effective problem solving (particularly within groups) is that people are afraid their ideas may appear foolish. In addition, group members often devote too much energy to defending a pet idea, instead of searching collectively for a better one.

To get a feeling for brainstorming, get together with several friends and pick a problem or issue that affects everyone. You might, for example, choose pollution, the threat of nuclear war, or world hunger. Explain the rules of brainstorming to the group and then, for 15 minutes, have the group generate possible solutions to the problem. You may have one member of the group take notes. After the session, evaluate the solutions. Did any unusual or especially creative ones surface? Keep this technique in mind and, the next time your group has a problem, suggest using it.

Although brainstorming was originally designed as a group problem-solving technique, it is also effective in solving individual problems. Try using it to generate possible solutions to any personal problem or situation you want to change. Again, follow the rules and be nonjudgmental and creative! You may find just the answer you have been looking for.

WHERE TO LOOK FOR MORE INFORMATION

Adams, J. L. (1974). *Conceptual blockbusting: A guide to better ideas.* San Francisco: W. H. Freeman.

Adams discusses brainstorming and a variety of other techniques for increasing creativity in thinking and problem solving.

Williams, S. (1984, April). Disk therapy. *Science 84.*

Williams discusses ELIZA and several other computer therapy programs.

ANSWERS

PROGRESS TEST 1

Multiple-Choice Questions

1. d (p. 283)
2. b (p. 282)
3. c (p. 271)
4. d (p. 273)

5. c (p. 287)
6. a (p. 288)
7. b (p. 289)
8. c (p. 291)

9. d (p. 294)
10. c (p. 290)
11. b (p. 276)
12. d (p. 273)

Matching Items

1. f (p. 282)
2. i (pp. 282, 283–284)
3. a (p. 288)
4. g (p. 288)

5. e (pp. 279–280)
6. j (pp. 280–281)
7. k (p. 275)
8. d (p. 272)

9. h (p. 276)
10. c (p. 275)
11. b (p. 288)

PROGRESS TEST 2

Multiple-Choice Questions

1. a (p. 283)
2. a (p. 287)
3. b (p. 288)
4. d (p. 290)

5. d (p. 293)
6. b (pp. 278–280)
7. a (p. 290)
8. c (p. 285)

9. d (p. 280)
10. a (p. 282)
11. d (p. 283)
12. d (p. 290)

True–False Items

1. False (p. 282)
2. True (pp. 273–274)
3. True (p. 273)
4. False (p. 280)

5. True (p. 276)
6. True (p. 275)
7. False (p. 287)
8. True (p. 288)

9. False (p. 295)
10. True (p. 286)

CHAPTER 12

Intelligence

CHAPTER OVERVIEW

An enduring controversy in psychology involves the definition and measurement of intelligence. Chapter 12 describes the historical origins of intelligence tests and discusses several important issues concerning their use. These include the methods by which intelligence tests are constructed and whether such tests are valid, reliable, and free of cultural bias. The chapter also discusses research that attempts to assess the extent of genetic, racial, and environmental influences on intelligence.

GUIDED STUDY

The text chapter should be studied one section at a time. Before you read, preview each section by skimming it, noting headings and boldface items. Then read the appropriate section objectives from the following outline. Keep these objectives in mind, and as you read the chapter section, search for the information that will complete each one. You may wish to write out answers for each objective as soon as you finish reading that section of the chapter.

The Measurement of Intelligence (pp. 302–314)

1. Discuss the contributions of Galton, Binet, and Terman in the effort to measure intelligence.

2. Explain how the intelligence quotient is computed.

3. Contrast aptitude and achievement tests and give examples of each.

4. Describe each of the following intelligence tests.

a. WAIS

b. SAT

c. DAT

5. Explain how an intelligence test is standardized.

6. Explain the concepts of reliability and validity and how each is measured.

7. Discuss whether intelligence tests are valid and reliable.

The Nature of Intelligence (pp. 315–321)

8. Identify several issues in the controversy over a definition of intelligence.

9. Describe the factor analysis approach to the measurement of intelligence, and evaluate the evidence for a general intelligence factor.

10. Describe the general strategy used in the information processing approach to the measurement of intelligence.

11. Discuss whether a person's IQ remains stable throughout life.

12. Discuss the relationship between intelligence and creativity.

Genes, Environment, and Intelligence
(pp. 322–330)

13. Summarize the evidence provided by twin and adoption studies for a genetic factor in intelligence.

14. Summarize the evidence for environmental influences in intelligence.

15. Explain why group or racial differences in IQ scores do not necessarily reflect genetic differences.

16. Evaluate whether intelligence tests are "biased."

17. List several reasons that cause most psychologists to believe that racial differences in IQ are due to environmental differences, rather than heredity.

CHAPTER REVIEW

When you have finished reading the chapter, complete the sentences that follow. Using your hand or a strip of paper, cover the correct answers in the margin and fill in each blank. Verify your answer by un-covering the correct one. As you proceed, evaluate your performance for each chapter section. *Do not continue with the next section until you understand why each margin term is the correct answer.* If you need to, review or re-read the appropriate chapter section in the text before continuing.

The Measurement of Intelligence (pp. 302–314)

1. The early Greek philosopher _____ concluded that individual differences were biologically determined.

Plato

2. Three persons who contributed greatly to the measurement of individual differences were _____,

_____, and _____ .

Galton

Binet; Terman

3. Galton formulated a plan for selectively breeding persons with superior traits; this was called _____ .

eugenics

4. The assumption behind this plan was that most important human traits are _____ .

inherited

5. Galton also attempted to equate intelligence with the size of a person's _____ .

head

6. The French psychologist who devised a test to predict the success of children in school was _____ .

Binet

7. The concept behind this test was to compare children's chronological ages with their _____ ages.

mental

8. Binet's test _____ (was/was not) designed to measure inborn intelligence.

was not

9. Lewis Terman's revision of Binet's test is called the

_____-_____ .

Stanford-Binet

10. This test enables one to compute an _____ _____ for an individual.

intelligence quotient

11. The IQ is computed as the ratio of _____ _____ to _____ _____.

mental age
chronological age

12. The resulting value is multiplied by _____ to remove decimal points.

100

13. Today's tests compute IQ on the basis of the individual's performance, as compared with others of _____ (the same/all) age(s).

the same

14. The test was designed so that a score of _____ is considered average.

100

15. Tests designed to predict ability to learn something new are called _____ tests.

aptitude

16. Tests designed to measure what you have already learned are called _____ tests.

achievement

17. The Stanford-Binet is classified as an _____ test.

aptitude

18. The most commonly used psychological test is the _____ _____ _____ _____.

Wechsler Adult Intelligence Scale

19. This test consists of _____ subtests.

eleven

20. It provides separate IQ scores for two categories of intelligence: _____ and _____.

verbal; performance

21. The test designed to predict a student's academic performance in college is the _____ _____ _____.

Scholastic Aptitude Test

22. This test _____ (does/does not) provide an overall intelligence score.

does not

23. Unlike the tests noted above, which assess general abilities, the _____ _____ _____ evaluates specific academic and nonacademic abilities.

Differential Aptitude Test

24. Three requirements of a good test are _____, _____, and _____.

standardization
reliability; validity

25. The administering of a test to a representative comparison group is called _____.

standardization

26. When scores on a test are compiled, they generally result in a bell-shaped, or _____, distribution.

normal

27. During the 1960s and 1970s, SAT scores in the United States showed a steady _____.

decline

28. Unlike the SAT, the Stanford-Binet and WAIS _____ (are/are not) periodically restandardized.

are

29. Since the 1930s, IQ scores on the WAIS have generally _____.

risen

30. If a test yields consistent results, it is said to be _____.

reliable

31. When a test is repeatedly administered to the same people, the psychologist is determining its _____-_____ reliability.

test-retest

32. When a person's scores for the odd- and even-numbered questions on a test are compared, the test's _____-_____ reliability is being assessed.

split-half

33. The Stanford-Binet, Wechsler, SAT, and DAT have reliabilities of about _____.

.90

34. Study courses for the SAT _____ (have/have not) been shown to have beneficial effects on test performance.

have

35. The degree to which a test measures what it is designed to measure is referred to as the test's _____.

validity

36. The degree to which a test predicts future performance is referred to as the test's _____ _____.

predictive validity

The Nature of Intelligence (pp. 315–321)

37. If by naming a concept you accept it as valid, you are committing the error called _____.

reification

38. Intelligence is generally defined as _____-directed and adaptive behavior.

goal

39. This definition indicates that the concept of a culture-free intelligence test _____ (is/is not) valid.

is not

40. One controversy in the area of intelligence measurement concerns whether intelligence is a general ability or a collection of _____ abilities.

specific

41. The statistical procedure used to identify groups of items that appear to measure a common ability is called _____ _____.

factor analysis

42. The developer of this technique, Charles Spearman, believed that a factor called *g*, or _____ _____, runs through the more specific factors.

general intelligence

43. Individuals who are mentally retarded yet possess one extraordinary skill are called _____ _____.

idiot savants

44. When solving a problem, highly intelligent persons spend more time _____ the problem than do those labeled less intelligent.

encoding

45. Researchers such as Hunt and Eysenck have found that those with high IQ scores tend to react _____ (faster/more slowly) than people with low IQ scores on various cognitive tasks.

faster

46. Before about age _____ a child's IQ test performance is not very predictive of adult IQ.

4

47. Individuals scoring below 70 on an IQ test and having difficulty adapting to daily life may be labeled _____ _____.

mentally retarded

48. This label applies to approximately _____ percent of the population.

1

49. Severe retardation is generally caused by a genetic defect such as that in _____ _____.

Down's syndrome

50. The ability to produce novel ideas is called _____.

creativity

51. In general, creative people tend to have _____ (high/low) IQ scores.

high

52. This relationship holds only up to a certain point—an IQ score of about _____.

120

Genes, Environment, and Intelligence
(pp. 322–330)

53. Intelligence is influenced by both _____ and _____.

genes; environment

54. The IQ scores of identical twins are _____ (more/less) similar than those of fraternal twins.

more

55. This may reflect more than genetic factors; identical twins are also treated more _____ than are fraternal twins.

similarly

56. Hereditarians offer in response the fact that the IQ scores of identical twins reared _____ are still more similar than those of fraternal twins.

separately

57. Kamin has reported that identical twins who have been separated are often placed in _____ environments.

similar

58. Researchers employing the technique of selective breeding _____ (have/have not) been successful in breeding animals that show special learning abilities.

have

59. Studies by Skeels and Hunt show that seemingly retarded children _____ (do/do not) show signs of recovery in IQ and behavior when placed in more nurturing environments.

do

60. On general tests of intelligence, black Americans score an average of 15 points _____ than white Americans.

lower

61. Japanese children average _____ (higher/lower) intelligence scores than American children.

higher

62. These results fail to indicate that the variation within a racial group is _____ (less/greater) than that between groups.

greater

63. The black-white gap in aptitude test performance has been _____ (increasing/decreasing), while the Japanese-American gap has been _____ (increasing/decreasing).

decreasing
increasing

64. Black children raised in middle-class white homes show _____ (an increase/no difference) in their IQ scores relative to average black children.

an increase

65. Most psychologists agree that, in terms of predictive validity, the major aptitude tests _____ (are/are not) racially biased.

are not

FOCUS ON PSYCHOLOGY:
BECOMING AN IDIOT SAVANT

As explained in the text, idiot savants are individuals who possess one incredible skill, but are often retarded in other areas. One area in which such persons often excel is mathematics. Steven Smith (1983) refers to individuals who can perform complex calcu-

lations in their heads as *mental calculators*. For example, Shyam Marathe determined that the twenty-third root of 24,242,900,770,553,981,941,874,678,-268,486,966,725,193 was 57—and he performed the calculation mentally, in only 50 seconds.

Although people once believed that the ability to perform complex mental calculations was a sign of superior intelligence, we now know that almost anyone willing to learn a few systematic steps can do the calculations. As an illustration, consider the digits 0 through 9, and their cubes.

Digit (root)	Cube
0	0
1	1
2	8
3	27
4	64
5	125
6	216
7	343
8	512
9	729

Except for 2, 3, 7, and 8, the last digit of each cube is the same as its root. For these four numbers, the last digit of the cube is equal to the root subtracted from 10. For example, the last digit of the cube of 8 is 2 (10 − 8). Once you have committed the ten cubes to memory, you can easily find the root of any perfect cube less than 1,000,000. In every case, the root will have only 1 or 2 digits. The last digit of the cube is either the root itself or the root subtracted from 10. Suppose you want to find the cube root of 274,625. The last digit is 5, which is also the second digit of its root. To find the first digit, you need to remember the table and one additional rule. Determine which two cubes the digits to the left of the comma fall between. These digits, 274, fall between the cubes of 6 and 7 in the table. The first digit of the cube root you seek is simply the smaller of the two. Therefore, the cube root of 274,625 is 65. Try using this technique to determine the cube roots of 10,648 and 132,651.

PROGRESS TEST 1

Circle your answers to the following questions and check them with the answer key at the end of the chapter. Be sure to consult the appropriate pages of the text in order to understand the correct answer for any missed question.

Multiple-Choice Questions

1. The English scientist who attempted to assess intelligence by measuring head size was:
   a. Galton.
   b. Binet.
   c. Terman.
   d. Wechsler.

2. A 6-year-old child has a mental age of 9. The child's IQ equals:
   a. 100.
   b. 125.
   c. 140.
   d. 150.

3. Which of the following tests consists of eleven subtests and yields separate IQ scores for verbal and performance categories?
   a. WAIS
   b. SAT
   c. DAT
   d. Stanford-Binet

4. Jack takes the same test of mechanical reasoning on two different days and gets very different scores. This suggests that the test:
   a. has not been standardized.
   b. has low validity.
   c. has low reliability.
   d. has no predictive validity.

5. Terman found that an intelligence test developed by Binet for French children did not work well with children in California. The test needed to be _____ for the new group.
   a. validated
   b. standardized
   c. reliability rated
   d. normally distributed

6. Which of the following disorders typically results in severe mental retardation?
   a. Korsakoff's syndrome
   b. jaundice
   c. Down's syndrome
   d. XYY syndrome

7. You would not use a test of hearing acuity as an intelligence test because it lacks:
   a. internal reliability.
   b. test-retest reliability.

c. content validity.
d. predictive validity.

8. In a study of black children raised in middle-class white homes, Scarr and Weinberg found that the IQ scores of the adopted black children were:
a. comparable to those of adopted white children.
b. lower than those of adopted white children.
c. higher than those of adopted white children.
d. higher than those of black children in general, but lower than those of adopted white children.

9. One reason that the similarity in IQ of identical twins raised separately is not conclusive proof of heredity's role in determining intelligence is that:
a. the similarity in their IQs before separation is not known.
b. separation from a twin is an extremely traumatic experience which may result in brain damage.
c. twins are often placed in adoptive homes that provide very similar environments.

d. the correlation between the IQ scores of such twins is only marginally significant.

10. Children in which country typically score higher on intelligence tests than do American children?
a. Uganda
b. Israel
c. France
d. Japan

11. Which of the following is a measure of the internal consistency of a test?
a. split-half reliability
b. test-retest reliability
c. internal validity
d. standardization

12. Which of the following best describes the relationship between creativity and intelligence?
a. Creativity increases with intelligence.
b. Creativity decreases with intelligence.
c. Creativity and intelligence are unrelated.
d. Up to a point, people with high IQ scores are more creative.

Matching Items

_____ 1. IQ
_____ 2. *g*
_____ 3. eugenics
_____ 4. idiot savant
_____ 5. factor analysis
_____ 6. aptitude test
_____ 7. achievement test
_____ 8. Stanford-Binet
_____ 9. SAT
_____ 10. validity
_____ 11. reliability

a. a test designed to predict a person's ability to learn something new.
b. a test designed to measure current knowledge.
c. the consistency with which a test measures performance.
d. the degree to which a test measures what it is designed to measure.
e. Terman's revision of Binet's original intelligence test.
f. an aptitude test designed to predict academic performance in college.
g. an underlying general intelligence factor.
h. the ratio of mental age to chronological age.
i. a mentally retarded individual who is extremely gifted in one ability.
j. a program for the selective breeding of the most intelligent individuals.
k. a statistical technique that identifies related items on a test.

FOCUS ON PSYCHOLOGY:
WOLF CHILDREN

The movie "The Wild Boy of Aveyron" depicts one case of a *feral child:* a human who has been raised by animals under conditions of extreme isolation. A few other incredible case studies, involving children abandoned in remote jungle regions being cared for by animals, have been reported. A number of these cases have been documented from diaries kept by missionaries in the jungles of India (Singh and Zingg, 1962). In one well-known case, the "wolf-boy" Sanichar lived for thirty years at an orphanage in Sikandra until his death in 1895. Sanichar became something of a celebrity, and was visited by people from all over the world, including several prominent scientists. Sanichar was believed to have lived for some time with wolves, as the following entry indicates.

> The boy was captured in 1867 by a shooting expedition in the unfrequented jungles of Bulandshahr. The hunters surprised a stray wolf, which they followed to a small mound of earth with a flat-topped rock sticking out of the ground. A small, strange-looking animal was asleep in the sun on the rock. To the amazement of the hunting party, it proved to be a boy, who leaped from the rock as soon as he saw the hunters and, running on all fours, disappeared into a cave along with the startled wolf.

The boy was later captured and sent to the orphanage, where he was studied by Mr. V. Ball of the Indian Geological Survey:

> He presented an appearance not uncommonly seen in ordinary idiots. His forehead was low, his teeth somewhat prominent, and his manner restless and fidgety. From time to time he grinned in a manner that was more simian than human, the effect of which was intensified by a nervous twitching of the lower jaw.

When Sanichar was 13 or 14 years of age and had been there for six years, the superintendent of the orphanage wrote:

> He has learnt to make sounds, speak he cannot; but he freely expresses his anger and joy; work he will at times a little; but he likes eating better. His civilization has progressed so far that he likes raw meat less, though he still will pick up bones and sharpen his teeth on them. . . .

The authenticity of these cases, and the particular experiences of the children, is of course controversial. If authentic, they strongly attest to the importance of early experiences in the development of intelligence, as well as many other aspects of human behavior.

PROGRESS TEST 2

Progress Test 2 should be completed during a final chapter review. Do so after you thoroughly understand the correct answers for the Chapter Review and Progress Test 1.

Multiple-Choice Questions

1. The test designed by Alfred Binet was designed specifically to:
a. measure inborn intelligence in adults.
b. measure inborn intelligence in children.
c. predict school performance in children.
d. identify mentally retarded children so that they could be institutionalized.

2. Which of the following tests is designed to evaluate specific skills, such as mechanical reasoning and clerical speed?
a. WAIS
b. SAT
c. DAT
d. Stanford-Binet

3. If a test designed to indicate which applicants are likely to perform the best on the job fails to do so, the test has:
a. low reliability.
b. low content validity.
c. low predictive validity.
d. poor standardization.

4. By creating a label such as "gifted," we begin to act as if all children are naturally divided into two categories, those gifted and those not gifted. This logical error is referred to as:
a. rationalization.
b. nominalizing.
c. factoring.
d. reification.

5. The formula for the intelligence quotient was devised by:
a. Galton.
b. Terman.

c. Binet.

d. Wechsler.

6. On the Wechsler intelligence test, scores form a bell-shaped distribution:

a. in which IQ scores increase with age.

b. called a normal distribution.

c. in which IQ scores decrease with age.

d. in which IQ scores are stable across different ages.

7. Skeels found that institutionalized children placed in nurturing foster homes:

a. showed no change in intelligence test performance compared with those remaining institutionalized.

b. eventually had to be reinstitutionalized due to their failure to adapt.

c. showed significant increases in IQ scores relative to those remaining institutionalized.

d. actually developed higher IQs than control subjects who had lived in foster homes since birth.

8. If you want to develop a test of musical aptitude in American children, which would be the appropriate standardization group?

a. children all over the world

b. American children

c. children of musical parents

d. children with known musical ability

9. How is "intelligence" most commonly defined?

a. verbal reasoning ability

b. spatial and mathematical reasoning ability

c. the capacity for goal-directed, adaptive behavior

d. performance on general achievement tests

10. By what age does a child's performance on an IQ test become stable?

a. 2

b. 4

c. 6

d. 7

11. Since the 1930s, IQ scores in the United States have:

a. remained stable.

b. decreased.

c. increased.

d. decreased in men and increased in women.

12. In his study of children with high IQs, Terman found that:

a. the children were more emotional and less healthy than a control group.

b. the children were ostracized by classmates.

c. the children were healthy, well-adjusted, and did well academically.

d. as adults they showed a greater incidence of alcoholism and suicide than a control group.

True–False Items

_____ 1. In the current version of the Stanford-Binet intelligence test, one's performance is compared only with those of the same age.

_____ 2. IQ scores in the United States have been dropping over the past 50 years.

_____ 3. Most of the major aptitude tests have higher validity than reliability.

_____ 4. People with high IQ scores tend to process sensory information more quickly.

_____ 5. The gap in IQ scores between black and white children is increasing.

_____ 6. The IQ scores of adopted children are more similar to those of their biological parents than their adoptive parents.

_____ 7. The consensus among psychologists is that most intelligence tests are extremely biased.

_____ 8. Most psychologists agree that intelligence is primarily determined by heredity.

_____ 9. Study courses for aptitude tests generally produce a small benefit in scores.

_____ 10. The variation in IQ within a racial group is generally larger than that between racial groups.

SAMPLE ESSAY QUESTIONS

1. Discuss whether IQ tests are valid and reliable. How are validity and reliability measured?

2. Discuss several of the ways psychologists have attempted to define intelligence. How is intelligence generally defined today?

3. What light do studies of identical and fraternal twins shed on the issue of the heritability of intelligence? For what reasons are these studies inconclusive?

4. Discuss racial differences in IQ test performance. Do these differences implicate genetic tendencies in intelligence?

5. Describe the contributions of Galton, Binet, and Terman to the measurement of intelligence.

PROJECT:

THE DOVE COUNTERBALANCE GENERAL
INTELLIGENCE TEST

Sociologist Adrian Dove found that he frequently had to translate the black street language of the Watts region in Los Angeles so that his colleagues could understand it. As a half-serious demonstration of how cultural bias in an intelligence test can discriminate against those of other cultures, Dove designed his own intelligence test, the Dove Counterbalance General Intelligence Test. Although the slang in the test is somewhat dated, it clearly demonstrates how a test can be biased against people with different cultural backgrounds. Ten of the test's 30 multiple-choice questions are listed below. See how well you do.

1. A "handkerchief head" is:
a. a cool cat
b. a porter
c. an Uncle Tom
d. a hoddi
e. a preacher

2. Which word is most out of place here?
a. splib
b. blood
c. gray
d. spook
e. black

3. A "gas head" is a person who has a:
a. fast-moving car
b. stable of "lace"
c. "process"

d. habit of stealing cars
e. long jail record for arson

4. "Bo Diddley" is a:
a. game for children
b. down-home cheap wine
c. down-home singer
d. new dance
e. Moejoe call

5. If a pimp is uptight with a woman who gets state aid, what does he mean when he talks about "Mother's Day?"
a. second Sunday in May
b. third Sunday in June
c. first of every month
d. none of these
e. first and fifteenth of every month

6. "Hully Gully" came from:
a. East Oakland
b. Fillmore
c. Watts
d. Harlem
e. Motor City

7. If a man is called a "blood," then he is a:
a. fighter
b. Mexican-American
c. Negro
d. hungry hemophile
e. Redman or Indian

8. What are the "Dixie Hummingbirds?"
a. part of the KKK
b. a swamp disease
c. a modern gospel group
d. a Mississippi Negro paramilitary group
e. deacons

9. If you throw dice and seven is showing on top, what is facing down?
a. seven
b. snake eyes
c. boxcars
d. little Joes
e. 11

10. "Jet" is:
a. an East Oakland motorcycle club
b. one of the gangs in "West Side Story"
c. a news and gossip magazine
d. a way of life for the very rich

Questions

1. Could you construct an intelligence test based on contemporary slang expressions that would be biased in favor of people with your own cultural background?

2. After reading Chapter 12, do you feel that most intelligence tests are culturally biased?

3. What procedures for test construction would you follow to create a culture-free intelligence test?

4. What important decisions about you have been made on the basis of standardized tests? Do you feel that these decisions were ever in error?

5. Do you think it is possible to assess intelligence accurately?

Answers to the Dove Test

1. c	5. e	9. a
2. c	6. c	10. c
3. c	7. c	
4. c	8. c	

WHERE TO LOOK FOR MORE INFORMATION

Smith, S. B. (1983). *The great mental calculators: The psychology, methods, and lives of calculating prodigies, past and present.* New York: Columbia University Press.

A fascinating account of persons with amazing abilities to perform complex mental calculations.

Singh, J. A. L., and Zingg, R. M. (1966). *Wolf-children and feral man.* Hamden, CT: Archon Books.

Written in diary form, this book documents the discovery by missionaries of several children abandoned in the wilderness.

ANSWERS

PROGRESS TEST 1

Multiple-Choice Questions

1. a (p. 303)
2. d (p. 304)
3. a (p. 307)
4. c (pp. 312–313)

5. b (pp. 310–312)
6. c (p. 320)
7. c (pp. 313–314)
8. a (p. 329)

9. c (p. 324)
10. d (p. 327)
11. a (p. 313)
12. d (p. 321)

Matching Items

1. h (p. 304)
2. g (p. 317)
3. j (p. 303)
4. i (p. 317)

5. k (pp. 316–318)
6. a (p. 306)
7. b (p. 306)
8. e (pp. 304–305)

9. f (p. 308)
10. d (pp. 313–314)
11. c (pp. 312–313)

PROGRESS TEST 2

Multiple-Choice Questions

1. c (p. 303)
2. c (pp. 308–309)
3. c (p. 314)
4. d (p. 315)

5. b (p. 304)
6. b (p. 311)
7. c (p. 325)
8. d (pp. 310–311)

9. c (p. 315)
10. d (p. 319)
11. c (p. 312)
12. c (p. 319)

True–False Items

1. True (p. 305)
2. False (p. 312)
3. True (p. 314)
4. True (p. 318)

5. False (p. 328)
6. True (p. 324)
7. False (pp. 329–330)
8. False (pp. 326–327)

9. True (p. 313)
10. True (p. 328)

PART FIVE

MOTIVATION AND EMOTION

CHAPTER 13

Motivation

CHAPTER OVERVIEW

No topic is more fundamental to psychology than motivation—the energizing and directing of behavior. Chapter 13 discusses three motives: hunger, sexuality, and the need to achieve. Research on hunger points to the interplay between biological and psychological factors in motivation. Sexual motivation in men and women is triggered less by biological factors and more by external incentives. Intrinsic motivation and a need for achievement demonstrate that a drive-reduction theory of motivation is an incomplete theory of human behavior. Such motives are in the service of no apparent physiological need, yet they may be no less forceful.

GUIDED STUDY

The text chapter should be studied one section at a time. Before you read, preview each section by skimming it, noting headings and boldface items. Then read the appropriate section objectives from the following outline. Keep these objectives in mind, and as you read the chapter section, search for the information that will complete each one. You may wish to write out answers for each objective as soon as you finish reading that section of the chapter.

Concepts of Motivation (pp. 339–341)

1. Define *motivation*.

2. Describe each of the following theories of motivation.

a. drive-reduction

b. incentive

c. hierarchy of needs

Hunger (pp. 341–350)

3. Discuss the relationship of each of the following to hunger.

a. stomach hunger pangs

b. blood sugar levels

c. external cues

4. Describe the role of the hypothalamus in regulating hunger and the body's set point.

5. Explain why obese people find it difficult to lose weight permanently.

6. Using the research discussed in the text, list several hints for those attempting to lose weight.

Sexuality (pp. 351–360)

7. Discuss psychological definitions of normal and abnormal sexual behavior.

8. Contrast the research techniques of Kinsey and Masters and Johnson.

9. Describe the stages of the sexual response cycle.

a. excitement phase

b. plateau phase

c. orgasm

d. resolution phase

10. Discuss the relationship of hormones to human and animal sexual motivation.

11. Discuss the relationship of actual and imagined external stimuli to sexual motivation.

12. Describe the similarities and differences between hunger and sexual motivation.

13. Describe several theories of the development of sexual orientation.

14. Discuss whether the social impact of sexual research has been positive or negative.

Achievement Motivation (pp. 360–364)

15. Explain the differences between intrinsic and extrinsic motivation.

16. Give several reasons that the drive-reduction theory is only a partial explanation of motivation.

17. Compare individuals with high and low needs for achievement.

18. Discuss how parental and situational factors foster the development of a need for achievement.

19. Describe the effects of rewards on intrinsic motivation.

CHAPTER REVIEW

When you have finished reading the chapter, complete the sentences that follow. Using your hand or a strip of paper, cover the correct answers in the margin and fill in each blank. Verify your answer by un-

covering the correct one. As you proceed, evaluate your performance for each chapter section. *Do not continue with the next section until you understand why each margin term is the correct answer.* If you need to, review or re-read the appropriate chapter section in the text before continuing.

1. To motivate is to _____ and _____ behavior toward goals.

energize
direct

Concepts of Motivation (pp. 339–341)

2. As a result of Darwin's influence, the role of _____ forces in behavior became more apparent.

biological

3. Instinct theorists failed to realize that simply naming a behavior does not _____ it.

explain

4. Instinct theory was replaced by _____-_____ theory.

drive-reduction

5. According to this theory, organisms experience physiological states of deprivation called _____.

needs

6. The psychological states of arousal that are created by this deprivation are referred to as _____.

drives

7. The aim of drive reduction is to maintain a constant internal state, called _____.

homeostasis

8. Another motivational theory was based on the realization that behavior is often not so much pushed by our drives as it is pulled by _____ in the environment.

incentives

9. To illustrate that some needs take precedence over others, Maslow constructed a _____ of needs.

hierarchy

10. From most to least pressing, Maslow's needs are:

_____ needs, _____ needs,   physiological; safety

_____ needs, _____ needs, and   belongingness; esteem

_____ _____ needs.   self-actualization

Hunger (pp. 341–350)

11. Cannon had individuals swallow a _____ so that   balloon
he could record their stomach contractions.

12. Using this technique, he discovered that there
_____ (is/is not) a correlation between stomach con-   is
tractions and self-reports of hunger.

13. When an animal or human has had its stomach removed, hunger
_____ (does/does not) continue.   does

14. Feelings of hunger are decreased when the sugar
_____ is injected into the bloodstream.   glucose

15. Blood sugar is lowered, and hunger increased, when
_____ is injected.   insulin

16. The brain area that plays a role in hunger and other bodily maintenance functions is the _____ .   hypothalamus

17. Animals will begin eating when the _____   lateral hypothalamus
_____ is electrically stimulated.

18. When this region is destroyed, hunger _____   decreases
(increases/decreases).

19. Animals will stop eating when the _____   ventromedial
_____ is stimulated.   hypothalamus

20. When this area is destroyed, animals _____   overeat
(overeat/undereat).

21. Keesey introduced the concept of a weight level the body is
programmed to stay at; this value he referred to as the

_____ _____ .   set point

22. Rodin refers to people whose eating is more affected by food stimuli than by internal cues as _____ .   externals

23. Rodin found that such individuals showed an increased blood
_____ reaction when confronted with the sight,   insulin
smell, and sound of a steak being grilled.

24. A person with excess body fat is said to be _____ .   obese

25. Obesity increases one's risk of having _____, high _____ _____, and certain types of cancer.

diabetes
blood pressure

26. Traditionally, obesity has been considered a _____ problem rather than a physiological disorder.

personality

27. The energy equivalent of a pound of fat is approximately _____ calories.

3500

28. The immediate determinant of body fat is the size and number of _____ _____ one has.

fat cells

29. In the obese, these cells may enlarge and _____.

multiply

30. Once the number of cells increases, it _____ (can/cannot) be decreased.

cannot

31. The rate of energy expenditure in the body is the _____ rate.

metabolic

32. Fat tissue has a _____ (lower/higher) metabolic rate than lean tissue.

lower

33. The result is that fat tissue takes _____ (more/less) food energy to maintain.

less

34. Obese persons tend to be _____ (more/less) responsive than nonobese people to external food cues.

more

35. Following a meal, obese people secrete more _____ than nonobese persons.

insulin

36. Physical activity accounts for approximately _____ of our usage of energy.

one-third

37. When food intake is reduced, the body compensates by _____ (raising/lowering) metabolism.

lowering

38. Evidence indicates that there probably _____ (is/ is not) a genetic component to weight set point.

is

39. One strain of rats, Zucker fatties, is genetically predisposed to obesity because its _____ tends to be lower than that of normal-weight rats.

metabolism

40. Studies show that most obese persons who lose weight _____ (do/do not) eventually gain it back.

do

41. The most effective way to boost your body's metabolism is through _____.

exercise

42. Certain foods, such as _____ fats, produce the most weight gain.

saturated

43. Fructose, the sugar found in fruits, causes a less rapid rise in insulin than does _____, which is found in table sugar.

sucrose

44. Starving oneself all day and eating one big meal at night tends to _____ (speed up/slow down) metabolism.

slow down

Sexuality (pp. 351–360)

45. Psychologists define "abnormal" sexual behavior as that which physically or emotionally _____ someone.

hurts

46. Although there is great diversity in sexual practices, there are commonalities such as favoring the _____-_____ position for intercourse.

face-to-face

47. This position may be favored because it provides the most effective stimulation of the woman's _____.

clitoris

48. In the 1940s and 1950s, biologist _____ surveyed the sexual practices of thousands of men and women.

Kinsey

49. One of his major findings was that there _____ (was/was not) great diversity in "normal" sexual behavior.

was

50. The two researchers who identified a four-stage sexual response cycle are _____ and _____.

Masters; Johnson

51. In order, the stages of the cycle are: the _____ phase, the _____ phase, _____, and the _____ phase.

excitement
plateau; orgasm
resolution

52. List the major physical changes that occur during each of these stages.

a. excitement phase

b. plateau phase

c. orgasm

d. resolution phase

excitement: genital areas become engorged with blood.
plateau: breathing, pulse, and blood pressure continue to rise.
orgasm: rhythmic muscle contractions occur.
resolution: the body gradually returns to its nonaroused state.

53. During resolution, males experience a _____ _____ during which they are not capable of another orgasm.

refractory period

54. The presence of the male hormone _____ determines whether a developing embryo becomes male or female.

testosterone

55. The hormone surge during puberty is responsible for the development of the _____ sex characteristics.

secondary

56. In females, hormones also control the _____ cycle, pregnancy, and the onset of _____ .

menstrual
menopause

57. The importance of testosterone to male sexual arousal is confirmed by the fact that sexual interest declines in animals if their _____ are removed.

testes

58. In most mammals, females are sexually receptive only during ovulation, when the hormone _____ has peaked.

estrogen

59. Hormonal levels affect sexual motivation by influencing the _____ of the brain.

hypothalamus

60. Drugs that inhibit the formation of testosterone, such as _____-_____ , may decrease the sexual motivation of males.

Depo-Provera

61. Normal hormonal fluctuations in humans _____ (do/do not) greatly affect sexual motivation.

do not

62. Unlike in animals, sexual motivation in women may be increased more by an increase in the hormone _____ than an increase in estrogen.

testosterone

63. Humans _____ (do/do not) automatically become aroused by odors emitted by the opposite sex.

do not

64. The only unlearned stimulus for human arousal is _____ .

touch

65. Studies by Heiman have shown that erotic stimuli _____ (are/are not) as arousing for women as for men.

are

66. A potential problem with erotic material is that sexual activity may not live up to the _____ one develops from such material.

expectations

67. In one study, male students rated an average woman as _____ (more/less) attractive after viewing beautiful women.

less

68. In men, nocturnal emissions are more likely if orgasm _____ (has/has not) occurred recently.

has not

69. A person's sexual attraction to the same or opposite sex is referred to as _____ _____ .

sexual orientation

70. A person's awareness of his or her own biological sex is called _____ _____ .

gender identity

71. The degree to which people display gender-related traits is called _____ _____ .

sex typing

72. In terms of sexual orientation, all cultures have been predominantly _____ .

heterosexual

73. Studies indicate that approximately _____ percent of men and _____ percent of women are exclusively homosexual.

2 to 4

1

74. A person's sexual orientation _____ (does/does not) seem to be voluntarily chosen.

does not

75. On the basis of a person's background, one _____ (can/cannot) predict what that person's sexual orientation will become.

cannot

76. Sex hormone levels _____ (do/do not) predict sexual orientation.

do not

77. Storms has suggested that sexual orientation develops during _____ , when the sex drive begins and erotic associations are formed.

puberty

78. This theory proposes that homosexuality is associated with _____ (early/late) sexual maturation.

early

79. One difficulty with this theory is that homosexuals usually recall developing their sexual orientation _____ (before/after) engaging in any homosexual behavior.

before

80. An inability to maintain an erection is referred to as _____ .

impotence

81. In females, an inability to experience orgasm is referred to as _____ _____ .

orgasmic dysfunction

82. Personality disorders _____ (have/have not) been linked with most types of sexual dysfunction.

have not

Achievement Motivation (pp. 360–364)

83. The drive theory of motivation is contradicted by the existence of many behaviors that appear to satisfy no apparent biological _____.

needs

84. The desire for accomplishment, mastering things and attaining a high standard, is referred to as a need for _____.

achievement

85. Psychologists Murray, McClelland, and Atkinson studied achievement motivation by having people create _____ about ambiguous pictures.

stories

86. Given a choice, people with a low need for achievement prefer tasks that are very _____ or that are very _____.

easy; difficult

87. People with a high need for achievement prefer tasks that are _____ difficult.

moderately

88. This is so that their success may be attributed to their own _____.

skill

89. In terms of performance in school and on intelligence tests, children who are first-born do slightly _____ (better/ worse) than later-born children.

better

90. Other studies have shown that _____-born children tend to be more socially relaxed and popular.

later

91. Achievement _____ (is/is not) improved by goal setting.

is

92. Motivation to perform a behavior for its own sake is referred to as _____ _____.

intrinsic motivation

93. Motivation based on external rewards and punishments is called _____ _____.

extrinsic motivation

94. Studies comparing the effects of intrinsic and extrinsic motivation on achievement indicate that _____ motivation is most beneficial.

intrinsic

95. Helmreich found that there is an _____ effect between competitiveness and an orientation toward hard work.

interaction

96. If one intrinsically enjoys hard work, competitiveness _____ (is/is not) advantageous.

is not

97. Studies have shown that when rewards are used to control an individual, intrinsic motivation is _____ (raised/lowered); when they provide informational feedback, intrinsic motivation is _____ (raised/lowered).

lowered

raised

98. Deci and Ryan found that rewarding children for participating in organized sports made them _____ (more/less) likely to participate in the future if the rewards were terminated.

less

FOCUS ON PSYCHOLOGY:
ANOREXIA NERVOSA AND THE OBLIGATORY RUNNER

Anorexia has been defined as "an intense fear of becoming obese, which does not diminish as weight loss progresses; a loss of at least 25 percent of original body weight; and a disturbance of body image." Dieting and slimness become all-consuming goals; when the anorexic cannot lose weight, anxiety, depression, and low self-esteem often result. The anorexic often continues to attempt to lose weight in spite of physical debility, which is typically denied, in some cases even to the point of death.

Yates, Leehey, and Shisslak (1983) have noted several similarities between anorexic women and unusually dedicated distance runners they call *obligatory runners*. For these individuals, running becomes an all-consuming goal; when they are unable to run, anxiety and depression typically result. Such runners often continue to run long distances (50 to 125 miles a week) in spite of illness, which is often denied, to the point of permanent disability or even death. Like anorexics, obligatory runners are typically hard-working, introverted overachievers, brought up in middle- to upper-class families. The commitment to running (or to becoming extremely thin) typically began when these individuals were experiencing identity confusion, anxiety, or depression. Their obsession may have provided a sense of control over their lives, along with a greater sense of personal identity. Yates et al. further note that obligatory runners also become very concerned about their weight, just as anorexic women are often athletic. "The runner's ideal of less than 5 percent body fat represents a degree of emaciation not commonly found in our culture, except among ballet dancers, gymnasts, models, and patients with anorexia. Yet should the obligatory runner, through strict privation, attain 5 percent body fat, he will aim for 4 percent."

The authors suggest that obligatory running and anorexia may represent attempts to establish an identity, attempts that are reinforced in several ways. Cultural ideals may promote the two disorders. This would explain why most obligatory runners are men, and most anorexics are women. Cultural ideals place a premium on beauty in women and athleticism in men. These values could have an unusually strong influence on the person experiencing identity confusion. In addition, Yates and his colleagues suggest that physiologically, running and anorexia may have the same built-in mechanisms for reinforcement. Both anorexics and runners often report experiencing an elation, or "high." Several laboratory studies have demonstrated unusually high levels of plasma endorphin in anorexic women. Although the research is not conclusive, there are many who believe that the "runner's high" is also explained by an increase in endorphin, or noradrenalin. Endorphins are believed to be potent painkillers, with mood-elevating properties as well. Endorphin production may therefore make anorexic and obligatory running behavior patterns very difficult to change.

Although similarities between anorexia and obligatory running are striking, these scientists are careful to point out that there are exceptions to these patterns. More research investigating these phenomena is clearly needed.

PROGRESS TEST 1

Circle your answers to the following questions and check them with the answer key at the end of this chapter. Be sure to consult the appropriate pages of the text to understand the correct answer for any missed question.

Multiple-Choice Questions

1. The concept of motivation refers to a hypothetical state that:
a. energizes behavior.
b. reduces a drive.
c. reduces a need.
d. energizes and directs behavior.

2. What is the difference between a drive and a need?
a. Needs are learned, drives are inherited.
b. Needs are physiological states, drives are psychological states.
c. Drives are generally stronger than needs.
d. Needs are generally stronger than drives.

3. One problem with drive-reduction theory is that:
a. some drives do not seem to be based on physiological needs.
b. it fails to explain any human motivation.
c. it cannot account for homeostasis.
d. it does not explain the hunger drive.

4. Which of the following needs are at the top of Maslow's hierarchy?
a. physiological needs
b. safety needs
c. belongingness needs
d. self-actualization needs

5. Injections of insulin will:
a. lower blood sugar and trigger hunger.
b. raise blood sugar and trigger hunger.
c. lower blood sugar and trigger satiety.
d. raise blood sugar and trigger satiety.

6. Electrical stimulation of the lateral hypothalamus will cause:
a. an animal to begin eating.
b. an animal to stop eating.
c. an animal to become obese.
d. an animal to begin copulating.

7. Recent evidence suggests that the lateral hypothalamus produces the effects it does because:

a. it interferes with testosterone and estrogen levels.
b. it affects the body's water balance.
c. it decreases the available amount of serotonin in the brain.
d. of its role in determining the body's weight set point.

8. Rodin found that, in response to the sight and smell of a steak being grilled:
a. obese people had a greater insulin response than nonobese people.
b. nonobese people had a greater insulin response than obese people.
c. externals had a greater insulin response than internals.
d. internals had a greater insulin response than externals.

9. Which of the following is *not* necessarily a reason obese people have trouble losing weight?
a. Fat tissue has a lower metabolic rate than lean tissue.
b. Obese people are more responsive to external cues.
c. Obese persons have a stronger insulin reaction to external cues.
d. Lack of willpower.

10. Who conducted the most comprehensive survey of the sexual behavior of American men and women?
a. Kinsey
b. Masters and Johnson
c. Byrne
d. Greer

11. The correct order of the stages of Masters and Johnson's sexual response cycle is:
a. plateau; excitement; orgasm; resolution.
b. excitement; plateau; orgasm; resolution.
c. excitement; orgasm; refractory; resolution.
d. plateau; excitement; orgasm; refractory.

12. The presence of _____ determines whether the developing embryo becomes male or female.
a. estrogen
b. progesterone
c. testosterone
d. Depo-Provera

Matching Items

_____ 1. intrinsic motivation
_____ 2. set point
_____ 3. drive
_____ 4. orgasmic dysfunction
_____ 5. sex typing
_____ 6. estrogen
_____ 7. homeostasis
_____ 8. sexual orientation
_____ 9. Depo-Provera
_____ 10. incentives
_____ 11. impotence

a. hormone secreted more by females than males
b. the body's tendency to maintain an optimum internal state
c. environmental stimuli that motivate behavior
d. a person's attraction to stimuli associated with members of the same or opposite sex
e. the motivation to perform a behavior for its own sake
f. psychological state arising from an underlying need
g. an inability to have or maintain an erection
h. a woman's inability to experience orgasm
i. the extent to which a person displays traits typical of his or her gender
j. a drug that inhibits the release of testosterone
k. the body's weight-maintenance setting

FOCUS ON PSYCHOLOGY:
WHY DID SEX EVOLVE?

According to one biologist, "At first glance, and second, and third, it appears that sex shouldn't have evolved." It is an inefficient and potentially dangerous method of reproduction. Asexual reproduction requires less energy and follows a basic biological law: that an individual must pass as many of its genes as possible on to the next generation. Furthermore, with asexual reproduction an individual organism is literally cloned. With sexual reproduction, on the other hand, the offspring produced have much weaker genetic ties.

Why then has sexual reproduction evolved? An early theory to explain this evolution was the Fisher-Muller hypothesis, which maintained that organisms reproducing asexually would eventually become extinct, since any harmful mutations would be passed on to every clone in the population. Moreover, Fisher and Muller proposed that sexual reproduction accelerates evolution by "encouraging" beneficial mutations. These conclusions, however, did not hold up under the scrutiny of other biologists. Since the 1960s, a number of alternative theories, none of which is universally accepted, have been proposed. George Williams, for example, has suggested the "best man hypothesis." According to this theory, sexual reproduction promotes genetic variability, which is particularly advantageous to populations living under changing environmental conditions. When conditions change, most of the population will survive because their genetic makeup enables them to adapt to the new conditions. Members of a genetically identical population may not do so well. A similar theory proposes that an entire population of organisms reproducing asexually could be wiped out by one disease; sexual reproduction may allow organisms to develop more defenses.

Unfortunately, none of the current theories is widely accepted. As a result, many believe that biologists are no closer to an acceptable answer now than 50 years ago. Some try to ignore the issue by noting that sexual reproduction may somehow be a prerequisite for the evolution of complex species such as the human, although they are unsure why. As Maranto and Brownlee (1984) have noted, the answer to the question "Why sex?" may simply be "Why not?"

PROGRESS TEST 2

Progress Test 2 should be completed during a final chapter review. Do so after you thoroughly understand the correct answers for the Chapter Review and Progress Test 1.

Multiple-Choice Questions

1. Sexual motivation in women is most influenced by:

a. the level of progesterone.

b. the level of estrogen.

c. the phase of the menstrual cycle.

d. social and psychological factors.

2. Homeostasis refers to:

a. the tendency to maintain a steady internal state.

b. the tendency to seek external incentives for behavior.

c. the body's innate weight level.

d. a theory of the development of sexual orientation.

3. Which of the following tends to foster a high need for achievement?

a. the use of frequent extrinsic controls on behavior

b. parents who discourage independence

c. the use of punishment for failures

d. rewards that provide feedback for appropriate behavior

4. Which of the following is true concerning the relationship between birth order and achievement?

a. First-born children have the highest need for achievement.

b. Middle-born children have the highest need for achievement.

c. Last-born children have the highest need for achievement.

d. There is no consistent relationship between achievement and birth order.

5. Why do people with a high need for achievement prefer tasks of moderate difficulty?

a. They are afraid of failing at more difficult tasks.

b. They want to avoid the embarrassment of failing at easy tasks.

c. Moderately difficult tasks present an attainable goal in which success is attributable to their own skill.

d. They have high extrinsic motivation.

6. The brain area that suppresses eating when stimulated is the:

a. lateral hypothalamus.

b. ventromedial hypothalamus.

c. lateral thalamus.

d. ventromedial thalamus.

7. Weight loss is difficult for obese people because:

a. fat tissue has a lower metabolic rate than lean tissue.

b. obese people are more responsive to external food cues.

c. obese people secrete more insulin following eating.

d. of all of the above.

8. Which of the following statements concerning homosexuality is true?

a. Homosexuals have abnormal hormone levels.

b. As children, most homosexuals were molested by an adult homosexual.

c. Homosexuals had a domineering opposite-sex parent.

d. The basis for sexual orientation is largely unknown.

9. A person on a diet initially loses weight rapidly, then much more slowly. This occurs because:

a. most of the initial weight loss is simply water.

b. when a person diets, metabolism decreases.

c. people begin to "cheat" on their diets.

d. insulin levels tend to increase with reduced food intake.

10. According to Maslow's theory:

a. the most basic motives are based on physiological needs.

b. needs must be satisfied in the order specified.

c. the highest motive is self-actualization.

d. all of the above are true.

11. Which of the following is inconsistent with the drive-reduction theory of motivation?

a. Some motives, such as sex, are difficult to satiate.

b. Some motives actually increase when gratified.

c. Monkeys will work puzzles even if not rewarded.

d. All of the above are true.

12. Which of the following best describes the relationship between competitiveness and a hard-work orientation?

a. Among those intrinsically motivated to work, more competitive individuals achieve more.

b. Among those intrinsically motivated to work, less competitive individuals achieve more.

c. Among those not intrinsically motivated to work, less competitive individuals achieve more.

d. There is no relationship between competitiveness and a hard-work orientation.

True–False Items

_____ 1. Once fat cells have been acquired, they are never lost.

_____ 2. According to Masters and Johnson, only males experience a refractory period in the cycle of sexual arousal.

_____ 3. Testosterone affects the sexual arousal of the male only.

_____ 4. Men tend to be more aroused than women by sexually explicit material.

_____ 5. Individuals with a high need for achievement also tend to have high intrinsic motivation.

_____ 6. Later-born children tend to be more socially popular than first-born children.

_____ 7. An injection of insulin increases neural activity in the ventromedial hypothalamus.

_____ 8. The body's set point is lowered by destruction of the lateral hypothalamus.

_____ 9. The number of fat cells one has is fixed at birth and remains constant thereafter.

_____ 10. One's sexual orientation appears not to be chosen voluntarily.

SAMPLE ESSAY QUESTIONS

1. Contrast the incentive and drive-reduction theories of motivation. What are some of the problems with the drive theory?

2. Discuss the following aspects of achievement motivation.

a. What factors contribute to its development?

b. How is achievement motivation related to preference in task difficulty?

c. What relationship is there between competitiveness and achievement?

3. Describe the phases of the sexual response cycle identified by Masters and Johnson.

4. Discuss the importance of stomach contractions, blood sugar, insulin, and the hypothalamus in regulating hunger.

5. Explain why obese people find it difficult to lose weight permanently.

PROJECT:
THE NEED FOR ACHIEVEMENT

Anthony Grasha (1983) suggests that one method of assessing need for achievement is to examine an individual's doodling and drawings. These are compared with drawings of people previously determined to have high or low needs for achievement. To test yourself, simply take a sheet of paper and mark out an area approximately 3 inches square. Relax and begin doodling within the square. Do so for 2 minutes. Draw whatever you feel like. After you have finished, use the six criteria listed below to assess your achievement motivation.

Grasha reports that the drawings of those with high need for achievement tended to have the following characteristics.

1. The drawings filled most of the square. Margins were narrow.

2. Diagonal lines were frequently used.

3. Geometrical shapes (triangles, circles) were common.

4. Curved, S-shaped lines were often present.

5. Repetitive, multiwave lines were not commonly found.

6. Figures were drawn clearly and distinctly.

To score your drawing, give yourself one point for meeting each of the criteria clearly demonstrated. Assign fractions of a point for partial fulfillment of a criterion. The closer your score is to the maximum of 6, the higher your level of achievement motivation. Low scores demonstrate weaker achievement motivation.

WHERE TO LOOK FOR MORE INFORMATION

Grasha, A. (1983). *Practical applications of psychology.* Boston: Little, Brown.

Grasha provides numerous examples of psychological principles in operation in our daily lives.

Maranto, G., and Brownlee, S. (1984, February). Why sex? *Discover.*

Maranto and Brownlee discuss various theories of the evolution of sexual reproduction.

Yates, A., Leehey, K., and Shisslak, C. M. (1983, February 3). Running—An analogue of anorexia? *The New England Journal of Medicine.*

ANSWERS

PROGRESS TEST 1

Multiple-Choice Questions

1. d (p. 337)
2. b (p. 339)
3. a (pp. 340–341)
4. d (p. 341)
5. a (p. 343)
6. a (p. 343)
7. d (p. 343)
8. c (p. 344)
9. d (pp. 344–347)
10. a (p. 352)
11. b (p. 353)
12. c (p. 354)

Matching Items

1. e (p. 362)
2. k (p. 343)
3. f (p. 339)
4. h (p. 359)
5. i (p. 356)
6. a (p. 354)
7. b (p. 340)
8. d (p. 356)
9. j (p. 354)
10. c (p. 340)
11. g (p. 359)

PROGRESS TEST 2

Multiple-Choice Questions

1. d (p. 354)
2. a (p. 340)
3. d (p. 363)
4. a (p. 362)
5. c (p. 361)
6. b (p. 343)
7. d (pp. 346–348)
8. d (p. 358)
9. b (p. 346)
10. d (p. 341)
11. d (pp. 339–340)
12. b (p. 363)

True–False Items

1. True (p. 346)
2. True (p. 353)
3. False (p. 354)
4. False (p. 355)
5. True (p. 363)
6. True (p. 362)
7. False (p. 343)
8. True (p. 343)
9. False (p. 346)
10. True (p. 357)

CHAPTER 14

Emotion

CHAPTER OVERVIEW

Emotions are responses of the whole individual that involve physiological arousal, expressive reactions, and conscious feelings and thoughts. Chapter 14 examines each of these components in detail, particularly as they relate to three specific emotions: fear, anger, and happiness. In addition, several theoretical issues are discussed and compared. These include the James-Lange, Cannon-Bard, and two-factor theories of emotion. Finally, the chapter discusses whether emotional feelings can occur without conscious thought, the significance of nonverbal expressions of emotion, and whether the polygraph actually detects lying.

GUIDED STUDY

Before you read, preview each section by skimming it, noting headings and boldface items. Then read the appropriate section objectives from the following outline. Keep these objectives in mind, and as you read the chapter section, search for the information that will complete each one. You may wish to write out answers for each objective as soon as you finish reading that section of the chapter.

The Physiology of Emotion (pp. 370–373)

1. Identify the physiological changes that occur during emotional arousal.

2. Describe the relationship between arousal and performance.

3. Discuss how the polygraph works and whether it can actually detect lying.

The Expression of Emotion (pp. 373–376)

4. Discuss whether nonverbal expressions of emotion are universally understood.

The Experiencing of Emotion (pp. 376–385)

5. Discuss individual differences in the emotion of fear, and whether it is a learned or biologically determined emotion.

6. Discuss whether expressing anger is cathartic.

7. Explain the following principles in the experience of happiness:
a. adaptation level
b. relative deprivation

8. Describe the opponent-process theory of emotion.

Theories of Emotion (pp. 386–389)

9. Describe the James-Lange and Cannon-Bard theories of emotion.

10. Explain Schachter's two-factor theory of emotion.

11. Contrast the positions of Zajonc and Lazarus concerning the role of cognition in emotion.

CHAPTER REVIEW

When you have finished reading the chapter, complete the sentences that follow. Using your hand or a strip of paper, cover the correct answers in the margin and fill in each blank. Verify your answer by uncovering the correct one. As you proceed, evaluate your performance for each chapter section. *Do not continue with the next section until you understand why each margin term is the correct answer.* If you need to, review or re-read the appropriate chapter section in the text before continuing.

1. Of all the species, the most emotional is the

_____ .   human

2. Three aspects of any emotion are: _____ arousal,   physiological

_____ expressions, and conscious _____   facial; thoughts

and feelings.

The Physiology of Emotion (pp. 370–373)

3. List the major physiological changes that each of the following undergo during emotional arousal:

a. heart   heart: heart rate increases
b. muscles   muscles: become tense
c. liver   liver: releases sugar
                                                                                      into bloodstream
d. breathing   breathing: rate increases
e. digestion   digestion: slows down
f. pupils   pupils: become dilated
g. blood   blood: tends to clot
                                                                                      more rapidly

4. These responses are activated by the _____ nervous system.   sympathetic

5. This system has neural centers running along the _____

cord.   spinal

6. In response to a signal from this system, hormones that increase heart rate and blood pressure are released by the _____   adrenal

glands.

7. These hormones are _____ and   epinephrine

_____ .   norepinephrine

8. When the need for arousal has passed, the body is calmed through

activation of the _____ nervous system.   parasympathetic

9. The neural centers for this division of the nervous system are at the

_____ and _____ of the spinal   top; bottom

cord.

10. Performance and thinking tend to be best when arousal is
_____.

moderate

11. High arousal may improve performance on _____ tasks.

easy or well-learned

12. Optimum arousal is lower for _____ tasks.

more difficult

13. The various emotions are associated with _____ (similar/different) forms of physiological arousal.

similar

14. Psychologists _____ (do/do not) generally believe that different brain circuits may underlie different emotions.

do

15. The brain region that produces terror or rage when activated is the _____ system.

limbic

16. The technical name for a lie detector is a _____.

polygraph

17. This device measures the _____ indicators of emotion.

physiological

18. Some of the responses measured include changes in
_____, _____ rate, _____ pressure, and _____.

breathing; pulse
blood; perspiration

19. One of the main skeptics about the validity of the lie detector is _____.

Lykken

20. He believes that, because general arousal is the same for all emotions, the polygraph cannot distinguish between the emotions of
_____, _____, and
_____.

anxiety; irritation
guilt

21. By his estimate, polygraph tests are inaccurate about _____ of the time.

one-third

22. A test that assesses a suspect's knowledge of details of a crime that only the guilty person should know is the _____ _____.

guilty knowledge test

The Expression of Emotion (pp. 373–376)

23. Emotions may be communicated verbally and/or through bodily expressions, referred to as _____ communication.

nonverbal

24. Gestures may have different meanings in different _____.

cultures

25. Studies by Ekman and Friesen indicate that facial expressions of emotion appear to be understood _____.

universally

26. Eibl-Eibesfeldt found that the same _____ (is/is not) true of children's facial expressions.

is

27. Darwin believed that human emotional expressions are a carryover from earlier stages of _____.

evolution

28. Darwin also believed that when an emotion is accompanied by an outward facial expression, the emotion is _____ (intensified/diminished).

intensified

29. In one study, students who were induced to smile _____ (did/did not) find cartoons more humorous.

did

30. Imitating another person's facial expressions seems to allow one to become more _____ with that person's feelings.

empathic

31. Ekman, Levenson, and Friesen found that imitating emotional facial expressions also resulted in _____ changes characteristic of emotional arousal.

physiological

The Experiencing of Emotion (pp. 376–385)

32. Although fear can cause panic, it is generally a very _____ emotion.

adaptive

33. Most human fears are acquired through _____.

learning

34. Some fears are acquired more quickly than others, suggesting that humans are _____ prepared for acquiring them.

biologically

35. One study found that identical twins raised apart _____ (did/did not) tend to show fearfulness for the same things.

did

36. Averill has found that most people become angry several times per _____.

week

37. Anger is most typically directed at _____ or loved ones.

friends

38. We become angry when we believe someone has willfully done us a misdeed. This illustrates the importance of our _____ appraisal of situations in emotion.

cognitive

39. According to one theory, expressing pent-up emotion is adaptive. This is the _____ hypothesis.

catharsis

40. Psychologists have found that retaliation against a tormentor may reduce aggression under certain circumstances. List these below.

a. _____

_____

_____

b. _____

_____

c. _____

_____

_____

Counterattack must be directed against the tormentor.

Retaliation must be justifiable.

The target of the counterattack must not be intimidating.

41. Two dangers of expressing anger are that it may become _____-forming, and it may actually _____ one's anger.

habit
increase

42. Psychologists have consistently found that people become more willing to offer help to others when they are _____.

happy

43. Since the 1950s, spendable income has doubled; personal happiness _____ (has/has not) changed.

has not

44. After experiencing a tragedy in their lives, most people _____ (do/do not) regain their previous degree of happiness.

do

45. The principle that happiness is relative to one's most recent experience is _____.

adaptation level

46. The principle that one's happiness is relative to others' is _____ _____.

relative deprivation

47. Dermer found that, after seeing the misfortunes of others, students expressed _____ (greater/less) satisfaction with their own lives.

greater

48. The statement "Every emotion triggers its opposite" reflects the _____-_____ theory of emotion.

opponent-process

49. This theory was proposed by _____.

Solomon

50. According to this theory, the opposing emotion is most intense immediately _____ an emotion-arousing event.

after

51. With repeated experience of the event, the primary emotion becomes _____ and the opposing emotion becomes _____.

weaker
stronger

52. List some factors that tend to be correlated with feelings of happiness.

_____

_____

_____

_____

_____

high self-esteem; satisfying love relationship; religious faith; socially outgoing; sleep well; exercise; employment

53. List some factors that appear to be unrelated to happiness.

_____

_____

_____

age; race; gender; education; intelligence; parenthood

Theories of Emotion (pp. 386–389)

54. According to the James-Lange theory, emotional states _____ (precede/follow) bodily arousal.

follow

55. Cannon argued that bodily arousal is too general to trigger different _____ .

emotions

56. In addition, bodily responses occur too _____ to differentiate emotions.

slowly

57. Cannon proposed that emotional stimuli in the environment are routed simultaneously to the _____ , which results in the emotion, and to the _____ nervous system, which causes the body's reaction.

cortex

sympathetic

58. Because another scientist simultaneously proposed similar ideas, this theory has come to be known as the _____-_____ theory of emotion.

Cannon-Bard

59. For victims of spinal cord injuries who have lost all feeling below the neck, the intensity of emotions tends to _____ .

decrease

60. This result tends to support the _____-_____ theory of emotion.

James-Lange

61. The two-factor theory of emotion proposes that emotion has two components: _____ arousal and a _____ label.

physical

cognitive

62. This theory was proposed by _____.

Schachter

63. Schachter and Singer found that physically aroused subjects who were told that an injection would cause arousal _____ (did/did not) respond emotionally to the accomplice's behavior.

did not

64. Physically aroused subjects who were not expecting arousal _____ (did/did not) become emotional in response to the accomplice's behavior.

did

65. Zajonc believes that the feeling of emotion _____ (can/cannot) precede our cognitive labeling of that emotion.

can

66. Emotional processing in the brain typically takes place in the _____ hemisphere.

right

67. Some stimuli could trigger emotion directly, due to the existence of a neural pathway between the eye and the _____ of the brain.

hypothalamus

68. The researcher who disagrees with Zajonc and argues that most emotions require cognitive processing is _____.

Lazarus

FOCUS ON PSYCHOLOGY:
ALEXITHYMIA—EMOTIONAL ILLITERACY

Psychiatrists estimate that about 10 percent of the population have almost no awareness of their emotions, and/or are unable to express their feelings in words. Harvard professor of psychiatry Peter Sifneos had found that some of his patients failed to improve, in part because they could not describe their feelings. He coined the term *alexithymia* (which means "without words for feelings") to describe such individuals. Sifneos points out that alexithymics are often intelligent and highly successful in their careers; only in terms of their feelings are they inadequate. Sifneos also discovered that many alexithymics have psychosomatic illnesses, such as eczema, colitis, and arthritis, which may be side effects of their alexithymia. Unable to release emotional tension by talking about it, the alexithymic manifests emotions physically.

Clinical psychiatrists at UCLA have recently discovered that split-brain patients show an unusually high incidence rate of alexithymia. In such patients, as you will recall from Chapter 2, the right and left hemispheres of the brains have been surgically disconnected by the severing of the corpus callosum (com-missurotomization). The belief that the right hemisphere is generally responsible for generating emotions, and the left for their verbal expression has led psychologists to the natural conclusion that those suffering from alexithymia may be "functionally commissurotomized." This is manifested in difficulty in expressing emotions verbally. Further research is needed into this interesting phenomenon, but at the very least these findings have important implications for the kinds of treatment to be used with alexithymics.

PROGRESS TEST 1

Circle your answers to the following questions and check them with the answer key at the end of this chapter. Be sure to consult the appropriate pages of the text to understand the correct answer for any missed question.

Multiple-Choice Questions

1. Which of the following describes the relationship between arousal and performance?
a. On all tasks, performance is optimum when arousal is low.

b. On all tasks, performance is optimum when arousal is high.

c. On easy tasks, performance is optimum when arousal is low.

d. On easy tasks, performance is optimum when arousal is high.

2. Which division of the nervous system is especially involved in emotional arousal?

a. somatic nervous system

b. peripheral nervous system

c. sympathetic nervous system

d. parasympathetic nervous system

3. Concerning emotions and their accompanying bodily responses, which of the following is true?

a. Each emotion has its own bodily response and underlying brain circuitry.

b. All emotions involve the same bodily response as a result of the same underlying brain circuitry.

c. Many emotions involve similar bodily responses, but each probably has its own underlying brain circuitry.

d. All emotions have the same underlying brain circuitry, but different bodily responses.

4. Which of the following supports Darwin's idea that our nonverbal emotional expressions evolved from those of our animal ancestors?

a. The nonverbal expressions of many emotions are the same in different cultures.

b. The emotional expressions of children are the same across cultures.

c. Blind children show the same emotional expressions as normal children.

d. All of the above support his idea.

5. Electrical stimulation of which brain region can produce terror or rage?

a. limbic system

b. hypothalamus

c. cortex

d. cerebellum

6. Just before a big exam, you can tell you are nervous because your pulse is racing and you are sweating. Which theory of emotion does this support?

a. Cannon-Bard theory

b. James-Lange theory

c. opponent-process theory

d. two-factor theory

7. Which of the following was not raised as a criticism of the James-Lange theory of emotion?

a. Bodily responses are too similar to trigger the various emotions.

b. Emotional reactions occur before bodily responses can take place.

c. People with spinal cord injuries at the neck continue to feel normal, full-intensity emotions.

d. People with spinal cord injuries at the neck typically experience less emotion.

8. Current estimates indicate that the polygraph is inaccurate approximately _____ of the time.

a. one-half

b. three-fourths

c. one-third

d. one-fourth

9. In the Schachter-Singer experiment, which subjects reported an emotional change?

a. those receiving adrenaline and expecting to feel physical arousal

b. those receiving a placebo and expecting to feel physical arousal

c. those receiving adrenaline but not expecting to feel physical arousal

d. those receiving a placebo and not expecting to feel physical arousal

10. Which of the following is true?

a. People with more education tend to be happier.

b. Highly intelligent people tend to be happier.

c. Women tend to be happier than men.

d. Those with high self-esteem tend to be happier.

11. Catharsis tends to reduce anger toward another:

a. if the anger is displaced onto a third individual.

b. only if it is justifiable and directed toward one's tormentor.

c. only if the other retaliates in turn.

d. in none of the above cases; catharsis never reduces anger.

12. Emotions are:
a. physiological reactions.   **c.** conscious feelings.
b. behavioral expressions.   **d.** all of the above.

Matching Items

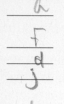

_____a_ **1.** the tendency to react only to *changes* from recent experience.

_____f_ **2.** we are sad because we cry

_____d_ **3.** emotional release

_____j_ **4.** the tendency to evaluate our situation against that of other people

_____b_ **5.** each emotional response triggers an opposing emotional response

_____c_ **6.** emotions have two components: physical arousal and a cognitive label

_____h_ **7.** an emotion-arousing stimulus causes cognitive and bodily responses simultaneously

_____i_ **8.** the division of the nervous system that is active when one is calm

_____e_ **9.** the division of the nervous system that is active when one is aroused

_____g_ **10.** a device that measures the physiological correlates of emotion

a. adaptation-level principle
b. opponent-process theory
c. two-factor theory
d. catharsis
e. sympathetic division
f. James-Lange theory
g. polygraph
h. Cannon-Bard theory
i. parasympathetic division
j. relative deprivation principle

FOCUS ON PSYCHOLOGY:
SOCIOPATHY, FEAR, AND CRIME

As the text explains, Schachter's cognitive-arousal theory proposes that physical arousal will intensify any emotion a person is experiencing. Individuals who have been labeled as *sociopaths* tend to be emotionally flat, and according to Schachter are overrepresented among prison inmates. Schachter wondered whether sociopaths were more likely to commit crimes because they were less fearful of being caught. As one test of this theory, Schachter had prison inmates who had been diagnosed as sociopaths tested on an avoidance task. Presumably motivated by fear, these individuals learned a response in order to avoid being shocked. Schachter found that sociopathic prisoners took much longer than nonsociopathic inmates

to learn the task. In a second experiment, reasoning that increased physical arousal might increase fear and improve avoidance learning, Schachter injected inmates with adrenaline and then tested their performance. The results showed a significant reduction in the amount of time it took the inmates to learn the task.

In a third experiment, college students were allowed to grade their own psychology exams, in complete privacy. Unknown to them, the experimenter had placed them under the influence of either adrenaline (which increases physical arousal) or chlorpromazine (a tranquilizer which decreases physical arousal). Supporting his hypothesis that tranquilized subjects should be less afraid, Schachter found the greatest incidence of answer changing in this group.

These three experiments suggest that by manipulating physiological arousal in certain populations of individuals, it may be possible for society to exert some control over crime. In Chapter 13 a study was mentioned in which the drug Depo-Provera was used to inhibit arousal in male sex offenders. Do you feel such techniques can be justified ethically?

PROGRESS TEST 2

Progress Test 2 should be completed during a final chapter review. Do so after you thoroughly understand the correct answers for the Chapter Review and Progress Test 1.

Multiple-Choice Questions

1. You are relaxing after eating a large, delicious dinner. Which division of your nervous system will be most active?
   a. sympathetic division
   b. parasympathetic division
   c. somatic division
   d. peripheral nervous system

2. Schachter's two-factor theory emphasizes:
   a. physiological arousal in emotion.
   b. social variables in emotion.
   c. both physical arousal and the cognitive label applied to it.
   d. the role of lower brain centers in emotion.

3. Dermer found that students who had seen others worse off felt greater satisfaction with their own lives; this is the principle of:
   a. relative deprivation.
   b. adaptation level.
   c. behavioral contrast.
   d. opponent processes.

4. Which theory of emotion emphasizes the simultaneous experience of bodily response and emotional feeling?
   a. James-Lange theory
   b. Cannon-Bard theory
   c. two-factor theory
   d. opponent-process theory

5. Expressing emotion with facial and behavioral reactions is called:
   a. subliminal communication.
   b. modeling.
   c. nonverbal communication.
   d. behavioral typing.

6. The polygraph directly measures:
   a. lying.
   b. brain rhythms.
   c. chemical changes in the body.
   d. physiological indicators of emotion such as blood pressure changes.

7. According to the opponent-process theory, as an emotion is repeatedly experienced:
   a. the primary emotional experience becomes stronger.
   b. the opposing emotional experience becomes weaker.
   c. both (a) and (b) occur.
   d. the primary emotional experience becomes weaker; the opposing emotional experience becomes stronger.

8. Which of the following is true?
   a. Gestures mean the same thing the world over.
   b. Facial expressions of emotion are culturally determined.
   c. Both (a) and (b) are true.
   d. The meaning of gestures varies from culture to culture.

9. Which theory of emotion proposes that an emotional experience takes place only after the body reacts?
   a. James-Lange theory
   b. Cannon-Bard theory
   c. two-factor theory
   d. opponent-process theory

10. For which of the following fears do humans appear biologically prepared?
    a. fear of electricity
    b. fear of cliffs
    c. fear of automobiles
    d. fear of flying

11. According to Hebb, the most emotional animal is the:
    a. dog.
    b. horse.
    c. chimpanzee.
    d. human.

12. Concerning the catharsis hypothesis, which of the following is true?

a. Most psychologists believe that catharsis, in the long run, does not reduce anger.

b. Most psychologists believe it is better to express anger than to keep it inside.

c. Expressing anger always calms a person down.

d. Psychologists agree that under no circumstances is catharsis beneficial.

True-False Items

F   **1.** The optimal level of arousal is higher for easy tasks than for difficult tasks.

F   **2.** Men are generally better than women at detecting nonverbal emotional expression.

F   **3.** The sympathetic nervous system triggers physiological arousal during an emotion.

T   **4.** The adrenal glands produce the hormones epinephrine and norepinephrine.

T   **5.** When a person imitates an emotional facial expression, the body may experience physiological changes characteristic of that emotion.

T   **6.** Paraplegics who have lost sensation only in their lower bodies experience a considerable decrease in the intensity of their emotions.

F   **7.** Wealthy people tend to be much happier than middle-income people.

T   **8.** Physical arousal can intensify emotion.

F   **9.** All emotions involve conscious thinking.

T   **10.** According to the two-factor theory, emotions are labeled cognitively *before* physical arousal occurs.

SAMPLE ESSAY QUESTIONS

1. Describe the physiological changes that take place during emotional arousal.

2. Explain and contrast the James-Lange, Cannon-Bard, and two-factor theories of emotion.

3. Discuss the research on nonverbal communication as it relates to the expression of emotion.

4. Explain how the polygraph works and discuss whether it is capable of detecting lying.

5. Discuss the principles of adaptation level and relative deprivation as they apply to happiness.

PROJECT:
SYMPATHETIC AROUSAL DURING
EMOTIONAL STATES

As noted in the text, the body reacts physically during emotional arousal. The sympathetic division of the autonomic nervous system is activated, adrenaline is secreted, and in response there are changes in heart rate, blood pressure, breathing, and skin resistance. The measurement of these responses by a polygraph forms the basis of the lie detector, or emotion-detection procedure. If you have contact with someone in the biology department, ask if you might be given a demonstration of how the polygraph works. It is also possible to measure directly several of these arousal responses without using elaborate equipment. You may do so on yourself, or you may experiment with several volunteers. In this project, you (and/or your volunteers) will need to know how to measure your own heart rate. This may be done easily by lightly pressing the tips of the index and middle fingers of one hand on the side of the neck, just below the jaw, and midway between the windpipe and the back of the neck. Have your subjects sit down and relax for a few minutes. Explain to them that you are investigating physical reactions that occur during emotions. Show them how to take their own pulses. Say "Begin," and have them count their heartbeats for one minute. Enter this baseline rate for each subject in the table on page 193.

Now ask your subjects to recall a frightening incident. Ask them to create a strong mental image of this situation. As they do so, have them again count their heartbeats for one minute. Record this second rate for each subject. If your subjects have difficulty concentrating on their frightening image while counting, put them in pairs and have them alternate taking each other's pulse and imagining their own scene.

Subject	Baseline Heart Rate	Heart Rate While Afraid	Difference in Heart Rate	Percent Change in Heart Rate
1	71	80	+9	12.7

Analyze your results in the following manner. For each subject, subtract the baseline heart rate from the heart rate while afraid. Ignore negative numbers; only the absolute difference is important. Note this difference in the appropriate column of the table. Next, for each subject, divide the difference in heart rate by the baseline heart rate. Note this value in the column labeled "Percent Change in Heart Rate." Using bar graphs, plot the percentage change in heart rate for each subject. An example of one subject is included in the right-hand column, along with a figure for plotting your results.

Questions to Consider

1. Were your subjects' heart rate changes very large? Were there occasions in which heart rate *decreased* in some subjects and *increased* in others? Why do you think this happened?

2. To what would you attribute the individual differences in heart rate change?

3. Have your subjects recall other incidents during which different emotions were felt. Are the different emotions characterized by specific heart rate changes?

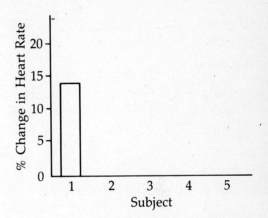

WHERE TO LOOK FOR MORE INFORMATION

Huyghe, P. (1984, March). Speechless. *Omni*.
    A discussion of the plight of individuals suffering from alexithymia.

Schachter, S. (1971). *Emotion, obesity, and crime*. New York: Academic Press.
    Schachter discusses his two-factor theory of emotion and the effects of physical arousal on fear and crime.

ANSWERS

PROGRESS TEST 1

Multiple-Choice Questions

1. d (p. 370)
2. c (p. 370)
3. c (p. 371)
4. d (p. 375)

5. a (p. 371)
6. b (p. 386)
7. c (p. 387)
8. c (p. 372)

9. c (p. 388)
10. d (p. 385)
11. b (p. 379)
12. d (p. 369)

Matching Items

1. a (p. 382)
2. f (p. 386)
3. d (p. 379)
4. j (p. 382)

5. b (p. 384)
6. c (p. 387)
7. h (p. 386)
8. i (p. 370)

9. e (p. 370)
10. g (p. 372)

PROGRESS TEST 2

Multiple-Choice Questions

1. b (p. 370)
2. c (p. 388)
3. a (p. 382)
4. b (p. 386)

5. c (p. 373)
6. d (p. 372)
7. d (p. 384)
8. d (p. 374)

9. a (p. 386)
10. b (p. 378)
11. d (p. 369)
12. a (p. 379)

True-False Items

1. True (p. 370)
2. False (p. 374)
3. True (p. 370)
4. True (p. 370)

5. True (p. 376)
6. False (p. 387)
7. False (p. 380)
8. True (p. 370)

9. False (p. 387)
10. False (p. 387)

PART SIX

PERSONALITY, DISORDER, AND WELL-BEING

CHAPTER 15

Personality

CHAPTER OVERVIEW

Personality refers to each individual's relatively distinctive and consistent pattern of thinking, feeling, and acting. This chapter examines the psychoanalytic, trait, humanistic, and social-cognitive perspectives on personality. Each perspective is described and then evaluated against the findings of current research. The psychoanalytic theory emphasizes the unconscious and irrational aspects of personality. The trait theory led to advances in techniques for measuring and describing personality. The humanistic theory draws attention to the concept of self and its potential for healthy growth. The cognitive-social learning perspective emphasizes the influence of the situation on behavior.

GUIDED STUDY

The text chapter should be studied one section at a time. Before you read, preview each section by skimming it, noting headings and boldface items. Then read the appropriate section objectives from the following outline. Keep these objectives in mind, and as you read the chapter section, search for the information that will complete each one. You may wish to write out answers for each objective as soon as you finish reading that section of the chapter.

1. Explain what is meant by personality.

The Psychoanalytic Perspective (pp. 396–405)

2. Describe each of the following aspects of personality according to Freud's theory.

 a. unconscious

 b. preconscious

 c. id

 d. ego

 e. superego

3. Describe the development of personality in each of the following psychosexual stages.

 a. oral stage

 b. anal stage

 c. phallic stage

 d. latency period

 e. genital stage

4. Explain the Oedipus complex and the process of fixation.

5. Describe each of the following defense mechanisms.

 a. repression

 b. regression

 c. reaction formation

 d. rationalization

 e. displacement

f. sublimation

g. projection

6. Explain how projective tests work and describe each of the following.

a. Thematic Apperception Test

b. Rorschach Test

7. Explain how each of the following "neo-Freudians" modified Freud's theory.

a. Carl Jung

b. Alfred Adler

c. Karen Horney

d. Erich Fromm

e. Erik Erikson

8. Discuss the shortcomings of psychoanalysis as a theory.

The Trait Perspective (pp. 405–410)

9. Explain how the trait perspective differs from the psychoanalytic perspective.

10. Describe the personality types proposed by the ancient Greeks and by William Sheldon.

11. Describe how Raymond Cattell and Hans Eysenck conceptualize personality.

12. Explain how the MMPI was developed and describe its structure.

13. Discuss whether personality traits are consistent over time and from situation to situation.

14. Compare the influence of traits and situations in determining behavior.

The Humanistic Perspective (pp. 411–417)

15. Contrast the humanistic perspective with that of Freud and behaviorism.

16. Explain the process of self-actualization.

17. Identify and describe the three conditions that promote growth, according to Carl Rogers.

18. Discuss the major criticisms of the humanistic perspective.

19. Contrast the effects of high and low self-esteem on behavior.

20. Explain what is meant by a self-serving bias; identify the evidence that points to its existence in most individuals.

The Social-Cognitive Perspective (pp. 417–421)

21. Define reciprocal determinism and explain the central idea of the social-cognitive theory.

22. Explain the difference between internal and external locus of control.

23. Explain what is meant by learned helplessness and how it is acquired.

24. Describe the Barnum effect and the techniques palm readers and astrologers use in order to appear to assess an individual's personality.

25. Identify the major contribution of each of the following to the understanding of personality.

a. the psychoanalytic perspective

b. the trait perspective

c. the humanistic perspective

d. the social-cognitive perspective

CHAPTER REVIEW

When you have finished reading the chapter, complete the sentences that follow. Using your hand or a strip of paper, cover the correct answers in the margin and fill in each blank. Verify your answer by un-

covering the correct one. As you proceed, evaluate your performance for each chapter section. *Do not continue with the next section until you understand why each margin term is the correct answer.* If you need to, review or re-read the appropriate chapter section in the text before continuing.

1. An individual's enduring response patterns across a variety of situations is that individual's _____.

personality

2. This definition reflects a person's consistent and distinctive ways of _____, _____, and _____.

thinking; feeling

acting

3. List the four major perspectives on personality discussed in this chapter.

a. _____   psychoanalytic

b. _____   trait

c. _____   humanistic

d. _____   social-cognitive

The Psychoanalytic Perspective (pp. 396–405)

4. The psychoanalytic perspective is based on the theory proposed by

_____.   Freud

5. Freud likened the mind to an _____ in that many   iceberg
of a person's thoughts, wishes, and feelings are in a hidden,
_____ region.   unconscious

6. Some of the thoughts in this region can be retrieved at will into
consciousness: these thoughts are said to be _____.   preconscious

7. Many of the memories in this region, however, are blocked, or
_____, from consciousness.   repressed

8. The technique used by Freud in which the patient relaxes and says
whatever comes to mind is called _____   free association

_____.

9. Freud called the analysis of painful unconscious memories

_____.   psychoanalysis

10. Freud believed a person's unconscious wishes are often reflected
in the person's _____.   dreams

11. Freud called the remembered content of dreams the

_____ _____.   manifest content

12. According to Freud, personality consists of three structures: the
_____, the _____, and the   id; ego
_____.   superego

13. The source of energy for the id is provided by instinctual drives
for survival, such as _____, _____,   hunger; thirst
and _____.   sex

14. The id is a reservoir of energy that is primarily _____   unconscious
(conscious/unconscious).

15. The id operates according to the _____ principle.   pleasure

16. The ego develops _____ (before/after) the id and consists of perceptions, thoughts, and memories that are mostly _____ (conscious/unconscious).

after

conscious

17. The ego operates according to the _____ principle.

reality

18. The ego mediates between the id and the superego, and is often called the _____ of personality.

executive

19. The personality structure that reflects moral values is the _____.

superego

20. A person with a _____ (strong/weak) superego may be self-indulgent; one with an unusually _____ (strong/weak) superego may be continually guilt-ridden.

weak

strong

21. According to Freud, the personality is formed as the child passes through a series of _____ stages.

psychosexual

22. During these stages, the id's energies are focused on different _____ zones.

erogenous

23. The first stage is the _____ stage, which takes place during the first 18 months of life.

oral

24. During this stage, the id's energies are focused on behaviors such as _____, _____, and _____.

sucking; biting

chewing

25. The second stage is the _____ stage, which lasts from about _____ months to _____ years.

anal

18

3

26. During this stage, the id's energies are focused on stimulation of the bowels, through _____ and _____.

elimination; retention

27. The third stage is the _____ stage, which lasts from ages _____ to _____.

phallic

3; 6

28. During this stage, the id's energies are focused on the _____.

genitals

29. Freud believed children in this stage develop sexual desires for the _____ (same/opposite)-sex parent.

opposite

30. Freud referred to these feelings as the _____.

Oedipus complex

31. During the next stage, sexual feelings are repressed: this phase is

called the _____ _____ and lasts
until _____ .

32. The final stage of development is called the _____

_____ .

33. According to Freud, it is possible for development to become locked in any of the stages; in such an instance, the person is said to be _____ .

34. The ego attempts to protect itself against anxiety through the use of _____ _____ .

35. The process underlying each of these mechanisms is

_____ .

36. Returning to an earlier stage of development is called

_____ .

37. When a person reacts in a manner opposite that of his or her true feelings, _____ _____ is said to have occurred.

38. When a person attributes his or her own feelings toward another person to that person, _____ has occurred.

39. When self-justifying explanations are offered instead of the real reasons for an action, _____ has occurred.

40. When impulses are directed toward an object other than the one that caused arousal, _____ has occurred.

41. The process in which impulses are displaced into socially accept-able achievements is called _____ .

42. Defense mechanisms are _____ (conscious/un-conscious) processes.

43. The theorists who established modified versions of psycho-analytic theory are called _____-_____ .

44. These theorists typically place _____ (more/less) emphasis on the conscious mind than Freud did.

45. Two theorists who placed greater emphasis on social rather than sexual factors in childhood are _____ and

_____ .

46. The theorist who believed that the ego had strivings of its own, such as love, truth, and freedom, was _____ .

latency period
adolescence
genital stage

fixated

defense mechanisms

repression

regression

reaction formation

projection

rationalization

displacement

sublimation
unconscious

neo-Freudians
more

Adler; Horney

Fromm

47. The theorist who proposed that development through psychosocial stages continued throughout life was _____ .

Erikson

48. Carl Jung suggested that part of the unconscious contains memories of universal experiences; this he called the _____ _____ .

collective unconscious

49. Henry Murray introduced the personality assessment technique called the _____ _____ Test.

Thematic Apperception

50. Tests such as this provide subjects with ambiguous stimuli for interpretation and are called _____ tests.

projective

51. The most widely used of these tests is the _____ test.

Rorschach

52. In this test, subjects are shown a series of _____ .

inkblots

53. Generally, the validity and reliability of projective tests are _____ (very good/not very good).

not very good

54. Freud's theory that personality is largely fixed during childhood _____ (has/has not) been confirmed by recent work in developmental psychology.

has not

55. Freud's theories of dreams and memory loss by repression generally _____ (have/have not) been supported by recent research.

have not

56. Recent research demonstrates that the unconscious mind is not filled with instinctual urges, but rather it is where _____ is processed without awareness.

information

57. A more general criticism of psychoanalysis is that as a theory it makes few predictions that are _____ .

testable

58. Another criticism is that Freud's theory "explains" any behavior because it provides explanations that are made _____ the fact.

after

The Trait Perspective (pp. 405–410)

59. Trait theorists are generally less concerned with explaining why we differ from one another and are more concerned with describing _____ we differ.

how

60. The ancient Greeks classified people according to four types: _____ , or depressed; _____ , or cheerful; _____ , or unemotional; and _____ , or irritable.

melancholic; sanguine
phlegmatic
choleric

61. Sheldon identified three body types: the jolly _____ type, the bold _____ type, and the high-strung _____ type.

endomorphic
mesomorphic
ectomorphic

62. Traits are defined as _____ to behave in certain ways.

predispositions

63. The psychologist who used factor analysis to identify clusters of personality traits is _____ .

Cattell

64. Eysenck believes that two personality dimensions are important: _____-_____ and emotional _____-_____ .

extraversion-introversion
stability-instability

65. Questionnaires that measure personality traits are called _____ _____ .

personality inventories

66. The most widely used of all personality tests is the _____ _____ _____ _____ .

Minnesota Multiphasic Personality Inventory

67. This test was developed by testing a large pool of items and selecting those that differentiated particular individuals; in other words, the test was _____ derived.

empirically

68. In number, the MMPI contains _____ different scales of items.

sixteen

69. Human behavior is influenced by our inner _____ and by the external _____ .

traits
situation

70. Forced to choose between the importance of inner traits and the influence of situations on behavior, most people would place more emphasis on _____ .

traits

71. A person's behavior observed on separate occasions is generally quite _____ (variable/consistent).

variable

72. An individual's score on a personality test _____ (is/is not) very predictive of his or her behavior in any given situation.

is not

73. Daryl Bem has found that people's self-assessments of their traits are generally _____ (accurate/inaccurate).

accurate

The Humanistic Perspective (pp. 411–417)

74. Two influential theories of humanistic psychology were proposed by _____ and _____ .

Maslow; Rogers

75. According to Maslow, humans are motivated by needs that are organized into a _____ .

hierarchy

76. Maslow refers to the process of fulfilling one's potential as

_____-_____.

self-actualization

77. List some of the characteristics of self-actualized people.

_____

_____

_____

_____

_____

_____

open, spontaneous,
loving, self-accepting,
have a few deep
relationships, and
have had mystical or
spiritual experiences

78. According to Rogers, a person nurtures growth in a relationship by being _____, _____ and

_____.

genuine; accepting
empathic

79. Accepting another despite his or her shortcomings characterizes

_____ _____ _____.

unconditional positive
regard

80. For both Maslow and Rogers, an important feature of personality is how an individual perceives him- or herself; this is the person's

_____-_____.

self-concept

81. Critics point out that the concepts of humanistic psychology are often vague and _____.

subjective

82. Critics also fear that humanistic psychology's emphasis on trusting one's own feelings may encourage _____ in behavior.

selfishness
(self-indulgence)

83. Since the 1940s, research on the self has greatly _____ (increased/decreased).

increased

84. List several characteristics of people with high self-esteem.

_____

_____

_____

_____

less depressed; less prone
to ulcers, insomnia,
conformity, and addiction

85. In a series of experiments, Amabile found that people who were made to feel insecure were _____ (more/less) critical of other persons.

more

86. Research has shown that most people have _____ (low/high) esteem for themselves.

high

87. The tendency of people to judge themselves favorably is called the _____-_____ bias.

self-serving

88. Credit for a personal success is generally accepted _____ (more readily/less readily) than is credit for failure.

more readily

89. When comparing their behavior to others', most people see their own behavior as _____ (above/below) average.

above

The Social-Cognitive Perspective (pp. 417–421)

90. The basic tenet of the social-cognitive perspective is that external events, in the form of _____ and _____, influence behavior through conditioning.

rewards
punishments

91. Social-cognitive theorists focus on how the individual and the _____ interact.

environment

92. The theorist who first labeled this perspective is _____.

Bandura

93. The two-way influence among personal factors, environmental factors, and behavior is referred to as _____ _____.

reciprocal
determinism

94. Individuals who believe they control their own destinies are said to possess an _____ _____ _____ _____.

internal locus of
control

95. Individuals who believe their fate is determined by forces they do not control are said to possess an _____ _____ _____.

external locus of
control

96. List several characteristics of people with internal locus of control.

_____

_____

_____

_____

_____

"internals" achieve
more in school, are
more independent,
better able to delay
gratification and cope
with stress

97. Seligman found that exposure to inescapable punishment produced a passive resignation in behavior, which he called

_____ _____.   learned helplessness

98. People become happier when they are given _____   more
(more/less) control over what happens to them.

99. The tendency of people to believe favorable descriptions of their
own personalities is called the _____ effect.   Barnum effect

100. This phenomenon is often used to advantage by palm readers
and _____.   astrologers

101. One criticism of the social-cognitive perspective is that it places
too much emphasis on the _____ in accounting for   situation
personality.

FOCUS ON PSYCHOLOGY:
THE CRIMINAL PERSONALITY

The early Greeks believed that phlegmatic, sanguine, melancholic, and choleric personalities were related to individual differences in bodily fluids. Although this theory has not been supported, some recent evidence indicates that body chemistry may be associated with personality type. At the National Institute of Mental Health, psychiatrist Gerald Brown has discovered biochemical differences in the brains of aggressive and nonaggressive animals. Aggressive animals have unusually low levels of the neurotransmitter serotonin, and the chemical 5-hydroxyindoleacetic acid (5-HIAA), a by-product of serotonin. More important, Brown has found that chronically aggressive and antisocial people also have low levels of 5-HIAA. The correlation between low 5-HIAA levels and aggression is so strong that Brown was able to predict with 85 percent accuracy which individuals of a group of servicemen would later be discharged for aggressive behavior.

Low levels of 5-HIAA have also been associated with a predisposition toward violent (but not nonviolent) suicide. One longitudinal study of individuals with low levels of 5-HIAA reported that after a two-year period, 25 percent of these individuals had committed suicide. Those with the lowest levels of 5-HIAA committed the most violent suicidal acts.

If body chemistry is at the root of behavior, should something be done to eliminate suicidal and criminal behavior? If a drug increases the body's production of serotonin, it might be used to suppress aggressive or suicidal tendencies. Some researchers are also experimenting with a form of nutrition therapy for antisocial behavior. In order to manufacture neurotransmitters, the brain requires certain nutrients. Serotonin, for example, is produced from tryptophan, an amino acid found in protein-rich foods. In one study, Stephen Schoenthaler found that when a nutritious diet was substituted for one based on high-sugar junk foods, fighting and other antisocial behaviors dropped 50 percent in 14 juvenile reform schools across the country.

Although many researchers believe that the evidence linking biochemistry to aggressiveness is strong, no national treatment program is currently under development, largely because of the ethical questions involved. What is your reaction to this issue? Do you believe a criminal personality may be biochemically produced?

PROGRESS TEST 1

Circle your answers to the following questions and check them with the answer key at the end of this chapter. Be sure to consult the appropriate pages of the text to understand the correct answer for any missed question.

Multiple-Choice Questions

1. The text defines personality as:
   a. the set of personal attitudes that characterize a person.
   b. an individual's enduring response patterns across a variety of situations.
   c. a predictable set of responses to environmental stimuli.
   d. an unpredictable set of responses to environmental stimuli.

2. Which of the following places the greatest emphasis on the unconscious mind?
   a. the humanistic perspective
   b. the social-cognitive perspective
   c. the trait perspective
   d. the psychoanalytic perspective

3. Which of the following is the correct order of psychosexual stages proposed by Freud?
   a. oral stage; anal stage; phallic stage; latency period; genital stage
   b. anal stage; oral stage; phallic stage; latency period; genital stage
   c. oral stage; anal stage; genital stage; latency period; phallic stage
   d. anal stage; oral stage; genital stage; latency period; phallic stage

4. According to Freud, defense mechanisms are methods of reducing:
   a. anger.
   b. fear.
   c. anxiety.
   d. lust.

5. Tests that provide ambiguous stimuli which the subject must interpret are called:
   a. personality tests.
   b. personality inventories.
   c. subjective scales.
   d. projective tests.

6. Neo-Freudians such as Jung, Adler, and Fromm believed that:
   a. Freud placed too great an emphasis on the conscious mind.
   b. Freud placed too great an emphasis on the instincts, sex, and aggression.
   c. the years of childhood were more important in the formation of personality than Freud had indicated.
   d. Freud's ideas about the id, ego, and superego as personality structures were not true.

7. Bill is muscular and physically strong. Sheldon would classify him as a(n):
   a. endomorphic type.
   b. mesomorphic type.
   c. ectomorphic type.
   d. dysmorphic type.

8. Which two dimensions of personality has Eysenck emphasized?
   a. extraversion-introversion and emotional stability-instability
   b. internal-external locus of control and extraversion-introversion
   c. internal-external locus of control and emotional stability-instability
   d. melancholic-phlegmatic and choleric-sanguine

9. Which of the following best describes the behavior of most people at different times and in different situations?
   a. Their behavior is highly variable.
   b. Their behavior is highly consistent.
   c. Their behavior seems consistent, but only to themselves.
   d. Their behavior seems consistent, but only to others.

10. The humanistic perspective on personality:
    a. argues against Freud's emphasis on negative impulses.
    b. emphasizes the growth potential of "healthy" individuals.
    c. discounted the behaviorist reduction of human experience to animal-level conditioning.
    d. emphasizes all of the above.

11. According to Rogers, the three conditions necessary to promote growth in personality are:
    a. honesty, sincerity, and empathy.
    b. high self-esteem, honesty, and empathy.
    c. genuineness, acceptance, and empathy.
    d. high self-esteem, acceptance, and honesty.

12. Which of the following is an example of the self-serving bias?

  a. attributing failure on a test to not studying long enough

  b. believing the boss fired you because you were unreliable

  c. feeling that people don't like you because you are too quiet

  d. believing that your skill in picking numbers caused you to win a drawing

Matching Items

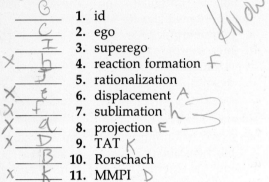

_____ **1.** id

_____ **2.** ego

_____ **3.** superego

_____ **4.** reaction formation

_____ **5.** rationalization

_____ **6.** displacement

_____ **7.** sublimation

_____ **8.** projection

_____ **9.** TAT

_____ **10.** Rorschach

_____ **11.** MMPI

  a. redirecting impulses to a less threatening object

  b. test consisting of a series of inkblots

  c. the conscious executive of personality

  d. a personality inventory

  e. disguising an impulse by imputing it to another person

  f. switching an unacceptable impulse into its opposite

  g. the unconscious repository of instinctual drives

  h. redirecting impulses into a more socially acceptable channel

  i. personality structure that corresponds to a person's conscience

  j. providing self-justifying explanations for an action

  k. a projective test consisting of a set of ambiguous pictures

---

FOCUS ON PSYCHOLOGY:
SELF-MONITORING

Snyder (1980) believes that an individual's self-concept is influenced by the impressions he or she conveys to other people in different situations. He further suggests that people have different abilities at *impression management*, the techniques by which social impressions are conveyed. Those who are more skillful tend to be acutely sensitive to the reactions of others and are easily able to adjust their behavior in order to produce the desired effect in each situation. Snyder calls such people *high self-monitoring* persons. They are actors who are easily able to convey a wide range of emotions using both verbal and nonverbal means of communication. *Low self-monitoring* persons are less concerned with adapting their behavior to different situations, tending instead to consistently express their true feelings and attitudes.

High self-monitoring persons are also more skilled than low self-monitoring persons in recognizing impression management in others. In one study, high-self monitoring persons were more accurate at identifying which of several actors was lying in order to deceive a panel of judges on a television game show.

Snyder's research has important implications for the study of the self. Most people assume that others are generally consistent in their expressions of attitudes, feelings, and their "true selves." While this may be true for low self-monitoring persons, high-self monitoring individuals have many selves, each of which is a social role, played under the appropriate circumstances. In the table on page 209 is an abbreviated version of Snyder's self-monitoring scale.

Scoring. Give yourself one point for each of questions 1, 5, and 7 that you answered F. Give yourself

Table 15.1 Snyder's Self-Monitoring Scale

These statements concern personal reactions to a number of different situations. No two statements are exactly alike, so consider each statement carefully before answering. If a statement is true, or mostly true, as applied to you, circle the T. If a statement is false, or not usually true, as applied to you, circle the F.

1. I find it hard to imitate the behavior of other people. T (F)
2. I guess I put on a show to impress or entertain people. (T) F
3. I would probably make a good actor. (T) F
4. I sometimes appear to others to be experiencing deeper emotions than I actually am. (T) F
5. In a group of people I am rarely the center of attention. T (F)
6. In different situations and with different people, I often act like very different persons. (T) F
7. I can only argue for ideas I already believe. T (F)
8. In order to get along and be liked, I tend to be what people expect me to be rather than anything else. T (F)
9. I may deceive people by being friendly when I really dislike them. T (F)
10. I'm not always the person I appear to be. (T) F

Source: Mark Snyder, "The many me's of the self-monitor." *Psychology Today*, March 1980, *13*(10), pp. 33–40, 92. Reprinted with permission of *Psychology Today* magazine. Copyright © 1980 American Psychological Association.

one point for each of the remaining questions that you answered T. Add up your points. If you scored 7 or above, you are probably a high self-monitoring individual; 3 or below, you are probably a low self-monitoring individual.

PROGRESS TEST 2

Progress Test 2 should be completed during a final chapter review. Do so after you thoroughly understand the correct answers for the Programmed Chapter Review and Progress Test 1.

Multiple-Choice Questions

1. Jill has a biting, sarcastic manner. According to Freud:
   a. she is projecting her anxiety onto others with her sarcasm.
   b. she is probably fixated in the oral stage.
   c. she is probably fixated in the anal stage.
   d. she is displacing her anxiety onto others.

2. The tendency to perceive one's own behavior favorably is called:
   a. reciprocal determinism.
   b. the fundamental attribution error.
   c. the self-serving bias.
   d. rationalization.

3. Which theory of personality emphasizes the interaction of environmental and internal personal factors?
   a. the psychoanalytic perspective
   b. the trait perspective
   c. the humanistic perspective
   d. the social-cognitive perspective

4. Seligman has found that humans and animals who are exposed to aversive events they cannot escape may develop:
   a. an internal locus of control.
   b. an external locus of control.
   c. learned helplessness.
   d. neurotic anxiety.

5. Research has shown that individuals who are made to feel insecure are subsequently:
   a. more critical of others.
   b. less critical of others.
   c. perceived as more likable.
   d. perceived as less likable.

6. According to Freud, a person who is overzealous in campaigning against pornography may be displaying:
   a. sublimation.   c. rationalization.
   b. displacement.   d. reaction formation.

7. The Minnesota Multiphasic Personality Inventory (MMPI) is:
   a. a projective test.
   b. an empirically derived projective test.
   c. an empirically derived objective test.
   d. no longer a widely used personality test.

8. Which of the following statements about trait theories is *not* correct?
   a. Traits are a useful way of explaining why people behave as they do.

b. Trait theories seek to describe how people behave.

c. Traits are predispositions to behave in certain ways.

d. Traits and situations interact in influencing behavior.

9. Which of the following statements is true?

a. People with internal locus of control achieve more in school.

b. "Externals" are better able to cope with stress than "internals."

c. "Internals" are less independent than "externals."

d. All the above are true.

10. Which of the following statements about self-esteem is *not* correct?

a. People who are negative about themselves are usually negative about others.

b. People with high self-esteem are less prone to drug addiction.

c. People with low self-esteem tend to be non-conformists.

d. People with high self-esteem suffer less from insomnia and ulcers.

11. Jack is completely at ease in his relationship with Sue, and does not fear that she will no longer love him if he does not act a certain way. Carl Rogers would say that the attitude conveyed by Sue toward Jack is one of:

a. mutual trust.

b. unconditional positive regard.

c. empathy.

d. coaction.

12. Which of the following is a common criticism of the humanistic perspective?

a. The concepts are vague and subjective.

b. The emphasis on the self encourages selfishness in individuals.

c. Humanism fails to appreciate the reality of evil in human behavior.

d. All of the above are common criticisms of humanism.

Matching Items

___G___ **1.** ectomorphic type	**a.** the id's demand for immediate gratification
___I___ **2.** Barnum effect	**b.** the child's sexual desires toward the opposite-sex parent
___H___ **3.** collective unconscious	**c.** bold and physically active behavior pattern
___J___ **4.** reality principle	**d.** stages of development proposed by Freud
___D___ **5.** psychosexual stages	**e.** relaxed and jolly behavior pattern
___A___ **6.** pleasure principle	**f.** the two-way interactions of behavior with personal and environmental factors
___K___ **7.** psychosocial stages	**g.** high-strung, solitary behavior pattern
___F___ **8.** reciprocal determinism	**h.** the repository of universal memories proposed by Jung
___C___ **9.** mesomorphic type	**i.** the tendency to accept general descriptions of personality as true for oneself
___B___ **10.** Oedipus complex	**j.** the process by which the ego seeks to gratify impulses of the id
___E___ **11.** endomorphic type	**k.** stages of development proposed by Erikson

SAMPLE ESSAY QUESTIONS

1. Describe Freud's theory of personality, including the relationship of personality structure to stages of personality development.

2. Discuss the theories of Maslow and Rogers and contrast their humanistic perspectives with that of Freud.

3. Compare and contrast the TAT and Rorschach projective tests with the MMPI.

4. Discuss the trait perspective and whether people's traits are consistent through time and across situations.

5. Contrast social-cognitive theory with psychoanalytic theory and the trait perspective.

PROJECT:
EVALUATING SHELDON'S TYPE THEORY

The text discusses Sheldon's theory that bodily types or physiques have corresponding personality types. To classify physiques, Sheldon devised a *somatotype* (body-type) index, consisting of ratings from 1 (low) to 7 (high) for each of three types of physique: *ectomorphy* (thin), *mesomorphy* (muscular), and *endomorphy* (fat). In order to determine the association of physique with personality, Sheldon constructed a list of 50 traits, interviewed a large group of men, and evaluated each on the list of traits. The findings revealed three clusters of traits. *Viscerotonia*, typical of endomorphs, includes traits such as love of physical comfort and relaxation, need for social approval and affection, sociability, slowness in reaction, and an even disposition. *Somatotonia*, typical of mesomorphs, includes traits such as assertiveness, enjoyment of adventure and physical activity, insensitivity to others' feelings, and aggressiveness. The third cluster, *cerebratonia*, is typical of ectomorphs and includes traits such as rapid reactivity, secretiveness, social restraint, and love of solitude.

According to Sheldon, an individual's physique shapes his or her personality in at least three ways. (1) A person's build determines what behaviors others expect. (2) A person's build limits the range of behaviors the individual is capable of. (3) There may be a common underlying cause (such as heredity) for both physique and personality.

Although the relationship between physique and personality is probably not as strong as Sheldon believed, it is clear that many people believe it to be true. To test Sheldon's theory, show the sketches provided here to several friends who are not in your psychology class. Explain that you are going to read aloud a list of twelve personality traits. For each trait, they are to decide to which of the three persons the trait probably applies. As you read each trait, have your subjects indicate their decision by saying aloud

"a," "b," or "c." As they do so, write their response next to the appropriate trait number.

Trait	Sheldon's Type	Subject's Response
1. enjoys solitude	a	
2. aggressive	b	
3. easygoing	c	
4. enjoys taking risks	b	
5. secretive	a	
6. seeks affection	c	
7. socially restrained	a	
8. loves comfort	c	
9. very physical	b	
10. reacts slowly	c	
11. insensitive to others	b	
12. reacts quickly	a	

Score the results by counting the number of times the subject's response agreed with Sheldon. By chance alone, each subject should get four of the twelve correct.

Questions to Consider

1. Was there agreement or disagreement with Sheldon's type theory?

2. What factors other than an actual physique-personality relationship could account for responses in agreement with Sheldon's theory?

3. Can you think of other personality traits or types that tend to be stereotypes of certain groups of people?

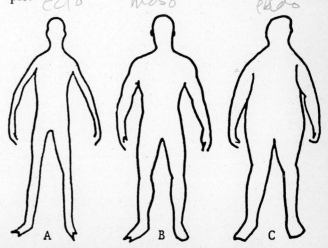

WHERE TO LOOK FOR MORE INFORMATION

Byrne, D., and Kelley, K. (1982). *An introduction to personality*, 3rd ed. Englewood Cliffs, NJ: Prentice-Hall.

A general introduction to personality research and theory.

The Mental Measurements Yearbook

Ask your school librarian for help in finding this one. This reference book provides reviews of most widely used personality tests.

Lindzey, G., Hall, C. S., and Manosevitz, M. (eds.) (1973). *Theories of personality: Primary sources and research*, 2nd ed. New York: Wiley.

This book is an edited collection of original writings from the major personality theorists.

Mischel, W. (1968). *Personality and assessment.* New York: Wiley.

This classic book discusses whether personality traits actually exist.

PROGRESS TEST 1

Multiple-Choice Questions

1. b (p. 395)
2. d (p. 396)
3. a (pp. 398–399)
4. c (p. 399)

5. d (p. 401)
6. b (p. 400)
7. b (p. 406)
8. a (p. 406)

9. a (p. 410)
10. d (p. 411)
11. c (p. 412)
12. d (p. 416)

Matching Items

1. g (p. 398)
2. c (p. 398)
3. i (p. 398)
4. f (p. 400)

5. j (p. 400)
6. a (p. 400)
7. h (p. 400)
8. e (p. 400)

9. k (p. 402)
10. b (p. 402)
11. d (p. 408)

PROGRESS TEST 2

Multiple-Choice Questions

1. b (p. 399)
2. c (p. 416)
3. d (p. 417)
4. c (p. 419)

5. a (p. 415)
6. d (p. 400)
7. b (p. 407)
8. a (p. 405)

9. a (p. 418)
10. c (p. 415)
11. b (p. 412)
12. d (p. 413)

Matching Items

1. g (p. 406)
2. i (p. 420)
3. h (p. 401)
4. j (p. 398)

5. d (p. 398)
6. a (p. 398)
7. k (p. 401)
8. f (p. 417)

9. c (p. 406)
10. b (p. 399)
11. e (p. 406)

CHAPTER 16

Psychological Disorders

CHAPTER OVERVIEW

Abnormal behavior is usually defined in terms of several criteria, including how atypical, undesirable, maladaptive, and unexplainable it is. Chapter 16 discusses neurotic, affective, schizophrenic, and personality disorders, as classified by the *Diagnostic and Statistical Manual of Mental Disorders* (DSM-III). Although this classification system follows a medical model, in which disorders are classified as illnesses, the chapter also discusses each disorder from a learning theory perspective, and as explained by the psychoanalytic perspective.

Your major task is to memorize each of several different types of disorders, their characteristics, and their causes from each of the above theoretical perspectives. Mentally completing the Chapter Review several times will be an effective way of rehearsing this material.

GUIDED STUDY

The text chapter should be studied one section at a time. Before you read, preview each section by skimming it, noting headings and boldface items. Then read the appropriate section objectives from the following outline. Keep these objectives in mind, and as you read the chapter section, search for the information that will complete each one. You may wish to write out answers for each objective as soon as you finish reading that section of the chapter.

Perspectives on Psychological Disorders (pp. 427–433)

1. Identify the four criteria that must be met in order to define behavior as disordered.

2. Contrast the legal definition of insanity with the psychological definition of disordered behavior.

3. Explain the differences in the medical and psychological perspectives of disordered behavior.

4. Explain the system by which psychological disorders are classified and discuss its diagnostic reliability.

Anxiety Disorders (pp. 433–438)

5. Describe the following anxiety disorders.

a. generalized anxiety disorder

b. phobic disorder

c. obsessive-compulsive disorder

6. Contrast the psychoanalytic and learning theory explanations of the following anxiety disorders.

a. generalized anxiety disorder

b. phobic disorder

c. obsessive-compulsive disorder

7. Discuss the characteristics and possible causes of anorexia nervosa and bulimia.

Somatoform Disorders (pp. 438–439)

8. Describe the following somatoform disorders.

a. conversion disorder

b. hypochondriasis

Dissociative Disorders (pp. 439–441)

9. Describe the following dissociative disorders.

a. amnesia

b. fugue

c. multiple personality disorder

Affective Disorders (pp. 441–448)

10. Discuss gender, cultural, and socioeconomic differences in suicide rates.

11. Summarize the known facts about depression, including its typical duration, changes that accompany depressive episodes, and who is at greatest risk.

12. Explain the psychoanalytic perspective on depression.

13. Present evidence that depression may have a genetic and biochemical basis.

14. Describe learned helplessness and discuss the cognitive-learning theory of depression.

Schizophrenic Disorders (pp. 448–453)

15. Describe the symptoms of schizophrenia.

16. Describe the following types of schizophrenia.

a. disorganized

b. catatonic

c. paranoid

d. undifferentiated

17. Explain the evidence that links dopamine to schizophrenia.

18. Explain the evidence for a genetic predisposition toward schizophrenia.

Personality Disorders (pp. 453–454)

19. Contrast personality disorders with clinical disorders such as schizophrenia.

20. Describe the antisocial personality.

Should People Be Labeled? The Power of Preconceptions (pp. 454–455)

21. Discuss the findings of experiments testing the effects of labels on a person's judgment.

CHAPTER REVIEW

When you have finished reading the chapter, complete the sentences that follow. Using your hand or a strip of paper, cover the correct answers in the margin and complete each sentence. Verify your answer by uncovering the correct one. *Do not continue with the next section until you understand why each margin term is the correct answer.* If you need to, review or re-read the appropriate chapter section in the text before continuing.

Perspectives on Psychological Disorders (pp. 427–433).

1. Abnormal behavior is that which is atypical and deviates from statistical _____.

norms

2. In order to be classified as disordered, behavior must be atypical and culturally _____.

disapproved

3. This definition emphasizes that standards of acceptability for behavior are _____ (variable/consistent).

variable

4. Some clinical psychologists define disorders as harmful behaviors that are _____.

maladaptive

5. Atypical behaviors are most likely to be labeled disordered when they cannot be justified _____.

rationally

6. The terms *sanity* and *insanity* are not psychological terms, but _____ terms.

legal

7. Under the present legal system, the insanity defense requires that the _____ (prosecution/defense) prove that the defendant is _____ (sane/insane).

prosecution

sane

8. Thousands of years ago, when a person acted abnormally, a hole was chipped in the person's _____ to allow evil spirits to escape.

skull

9. The view that psychological disorders are diseases is the basis of the _____ perspective.

medical

10. One of the first reformers to advocate this position and call for providing more humane living conditions for the mentally ill was _____.

Pinel

11. Another term for mental illness is _____.

psychopathology

12. One critic who has argued against this model is psychiatrist ___*Szasz*___.

Szasz

13. He has argued that mental illnesses are not defined medically, but rather ___socially___.

socially

14. Freud's theory is _____ (consistent/inconsistent) with the idea that behavior disorders are internal sicknesses.

consistent

15. Other psychologists who argue against the medical model believe that all behavior arises from the interaction of _____ and _____ influences, and past and present _____.

genetic

physiological

experiences

16. The most widely used system for classifying psychological disorders is the _____ _____ _____ _____ _____ _____.

Diagnostic and Statistical Manual of Mental Disorders

17. This system is abbreviated as ___DSM III___.

DSM-III

18. In number, there are more than ___200___ specific psychological disorders.

200

19. These disorders are grouped into _____ major categories.

15

20. Using DSM-III, diagnoses of specific disorders _____ (have/have not) been very reliable.

have not

21. Diagnoses based on broad categories rather than specific disorders have been _____ (higher/lower) in reliability.

higher

22. DSM-III has a new system that bases diagnoses on behaviors that are _____.

observable

Anxiety Disorders (pp. 433–438)

23. Physically unexplained disorders that allow a person to continue functioning rationally and socially are diagnosed as _____ disorders.

neurotic

24. Freud called these disorders _____.

neuroses

25. According to Freud, these disorders result from unconscious conflicts that cause the person to feel _____.

anxiety

26. In number, DSM-III identifies _____ major types of these disorders.

three

27. When a person feels anxious for no apparent reason, he or she is diagnosed as suffering the _____ _____.

generalized anxiety disorder

28. When a person has an irrational fear of a specific object or situation, the diagnosis is a(n) _____ disorder.

phobic

29. When a person cannot control repetitive thoughts and actions, a(n) _____-_____ disorder is diagnosed.

obsessive-compulsive

30. In the generalized anxiety disorder, the body reacts physiologically with arousal of the _____ nervous system.

autonomic

31. In some instances, the anxiety of this disorder may intensify dramatically and be accompanied by trembling or fainting; this is called a _____ _____.

panic attack

32. The psychoanalyst's interpretation of this type of disorder is that the _____'s defense mechanisms are weak.

ego

33. Learning theorists have produced a similar disorder in animals by exposing them to unpredictable _____.

shocks

34. Psychoanalysts argue that phobias result when a person's anxiety over his or her own impulses is not completely _____.

repressed

35. Learning theorists believe phobias are fears that are

_____.

conditioned

36. According to this view, phobias _____ (can/cannot) be unlearned.

can

37. Certain fears may be based on _____ predispositions.

biological

38. According to the Freudian view, compulsive behaviors are seen as helping suppress _____ over forbidden impulses; according to learning theory, these behaviors persist because they are _____ by a reduction in anxiety.

anxiety

reinforced

39. The condition in which a person fears becoming obese and becomes extremely thin is called _____

_____.

anorexia nervosa

40. This disorder most often affects _____ (males/females) during _____.

females
adolescence

41. The eating disorder in which periods of excessive overeating are followed by self-induced vomiting is called _____.

bulimia

42. Families of bulimic patients have an abnormally high incidence of disorders such as _____, _____, and _____.

alcoholism, obesity, depression

43. The families of anorexic patients are often very protective and emphasize _____.

achievement

Somatoform Disorders (pp. 438–439)

44. When a neurotic symptom is expressed bodily, as in vomiting, dizziness, or blurred vision, the diagnosis is a(n) _____ disorder.

somatoform

45. Freud believed that the _____ disorder resulted when anxiety was converted into a physical symptom.

conversion

46. When normal aches and pains are interpreted as serious illnesses, the person is said to suffer from _____.

hypochondriasis

Dissociative Disorders (pp. 439–441)

47. A person whose consciousness has become separated from his or her previous memories and feelings is suffering from a(n) _____ disorder.

dissociative

48. Dissociative disorders are relatively _____ (common/uncommon).

uncommon

49. In response to intolerable stress, a person may develop a forgetfulness that is called _____.

amnesia

50. The forgetfulness of amnesia is usually for _____ (all/selective) memories.

selective

51. When the individual not only loses memory but also runs away, _____ has occurred.

fugue

52. A person who develops two or more distinct personalities is suffering from _____ _____ disorder.

multiple personality

53. Nicholas Spanos has argued that people with multiple personalities may merely be playing different _____.

roles

Affective Disorders (pp. 441–448)

54. The _____ disorders are characterized by emotional extremes.

affective

55. When a person experiences prolonged depression, the disorder is called _____ _____.

major depression

56. When a person's mood alternates between depression and the hyperactive state of _____, a _____ disorder is diagnosed.

mania; bipolar

57. Research suggests that major depression will be suffered at some time by approximately _____ percent of men; for women, the projected incidence is _____ (higher/lower).

10
higher

58. A depressed mood that has lasted _____ weeks or longer is considered abnormal.

two

59. Two countries that have suicide rates much lower than the United States are _____ and _____.

Ireland; Israel

60. Three countries that have suicide rates higher than the United States are _____, _____, and _____.

Austria; Denmark Switzerland

61. In the United States, the suicide rate is higher among _____ (blacks/whites).

whites

62. Among men and women, _____ (men/women) attempt suicide more often, while _____ (men/women) are more likely to succeed.

women
men

63. List several other groups of people who have high suicide rates.

_____

_____

_____

suicide rates are highest among the rich, the irreligious, unmarried, widowed, and divorced

64. Depressed persons usually _____ (do/do not) recover.

do

65. The bipolar disorder occurs in approximately _____ percent of men and women.

1

66. List several of the behavioral and cognitive changes that accompany depression.

_____

_____

_____

inactivity, lack of motivation, sensitivity to negative happenings, expectation of negative outcomes

67. According to Lewinsohn, _____ (males/females) are at the greatest risk for depression.

females

68. Most depressive episodes last less than _____ months.

three

69. Stressful events usually _____ (do/do not) precede a depressive episode.

do

70. According to the psychoanalytic perspective, depression results when the anger triggered by some loss is _____.

internalized

71. Affective disorders _____ (do/do not) tend to run in families.

do

72. Studies of twins show that if one member of an _____ (identical/fraternal) twin pair suffers major depression, there is a _____ percent chance that the other twin will, too.

identical
40

73. In persons suffering from bipolar depression, the supply of the neurotransmitter _____ has been found to be abnormally _____ (high/low) during mania, but too _____ (high/low) during depression.

norepinephrine
high
low

74. Drugs that relieve depression tend to _____ (increase/decrease) levels of this neurotransmitter.

increase

75. Two other neurotransmitters that are being studied in relation to depression are _____ and _____.

serotonin; acetylcholine

76. Aaron Beck has suggested that depression may be linked with beliefs that are _____-_____.

self-defeating

77. After experiencing uncontrollable events, individuals may come to feel that their actions are futile; this feeling is called _____ _____.

learned helplessness

78. Depressed people are more likely to attribute failures to _____ (the situation/themselves).

themselves

79. Depressed people _____ (do/do not) overestimate others' judgments of them.

do not

80. Research by Peter Lewinsohn suggests that depressing thoughts _____ (do/do not) usually precede a depressed mood.

do not

81. A depressed person tends to elicit social _____ (empathy/rejection).

rejection

82. The four types of loneliness that have been identified include feeling _____, _____, _____, and _____.

excluded, unloved, constricted, alienated

Schizophrenic Disorders (pp. 448–453)

83. Disorders in which a person has irrational ideas and faulty perceptions are called _____ disorders.

psychotic

84. In which age groups does schizophrenia typically first occur? _____ _____ _____ _____.

adolescents and young adults

85. In which socioeconomic class is the incidence of schizophrenia highest? _____ _____ _____.

lower socioeconomic class

86. Translated literally, schizophrenia means _____ _____.

split mind

87. Three manifestations of schizophrenia are disorganized _____, disturbed _____, and inappropriate _____ and _____.

thinking, perceptions, emotions, actions

88. The distorted false beliefs of schizophrenics are called _____.

delusions

89. Schizophrenics are easily distracted and are believed to have an impaired capacity for selective _____.

attention

90. The hallucinations of schizophrenics usually involve the _____ sense.

auditory

91. List and briefly describe the four types of schizophrenia.

Type | Distinguishing Characteristics

1. _____ _____

_____

_____

_____

2. _____ _____

3. _____ _____

4. _____ _____

_____

Disorganized: Incoherent speech and inappropriate or silly emotions. Catatonic: Bizarre physical movements. Paranoid: Delusions of persecution or grandeur. Undifferentiated: Behaviors that do not fit any other category.

92. The brain tissue of schizophrenic patients has been found to have an abnormally high density of receptors for the neurotransmitter _____.

dopamine

93. Drugs that block these receptors have been found to _____ (increase/decrease) schizophrenic behaviors.

decrease

94. Brain scans have shown that many schizophrenics have a shrinkage of brain tissue and abnormal patterns of brain _____.

metabolism

95. Such persons also have a reduced quantity of an enzyme that converts _____ into norepinephrine.

dopamine

96. Among individuals having a schizophrenic identical twin, there is a _____ percent chance that they will become schizophrenic also.

50

Personality Disorders (pp. 453–454)

97. Character problems that need not involve anxiety or depression are called _____ disorders.

personality

98. An individual who seemingly has no conscience, lies, steals, is generally irresponsible, and may be criminal is said to have a(n) _____ personality.

antisocial

99. Previously, this person was labeled a _____ or _____ .

sociopath
psychopath

100. When awaiting electric shocks, such persons show _____ (more/less) arousal of the autonomic nervous system than do normal people.

less

101. This finding suggests that antisocial persons are _____ (more/less) fearless than normal persons.

more

102. Studies of the children of convicted criminals suggest that there may be a _____ predisposition to such traits.

genetic

Should People Be Labeled? The Power of Preconceptions (pp. 454–455)

103. One danger of applying diagnostic labels is that labels can make people see a person differently by creating _____ .

preconceptions

104. In one study, people who had been labeled psychiatric patients were _____ (more/less) likely to be perceived as abnormal than people who were not labeled.

more

FOCUS ON PSYCHOLOGY:
CHILDHOOD PSYCHOPATHOLOGY AND
HOME MOVIES

Although the parents of psychotic children typically do not recall their children's early development as being abnormal, clinical psychologists have long wondered whether these memories are accurate. Children diagnosed as psychotic at age 3 or 4 often are normal at birth. During the years prior to diagnosis as psychotic, then, these children must have experienced some abnormal developmental influence. Research studies of the early development of psychotic children have been hampered by lack of an objective method of verifying the accuracy of the parents' memories.

In an ingenious study, Massier and Rosenthal (1984) studied the early development of a group of children later diagnosed as psychotic by analyzing home movies filmed by their parents. The behavior of these children, especially in interacting with siblings and parents, was compared to that of a group of normal children, also documented in family movies. The most striking finding of this experiment was that, although most of the children were not diagnosed as disordered until they averaged 3 years of age, signs of abnormal behavior were apparent at a much earlier age. By the time the children were 6 months old, abnormal parent-child interactions were common. These interactions were characterized by a general lack of responsiveness of parent and child to one another, as if the two individuals were "out of sync." When social interactions occurred, they tended to be of necessity, and were carried out in a "lifeless, joyless manner."

Confirming the research findings of other psychologists, these authors found that the parents of these children did not recall any abnormalities in either the child or their social interactions. As McLeod (1984) has noted, in family life even "small failures of communication can build up into damaging patterns of interaction." Such patterns may have profound consequences for a child's intellectual and emotional health.

PROGRESS TEST 1

Circle your answers to the following questions and check them with the answer key at the end of the chapter. Be sure to consult the appropriate pages of the text to understand the correct answer for any missed question.

Multiple-Choice Questions

1. According to the medical model, psychological disorders are:
   a. learned responses to anxiety.
   b. sicknesses.
   c. the external expressions of anxiety.
   d. the result of unconscious strivings that have not been gratified.

2. Sue has an intense, irrational fear of snakes. She is suffering from a(n):
   a. generalized anxiety disorder.
   b. obsessive-compulsive disorder.
   c. phobic disorder.
   d. somatoform disorder.

3. The eating disorder in which a person has repeated "binge-purge" eating episodes is:
   a. bulimia.
   b. anorexia nervosa.
   c. hypochondriasis.
   d. the conversion disorder.

4. While mountain climbing, Jack saw his best friend killed by an avalanche. The stress caused Jack to forget who he was. This illustrates:
   a. a fugue state.
   b. the conversion disorder.
   c. a somatoform disorder.
   d. dissociative amnesia.

5. Which of the following has been called the "common cold" of psychological disorders?
   a. depression
   b. schizophrenia
   c. hypochondriasis
   d. neurosis

6. Which of the following is *not* true concerning depression?
   a. Stressful events tend to precede depression.

b. Most depressive episodes last less than three months.
   c. Depression is more common in males than in females.
   d. Most people recover from depression without professional therapy.

7. Which of the following is *not* true regarding schizophrenia?
   a. It affects men and women about equally.
   b. It occurs more frequently in the lower socio-economic classes.
   c. It occurs more frequently in industrialized countries.
   d. It usually appears during adolescence or early adulthood.

8. Schizophrenia that involves bizarre physical movements is called:
   a. disorganized.
   b. catatonic.
   c. paranoid.
   d. undifferentiated.

9. The effect of drugs that block receptors for dopamine is to:
   a. alleviate schizophrenic symptoms.
   b. alleviate depression.
   c. increase schizophrenic symptoms.
   d. increase depression.

10. Bob is unable to keep a job and has been in jail most of his life—for stealing, sexual assault, and spouse abuse. Bob would probably be diagnosed as having:
    a. a conversion disorder.
    b. disorganized schizophrenia.
    c. undifferentiated schizophrenia.
    d. an antisocial personality.

11. Behavior is classified as disordered when it is atypical and:
    a. undesirable.
    b. maladaptive.
    c. unexplainable.
    d. all of the above.

12. The terms *sanity* and *insanity* refer to:
    a. legal definitions.
    b. psychotic disorders only.
    c. personality disorders only.
    d. both psychotic and personality disorders.

Matching Items

_f_ **1.** fugue _f_

_D_ **2.** psychotic disorder _d_

_A_ **3.** affective disorder _a_

_i_ **4.** dissociative disorder _i_

_G_ **5.** neurotic disorder _g_

_B_ **6.** mania _B_

_K_ **7.** obsessive-compulsive disorder _k_

_J_ **8.** schizophrenia _j_

_C_ **9.** somatoform disorder _c_

_e_ **10.** anorexia nervosa _e_

_h_ **11.** hypochondriasis _h_

a. a psychological disorder of feelings and mood

b. an extremely elevated mood

c. a neurotic disorder in which symptoms take a bodily form

d. a psychological disorder in which the person loses contact with reality

e. an eating disorder in which a person starves himself or herself

f. a dissociative disorder in which the person flees his or her home

g. an anxiety disorder in which the person continues to think rationally

h. a disorder in which normal physical sensations are misinterpreted as symptoms of a disease

i. an anxiety disorder such as fugue, amnesia, or multiple personality

j. a group of disorders marked by disorganized thinking, disturbed perceptions, and inappropriate emotions

k. a disorder that is characterized by repetitive thoughts and actions

FOCUS ON PSYCHOLOGY:
THE BICAMERAL MIND

The human brain possesses right and left cerebral hemispheres, each of which is specialized for different functions. The left hemisphere is more adept at performing tasks that require the use of language and analytical logic. The right hemisphere is somewhat better at tasks requiring spatial skills and the use of synthetic or introspective reasoning. In the normal individual, the right and left hemispheres work together in an integrated fashion.

Psychologist Julian Jaynes has proposed that the brains of our ancestors had a more primitive organization in which the two hemispheres functioned independently of one another. Jaynes believes that before the second millennium B.C., these early humans looked more to the voices of gods than to their own powers of reasoning for guidance. These people heard voices that warned, comforted, and directed them. Jaynes believes that in this early "preconscious" stage of human development, such voices actually did exist, and originated in the right hemi-

sphere of the brain. Although few scientists have taken this theory seriously, Jaynes draws support from ancient writings and rituals, including the worship of idols. Jaynes suggests that people worshiped idols as the mouthpieces of gods because the auditory hallucinations emanating from their own minds were projected onto the idols.

The crux of the theory is that the brain's normal organization may be altered in response to environmental pressures. Jaynes points out that the human brain is characterized by _plasticity_—in response to an injury in one area of the brain, specialized functions may be shifted to another area. In addition, studies have shown the developing nervous system of an animal may be dramatically affected by whether its early environment is enriched or deprived.

Jaynes has proposed that, like our ancestors, schizophrenics may have preconscious, bicameral minds. He sees parallels in their behavior, including the experiencing of auditory hallucinations, the loss of identity, and the feeling of being controlled by an external force. Although there is no widely accepted neurological theory of schizophrenia, Jaynes suggests that bicameral brain organization may occur in response to abnormal or disturbed environmental pressures during early development.

Although some clinicians have found this theory to be a useful way of conceptualizing schizophrenia, others have suggested that it is simply an example of *pseudoscience*—an unsupported and untestable theory based on nothing more than ancient legends and myths.

PROGRESS TEST 2

Circle your answers to the following questions and check them with the answer key at the end of the chapter. Be sure to consult the appropriate pages of the text to understand the correct answer for any missed question.

Multiple-Choice Questions

1. Which of the following is true concerning disordered behavior?
   a. Standards of acceptable behavior vary in different countries.
   b. Standards of acceptable behavior have not changed over the years.
   c. Behavior that is atypical is always considered abnormal.
   d. Behavior that cannot be rationally explained is always considered abnormal.

2. Our early ancestors thought that disordered behavior was caused by:
   a. anxiety.
   b. evil spirits.
   c. brain injury.
   d. laziness.

3. Psychiatrist Thomas Szasz has argued that:
   a. the medical model is correct.
   b. for every behavioral disorder, a specific biochemical mechanism can be identified.
   c. mental illnesses are socially, not medically, defined.
   d. disordered behavior typically results from stress.

4. The most widely used system of classifying disordered behavior is:

a. The Diagnostic and Statistical Manual of Mental Disorders.
b. The World Health Organization's International Classification of Diseases.
c. The Mental Measurements Yearbook.
d. The Psychiatric Reference Book.

5. Sharon is continually tense, jittery, and apprehensive, for no specific reason. She would probably be diagnosed as suffering a(n):
a. phobic disorder.
b. conversion disorder.
c. obsessive-compulsive disorder.
d. generalized anxiety disorder.

6. According to the learning perspective, phobias are:
a. conditioned fears.
b. irrational responses to repressed impulses.
c. biological predispositions.
d. symptoms of stress that has been displaced.

7. Jason is so preoccupied with staying clean that he showers as many as ten times each day. Jason would be diagnosed as suffering from a(n):
a. somatoform disorder.
b. conversion disorder.
c. personality disorder.
d. obsessive-compulsive disorder.

8. If a person experiences blindness, paralysis, or some other physical ailment for which no physiological cause can be found, the diagnosis would be:
a. hypochondriasis.
b. a conversion disorder.
c. neurosis.
d. schizophrenia.

9. Learned helplessness has been suggested as a possible cause for:
a. schizophrenia.
b. depression.
c. dissociative disorders.
d. antisocial behavior.

10. Which neurotransmitter is present in overabundant amounts during the manic phase of bipolar depression?
a. dopamine
b. cholinesterase
c. epinephrine
d. norepinephrine

11. The text suggests that the disorganized thoughts of schizophrenics may be attributed to a breakdown in:
a. attention.
b. memory storage.
c. motivation.
d. memory retrieval.

12. Which of the following statements concerning the labeling of disordered behaviors is true?

a. The labels are often unreliable for specific disorders.
b. Normal people who simulate symptoms of psychoses have been diagnosed as schizophrenic.
c. Labels create preconceptions that can bias a person's perceptions.
d. All of the above are true.

Matching Items

_____ 1. multiple personality
_F___ 2. neuroses
_A___ 3. paranoid
_K___ 4. conversion disorder
_C___ 5. antisocial personality
_D___ 6. undifferentiated
_B___ 7. medical model
_H___ 8. bipolar disorder
_E___ 9. psychological perspective
_I___ 10. catatonic
_G___ 11. disorganized

a. a type of schizophrenia characterized by delusions of grandeur
b. a theory that considers disordered behavior to be similar to physical illness
c. an individual who seems to have no conscience
d. a type of schizophrenia characterized by bizarre physical movements
e. a theory that argues against attributing disordered behavior to internal causes
f. a Freudian term for disorders in which unconscious conflicts cause anxiety
g. a type of schizophrenia characterized by disorganized speech and inappropriate emotions
h. a type of dissociative disorder
i. a type of schizophrenia with symptoms that are not confined to any one of the other types
j. a type of affective disorder
k. a type of somatoform disorder

SAMPLE ESSAY QUESTIONS

1. Discuss the criteria by which disordered behaviors are defined.

2. Contrast the medical and psychological perspectives on disordered behavior.

3. Discuss the anxiety disorders and give an example of each type.

4. Discuss the affective disorders and give an example of each type.

5. Define schizophrenia and discuss the influence of biochemical, genetic, and psychological factors on its development.

PROJECT:
CLASSIFYING DISORDERED BEHAVIOR

The following paragraphs describe various kinds of disordered behavior. For each case, see if you can classify the disorder into the appropriate category from DSM-III. The *neurotic disorders* include obsessive-compulsive, phobic, generalized anxiety, somatoform, and dissociative disorders such as amnesia, fugue, and multiple personality. The *affective disorders* include major depression and the bipolar disorders. *Schizophrenic disorders* include catatonic, paranoid, disorganized, and undifferentiated types. The *personality disorders* include antisocial behavior. The correct answers can be found at the end of the chapter.

1. Jack has been in one type of trouble or another ever since he was 8 years old, beginning with truancy from school, fighting, and lying. His lack of conscience has expressed itself in adulthood in various criminal behaviors. He has been divorced four times, accused of abusing and neglecting his children, and fired from more jobs than he can remember. Although considered to be an intelligent person, he seems completely amoral.

CLASSIFICATION: _____

2. Sarah has an abnormal, and irrational fear of taking exams. She is a bright, conscientious student who usually studies hard, and is better prepared for tests than most of her classmates. Her anxiety is so extreme that she begins panicking as soon as an exam date is announced. The night before an exam, she typically becomes nauseous and can neither eat nor sleep. It is difficult to understand how this fear of exams was acquired; Sarah has a very high grade-point average and does not generally fear other situations.

CLASSIFICATION: _____

3. Jason is a college sophomore, believed by his friends to be a perfectionist. He spends hours each day grooming. It is not unusual for him to take ten showers in one 24-hour period. Combing his hair requires at least an hour of careful attention. He insists that every piece of furniture, every book, and every article of clothing in his dormitory room be kept in its one proper place. Even more troubling than these rigid, repetitive behaviors are the unwanted thoughts Jason experiences. He is mentally preoccupied with scheduling each second of his life for maximum efficiency. It is not unusual for Jason to mentally plan and re-plan each day several times. So compelling are these thoughts and rituals that Jason has little time for any other activities.

CLASSIFICATION: _____

4. Sandy was referred to a psychiatrist after she was arrested for disorderly behavior in a restaurant. Claiming that she heard a voice that commanded her to warn others that eating was harmful, Sandy attempted to convince others not to eat. The psychiatrist was often unable to make sense of anything Sandy said. Her speech and thinking are fragmented and jump from one idea to another in a random, "word salad" fashion. In addition to hallucinations and incoherent speech, Sandy's emotional reactions are often inappropriate. When asked about her mother's recent death, she breaks into a fit of laughter; when others laugh, she often appears sad or angry.

CLASSIFICATION: _____

5. For most of the last 3 years Bill's emotional life has regularly alternated between two states. In one he is elated, animated, over-talkative, uninhibited, and seems never to sleep or slow down. During one of these "up" phases, Bill chartered a plane, flew to Las Vegas, and spent several thousand dollars gambling, overtipping, and throwing parties for everyone he saw. During the second, "down" phase, Bill lives in slow motion. He feels extremely discouraged, worthless, and isolated from others. He can derive pleasure from nothing. He suffers from insomnia, almost never eats, and has trouble concentrating on his work.

CLASSIFICATION: _____

6. Jane's problem is that, although doctors can find nothing wrong with her (she is, in fact, quite healthy), she interprets the smallest ache or pain as a symptom of a major disease. Once when she experienced a headache she convinced herself that she had a brain tumor. Jane spends a small fortune on pills and medications she does not need. She has had over two dozen physicians in the past year. As each catches on to Jane, she is forced to find another who will heap more attention and concern on her.

CLASSIFICATION: _____

7. Tom was a business executive with a wife, two children, and a lovely home in a good neighborhood. Although he tended to keep his problems to himself, the stress of his failing business and impending bankruptcy became overwhelming. One day he simply failed to return to his home. Twenty-one months later, he "awakened" in a small tavern in another country. He was wearing the military uniform of a Third World country. Tom has no idea what happened to him during these months.

CLASSIFICATION: _____

8. Sue was rushed by her family to the emergency room the day she awakened unable to see. An eye examination revealed that she could not, in fact, see. After a thorough examination, the ophthalmologist could find no physical reason for her blindness. When her blindness persisted, she was referred to a psychiatrist. After uncovering a recent trauma in Sue's life that she was abnormally anxious about, the psychiatrist became convinced that her blindness was a symptom of anxiety.

CLASSIFICATION: _____

WHERE TO LOOK FOR MORE INFORMATION

Meyer, R., and Salmon, P. (1984). *Abnormal psychology*. Newton, MA: Allyn & Bacon.

A recent text on disordered behavior that includes cross-cultural perspectives.

Rodgers, J. E. (1982, July). Roots of madness. *Science 82*.

Rodgers argues that, despite biochemical theories, disordered behavior remains a psychological problem.

Rosenhan, D. L. (1973, January). On being sane in insane places. *Science, 179,* pp. 250–58.

This article describes the experiment in which normal imposters tried to be admitted into mental institutions. Although some of the patients saw through them, the staff did not.

ANSWERS

PROGRESS TEST 1

Multiple-Choice Questions

1. b (p. 431)
2. c (pp. 434–435)
3. a (p. 437)
4. d (p. 439)
5. a (p. 441)
6. c (p. 441)
7. c (p. 448)
8. b (p. 450)
9. a (p. 451)
10. d (pp. 453–454)
11. d (p. 429)
12. a (p. 429)

Matching Items

1. f (p. 439)
2. d (p. 448)
3. a (p. 441)
4. i (p. 439)
5. g (p. 433)
6. b (p. 441)
7. k (p. 436)
8. j (p. 448)
9. c (p. 438)
10. e (p. 437)
11. h (p. 439)

PROGRESS TEST 2

Multiple-Choice Questions

1. a (p. 428)
2. b (p. 430)
3. c (p. 431)
4. a (p. 432)
5. d (p. 433)
6. a (p. 435)
7. d (p. 436)
8. b (p. 438)
9. b (p. 445)
10. d (p. 445)
11. a (p. 448)
12. d (pp. 454–455)

Matching Items

1. h (p. 440)
2. f (p. 433)
3. a (p. 450)
4. k (p. 438)
5. c (p. 453)
6. i (p. 450)
7. b (p. 431)
8. j (p. 443)
9. e (p. 431)
10. d (p. 450)
11. g (p. 450)

PROJECT

1. antisocial personality
2. phobic disorder
3. obsessive-compulsive disorder
4. disorganized schizophrenia
5. bipolar disorder
6. hypochondriasis
7. fugue
8. somatoform disorder

CHAPTER 17

Therapy

CHAPTER OVERVIEW

This chapter discusses the major psychotherapies and biomedical therapies for maladaptive behavior. The psychotherapies include psychoanalysis; the humanistic perspectives of person-centered, Gestalt, and group therapy; and behavior therapies based on classical conditioning, operant conditioning, and a cognitive-behavior perspective. Although people who are untreated often improve, those receiving psychotherapy tend to improve somewhat more, regardless of the specific type of therapy they receive.

The biomedical therapies include the seldom-used procedures of psychosurgery, such as lobotomy, and the more frequently administered electroconvulsive therapy. The most widely used biomedical therapies involve the administration of antipsychotic, antianxiety, and antidepressant drugs.

This chapter does not present too many difficult terms or concepts. You will do best by carefully answering the chapter objectives and sample essay questions listed here.

GUIDED STUDY

The text chapter should be studied one section at a time. Before you read, preview each section by skimming it, noting headings and boldface items. Then read the appropriate section objectives from the following outline. Keep these objectives in mind and, as you read the chapter section, search for the information that will complete each one. You may wish to write out answers for each objective as soon as you finish reading that section of the chapter.

The Psychological Therapies (pp. 462–484)

1. Discuss the psychoanalytic method of psychotherapy and explain the significance of each of the following:
   a. insight
   b. resistance
   c. interpretation
   d. latent content
   e. transference

2. Identify several criticisms of psychoanalytic therapy.

3. Describe the ways that humanistic therapies differ from psychoanalysis.

4. Discuss Carl Rogers' person-centered therapy and describe active listening.

5. Explain what Gestalt therapy aims to accomplish.

6. Identify the advantages of group over individual therapies.

7. Explain how the underlying assumptions of behavior therapies differ from those of psychoanalysis and humanistic therapies.

8. Describe each of the following classical conditioning techniques.

a. counterconditioning

b. systematic desensitization

c. aversive conditioning

9. Explain the central idea behind behavior modification and token economies.

10. Identify and discuss two major criticisms of behavior modification.

11. Explain the cognitive-behavior perspective on psychotherapy.

12. Describe the following cognitive-behavior therapies.

a. rational-emotive therapy

b. Beck's cognitive therapy for depression

c. Meichenbaum's self-instructional training

13. Discuss whether psychotherapy is effective from the perspective of clients and clinicians.

14. Discuss the findings of controlled research studies on the effectiveness of psychotherapy.

15. Explain the statement, "Under appropriate circumstances psychotherapy has a great deal to offer."

16. Identify the common ingredients among different psychotherapies.

The Biomedical Therapies (pp. 484–488)

17. Describe the following biomedical therapies.

a. psychosurgery

b. lobotomy

c. electroconvulsive therapy

18. In each of the following categories, identify the drugs most commonly used in therapy, and how they produce their effects on maladaptive behavior:

a. antipsychotic drugs

b. antianxiety drugs

c. antidepressant drugs

19. Discuss the effectiveness of aerobic exercise as a biomedical therapy.

Treating the Social Roots of Disorder (pp. 488–490)

20. Contrast the emphases of community-based therapies with those of the psychotherapies and biomedical therapies.

21. Discuss the central assumptions of preventive mental health programs.

CHAPTER REVIEW

When you have finished reading the chapter, complete the sentences that follow. Using your hand or a strip of paper, cover the correct answers in the margin and fill in each blank. Verify your answer by uncovering the correct one. As you proceed, evaluate your performance for each chapter section. *Do not continue with the next section until you understand why each margin term is the correct answer.* If you need to, review or re-read the appropriate chapter section in the text before continuing.

1. Therapies are divided into two types: _____ and _____ therapies.

psychotherapies
biomedical

The Psychological Therapies (pp. 462–484)

2. Many therapists use a blend of therapies, and so they describe themselves as _____ .

eclectic

3. The major psychotherapies are based on three perspectives: the _____ , the _____ , and the _____-_____ perspectives.

psychoanalytic; humanistic
cognitive-learning

4. Psychoanalysis aims to bring into conscious awareness feelings that have been _____ .

repressed

5. By working through a problem, a person gains _____ into its origins.

insight

6. Freud's technique, in which a client says whatever comes to mind, is called _____ _____ .

free association

7. When a person omits shameful or embarrassing material during free association, _____ is occurring.

resistance

8. Insight is facilitated by the analyst's _____ of the meaning of resistances.

interpretation

9. Freud referred to the hidden meaning of a dream as its

_____ _____ .

latent content

10. When strong feelings from other relationships are developed toward the therapist, _____ has occurred.

transference

11. One criticism of psychoanalysis is that it provides after-the-fact interpretations that are _____ (difficult/easy) to disprove.

difficult

12. Humanistic therapies attempt to help people grow in their own _____-_____ .

self-awareness

13. List several ways that humanistic therapy differs from psychoanalysis.

_____

_____

_____

_____

_____

_____

_____

humanistic therapy focuses on the present, on becoming aware of feelings, on what is conscious, on taking responsibility for one's feelings, and on promoting growth

14. The humanistic therapy that is based on Rogers' theory is called _____-_____ , or _____-_____ , therapy.

client-centered
person-centered

15. It is so named because the therapist does not provide _____ of the person's problems.

interpretations

16. In order to promote growth in the person, humanistic therapists exhibit _____ , _____ , and _____ .

genuineness
acceptance; empathy

17. Rogers' technique of restating and clarifying what a person is saying is called _____ _____ .

active listening

18. The computer program based on this listening technique is

_____ .

ELIZA

19. Another type of humanistic psychotherapy is _____ therapy.

Gestalt

20. This technique was developed by _____ .

Perls

21. The word *gestalt* means _____ .

whole

22. Gestalt therapy focuses on bringing unconscious feelings to awareness, as _____ emphasized, and taking responsibility for oneself in the present, as emphasized by _____ therapies.

psychoanalysis

humanistic

23. Humanistic growth _____ have the advantages of saving the individual money and of allowing clients to experience social support from others.

groups

24. T-groups refer to groups of individuals participating in _____ training.

sensitivity

25. Rogers and other therapists developed a form of intensive group therapy known as the _____ group.

encounter

26. Psychoanalytic and humanistic therapists emphasize the importance of self-_____ in successful therapy.

awareness

27. In contrast, _____ therapists believe that simply being aware of a problem may not eliminate it.

behavior

28. Behavior therapists do not attempt to change an individual's _____ , but to alter specific _____ .

personality; symptoms

29. One type of behavior therapy is based on Pavlov's research on _____ _____ .

classical conditioning

30. The technique in which a new, incompatible response is substituted for a maladaptive one is called _____ .

counterconditioning

31. Two examples of this technique are _____ _____ and _____ _____ .

systematic desensitization; aversive conditioning

32. The technique of systematic desensitization has been most fully developed by the therapist _____ .

Wolpe

33. The assumption behind this technique is that one cannot simultaneously be _____ and relaxed.

anxious

34. The first step in systematic desensitization is the construction of a _____ of anxiety-arousing stimuli.

hierarchy

35. The second step involves training in _____.

relaxation

36. In the final step, the person is trained to associate the _____ state with the _____- arousing stimuli.

relaxed; anxiety

37. In aversive conditioning, the therapist attempts to substitute a _____ (positive/negative) response for one that is currently _____ (positive/negative).

negative

positive

38. In this technique, unwanted behaviors become associated with _____ consequences.

unpleasant

39. Therapies that influence behavior by controlling its consequences are called _____ _____.

behavior modification

40. Such therapies are based on principles of _____ conditioning.

operant

41. One application of this form of therapy to institutional settings is the _____ _____.

token economy

42. One criticism of behavior modification is that once rewards are removed, the new behaviors will _____, since the person has not developed _____ motivation for them.

disappear

intrinsic

43. A second criticism concerns whether one person controlling another's behavior is _____.

ethical

44. Behavior therapies are generally most successful with problems that are _____ (specific/generalized).

specific

45. Therapists who teach people more constructive ways of thinking are using _____-_____ therapy.

cognitive-behavior

46. The technique that attempts to eliminate irrational thinking is _____-_____ therapy.

rational-emotive

47. The creator of this technique is _____.

Ellis

48. A technique that attempts to reverse the negative attitudes associated with depression was developed by _____.

Beck

49. In _____-style therapy, people are taught to make more adaptive attributions concerning their successes and failures.

attributional

50. Meichenbaum helps people change maladaptive statements about themselves by using _____-_____ training.

self-instructional

51. In the past thirty years, the number of Americans who have been in contact with some form of psychotherapy has _____ (increased/decreased).

increased

52. Before the 1950s, the main providers of the therapy were

_____.

psychiatrists

53. Today, most psychotherapy is done by _____ psychologists, social workers, counselors, and nurses.

clinical

54. Most psychotherapy clients are _____ (satisfied/ dissatisfied) with the outcome of their therapy.

satisfied

55. In one long-term study of 500 Massachusetts boys, it was found that those in the group that received intensive counseling _____ (did/did not) have significantly fewer problems than a control group.

did not

56. One skeptic of the effectiveness of psychotherapy, who found that about the same number of treated and untreated persons recovered from neurotic disorders, is _____.

Eysenck

57. The number of people who improve without treatment is referred to as the _____ _____ rate.

spontaneous remission

58. A new statistical technique for evaluating the outcomes of many different studies of the effectiveness of psychotherapy is called _____-_____.

meta-analysis

59. Overall, the results of such analyses indicate that psychotherapy is _____ (somewhat effective/ineffective).

somewhat effective

60. Psychotherapy tends to be most effective with _____ (mature/immature) clients.

mature

61. Psychotherapy tends to be most effective with problems that are _____ (specific/generalized).

specific

62. Comparisons of the effectiveness of different types of therapy reveal _____ (clear/no clear) differences.

no clear

63. With phobias, compulsions, and other specific behavior problems, _____ therapies have been the most effective.

behavior

64. For depression, the _____-_____ therapies have been the most successful.

cognitive-behavior

65. List some of the benefits provided by all forms of psychotherapy.

_____

_____

_____

hope for demoralized persons; a new perspective; a warm, caring relationship

66. The beneficial effect of a person's belief in treatment is called the _____ effect.

placebo

67. Several studies have shown that treatment for mild problems offered by _____ is often as effective as that offered by professional therapists.

paraprofessionals

The Biomedical Therapies (pp. 484–488)

68. The biomedical therapy in which a portion of brain tissue is removed or destroyed is called _____.

psychosurgery

69. In the 1930s, Moniz developed an operation called a _____.

lobotomy

70. In this technique, the _____ lobe of the brain is disconnected from the rest of the brain.

frontal

71. A person who has received this operation is said to be _____.

lobotomized

72. Today, most psychosurgery has been replaced by the use of _____ or some other form of treatment.

drugs

73. The therapeutic technique in which the patient receives an electric shock to the brain is referred to as _____ therapy, abbreviated as _____.

electroconvulsive
ECT

74. This technique _____ (is/is not) widely used today.

is

75. ECT is most often used with patients suffering from severe _____.

depression

76. One theory of how ECT works suggests that it causes an increase in the neurotransmitter _____.

norepinephrine

77. The most widely used biomedical treatment involves the use of _____ therapies.

drug

78. The field that studies the effect of drugs on the mind and behavior is _____ .

psychopharmacology

79. When neither the subjects nor the experimenter are aware of which condition a given individual is in, a _____-_____ experiment is being conducted.

double-blind

80. One effect of _____ drugs is to decrease responsiveness to irrelevant stimuli in patients suffering from _____ .

antipsychotic

schizophrenia

81. Such drugs do so by blocking the receptor sites for the neurotransmitter ___dopamine___ .

dopamine

82. One side effect of antipsychotic drugs is that they may produce muscular coordination problems similar to those in persons with _____ disease.

Parkinson's

83. Valium and Librium are classified as _____ drugs.

anti-anxiety

84. These drugs depress activity in the _____ _____ _____ .

central nervous system

85. Drugs prescribed to alleviate depression are called _____ drugs.

antidepressant

86. These drugs work by increasing levels of the neurotransmitter _____ .

norepinephrine

87. In order to stabilize the mood swings of bipolar disorder, the drug _____ is often prescribed.

lithium

88. Recent studies have shown that mild depression can be relieved through a program of _____ exercise.

aerobic

Treating the Social Roots of Disorder (pp. 488–490)

89. Unlike the psychotherapies and biomedical therapies, which focus on treatment of the _____ , therapies such as _____ therapy concentrate on the social context in which the individual exists.

individual
family

90. Psychologists such as George Albee believe many psychological disorders can be prevented through the establishment of halfway houses, crisis intervention, and other _____ mental health programs.

preventive

FOCUS ON PSYCHOLOGY:
PERCEPTIONS OF HUMANISTIC AND BEHAVIOR THERAPIES

Your text indicates that comparisons of the effectiveness of different psychotherapies have not shown any one approach to be consistently more effective than others. Different therapies may be most effective with different problems. Several studies have examined the general public's impressions of the effectiveness of particular treatment procedures. Generally, these studies have found that humanistic psychotherapies are perceived more favorably than are behavior therapies.

Henry McGovern, Charles Fernald, and Lawrence Calhoun recently surveyed the reactions to humanistic and behavior therapies of 15 mental health professionals and 180 students at the University of North Carolina. Surprisingly, both students and professionals perceived the behavior therapies as somewhat more effective than humanistic therapy. Humanistic therapies were, however, rated as being warmer and more friendly than behavior therapies. In summary, both behavior and humanistic therapies are perceived favorably, but from different perspectives. Why do you think this is the case? Based on your own experience, and after having read Chapter 17, what is your perception of the various psychotherapies discussed? Which type of therapy would you recommend to a friend for reducing test anxiety? Why? Which therapy would you recommend for treatment of a bipolar disorder? Of schizophrenia?

Reference: McGovern, H. N., Fernald, C. D., and Calhoun, L. G. (1980). Perceptions of behavior and humanistic therapies. *Journal of Community Psychology,* 8(2), pp. 152–54.

PROGRESS TEST 1

Circle your answers to the following questions and check them with the answer key at the end of this chapter. Be sure to consult the appropriate pages of the text to understand the correct answer for any missed question.

Multiple-Choice Questions

1. Electroconvulsive therapy is most useful in the treatment of:

a. schizophrenia.
b. depression.
c. conversion disorders.
d. neuroses.

2. During his session of psychoanalysis, Joe hesitates while describing a highly embarrassing thought. Freud would say that this hesitation is an example of a(n):
a. transference.
b. insight.
c. mental repression.
d. resistance.

3. During her sessions of psychoanalysis, Jane developed strong feelings of hatred for her therapist. The analyst believes that Jane is showing _____ of her feelings toward her father.
a. transference
b. projection
c. sublimation
d. resistance

4. Which of the following is *not* a common criticism of psychoanalysis?
a. It provides after-the-fact explanations.
b. It provides interpretations that are hard to disprove.
c. It generally is very expensive.
d. Almost no one shows any improvement after psychoanalysis.

5. The computer program ELIZA was designed to simulate a:
a. psychoanalyst.
b. behavior therapist.
c. cognitive-behavior therapist.
d. humanistic therapist.

6. Which of the following is *not* necessarily an advantage of group over individual therapies?
a. They tend to take less time.
b. They tend to cost less.
c. They are more effective.
d. They allow the client to test new behaviors in a social context.

7. Today most psychotherapy is performed by:
a. clinical psychologists, social workers, and counselors.
b. psychiatrists.

c. psychoanalysts.

d. neurologists.

8. Which of the following is true concerning clients' perceptions of psychotherapy?

a. Most believe that all therapists are greedy charlatans.

b. Most are satisfied that their therapy has been effective.

c. Most believe they would have improved on their own anyway.

d. The effectiveness of psychoanalysis tends to be rated higher than any other form of therapy.

9. Which of the following best describes the results of the Cambridge-Somerville Youth Study?

a. Predelinquent boys who received counseling had fewer problems as adults than untreated predelinquent boys.

b. Predelinquent boys who did not receive counseling had fewer problems as adults.

c. Behavior therapy focusing on specific problems was more beneficial than psychoanalysis.

d. Psychoanalysis was more effective than behavior therapy.

10. The results of meta-analysis of the effectiveness of different psychotherapies reveal that:

a. no single type of therapy is consistently superior.

b. behavior therapies are most effective in treating specific problems, such as phobias.

c. cognitive-behavior therapies are most effective in treating depressed emotions.

d. all of the above are true.

11. The antipsychotic drugs appear to produce their effects by blocking the receptor sites for:

a. dopamine.

b. epinephrine.

c. norepinephrine.

d. serotonin.

12. Recent research has shown that aerobic exercise can be effective in reducing:

a. depression.

b. psychotic behavior.

c. manic behavior.

d. compulsive behavior.

Matching Items

Match each type of therapy with its defining feature.

_____ e 1. cognitive-behavior therapy
_____ k 2. behavior therapy
_____ b 3. systematic desensitization
_____ d 4. rational-emotive therapy
_____ g 5. person-centered therapy
_____ f 6. gestalt therapy
_____ a 7. aversive conditioning
_____ h 8. psychoanalysis
_____ c 9. preventive mental health
_____ i 10. biomedical therapy
_____ j 11. self-instructional training

a. associates unwanted behavior with unpleasant experiences

b. associates a relaxed state with anxiety-arousing stimuli

c. places emphasis on the social context of psychological disorders

d. attempts to eliminate irrational thinking

e. category of therapies that teach people more adaptive ways of thinking and acting

f. helps people express their true feelings and assume responsibility for them

g. therapy developed by Carl Rogers

h. therapy based on Freud's theory of personality

i. treatment with psychosurgery, electroconvulsive therapy, or drugs

j. attempts to replace negative "self-talk" with more adaptive responses

k. category of therapies derived from principles of classical and operant conditioning

FOCUS ON PSYCHOLOGY:
FREE ASSOCIATION

One psychoanalytic technique is *free association,* in which the client is encouraged to say every thought that comes to mind, no matter how embarrassing, irrelevant, or foolish it seems. These seemingly random thoughts are believed to help the analyst gain insight into the client's underlying psychological problems. It is common, however, for the client to *resist* mentioning or elaborating on certain themes, presumably in an effort to block anxiety-laden material from consciousness. It is the analyst's job to help the client interpret these resistances and the stream of consciousness that occurs during free association.

You may find it enjoyable to try the process for yourself, even without the aid of a professional psychoanalyst. Try using free association twice, once in the presence of a close friend, and once while speaking into a tape recorder. First find a quiet place where you will not be disturbed. To get the ball rolling, think of some specific incident that occurred recently. From this point on, say aloud *everything* that comes to mind. Don't hold back for any reason, no matter how silly or embarrassing a thought may be. Continue associating for about 10 minutes.

How difficult was it for you to freely associate? Was it easier to talk into the tape recorder than to another person? Can you identify any points at which you consciously resisted speaking about a thought? Is there any organizational unity to the stream of thoughts that occurred to you? How useful do you think free association is as a therapy technique?

PROGRESS TEST 2

Progress Test 2 should be completed during a final chapter review. Do so after you thoroughly understand the correct answers for the Chapter Review and Progress Test 1.

Multiple-Choice Questions

1. Carl Rogers is a _____ therapist who was the creator of _____ therapy.
   a. behavior; desensitization
   b. psychoanalytic; insight
   c. humanistic; person-centered
   d. cognitive-behavior; rational-emotive

2. Using techniques of classical conditioning to develop an association between unwanted behavior and an unpleasant experience is known as:
   a. aversive conditioning.
   b. systematic desensitization.
   c. transference.
   d. electroconvulsive therapy.

3. Which type of psychotherapy emphasizes the individual's inherent potential for self-fulfillment?
   a. behavior therapy
   b. psychoanalysis
   c. humanistic therapy
   d. biomedical therapy

4. Which type of psychotherapy emphasizes clients expressing their true feelings and taking responsibility for them?
   a. psychoanalysis
   b. Gestalt therapy
   c. behavior therapy
   d. cognitive-behavior therapy

5. Which type of psychotherapy focuses on changing symptoms rather than a client's personality?
   a. behavior therapy
   b. cognitive-behavior therapy
   c. humanistic therapy
   d. psychoanalysis

6. The technique of counterconditioning is based on principles of:
   a. observational learning.
   b. classical conditioning.
   c. operant conditioning.
   d. behavior modification.

7. In which technique does the client learn to associate a relaxed state with a hierarchy of anxiety-arousing situations?
   a. rational-emotive therapy
   b. self-instructional training
   c. counterconditioning
   d. systematic desensitization

8. Applications of operant conditioning to the treatment of maladaptive behavior are called:
a. behavior modification.
b. counterconditioning.
c. systematic desensitization.
d. rational-emotive therapy.

9. Which of the following is *not* a common criticism of behavior therapy?
a. Clients may not develop intrinsic motivation for their new behaviors.
b. Behavior control is unethical.
c. Although one symptom may be eliminated, another may replace it unless the underlying problem is treated.
d. All of the above are criticisms of behavior therapy.

10. Which type of therapy focuses on eliminating irrational thinking?
a. Gestalt therapy

b. person-centered therapy
c. rational-emotive therapy
d. self-instruction training

11. Antidepressant drugs are believed to produce their effects by increasing the availability of neurotransmitters such as:
a. dopamine.
b. serotonin.
c. norepinephrine.
d. acetylcholine.

12. Which type of therapy is based on the assumption that many psychological disorders could be prevented by changing oppressive, esteem-destroying environments?
a. humanistic therapy
b. behavior therapy
c. family therapy
d. Gestalt therapy

Matching Items

_____ e __ 1. active listening
_____ I __ 2. token economy
_____ F __ 3. placebo effect
_____ B __ 4. lobotomy
_____ D __ 5. lithium
_____ C __ 6. meta-analysis
_____ J __ 7. psychopharmacology
_____ K __ 8. double-blind procedure
_____ A __ 9. chlorpromazine
_____ G __ 10. Valium
_____ H __ 11. free association

a. antipsychotic drug
b. type of psychosurgery
c. procedure for statistically combining the results of many experiments
d. antidepressant drug
e. empathic technique based on person-centered therapy
f. the beneficial effect of a person's expecting that treatment will be effective
g. antianxiety drug
h. technique of psychoanalytic therapy
i. an operant conditioning procedure
j. the study of the effects of drugs on the mind and behavior
k. experimental procedure in which both patient and staff are unaware of a patient's treatment condition

SAMPLE ESSAY QUESTIONS

1. Compare and contrast psychoanalysis with humanistic therapy and behavior therapy.

2. Discuss whether psychotherapy is effective from the perspective of clients, clinicians, and the results of meta-analysis.

3. Discuss the use of drugs in biomedical therapy.

4. Identify the common ingredients of various psychotherapies.

5. Explain how psychotherapies, biomedical therapies, and community-based therapies differ in their treatment of psychological disorders.

PROJECT:
SELF-MODIFICATION

Principles of operant conditioning have been effectively applied as therapy techniques to a variety of behaviors. Robert Williams and James Long (1979) have illustrated how behavior modification techniques may be used to control one's own behavior. This may be done in order to eliminate undesirable behaviors such as smoking, or to establish more adaptive ones, such as exercising, studying more regularly, or managing money more effectively. If you have read the opening chapter of this study guide, "How to Manage Your Time Efficiently and Study Effectively," you will recognize the application of this self-management program to studying and time management. The fundamental theme of this program is that behavior is changed by altering the environment, "not simply by wanting to change or by talking about the need for change."

Step 1: Selecting a Goal

Many attempts to change behavior fail because inappropriate goals have been established. Select a goal, one that is measurable in behavioral terms (so that you can detect your progress) and attainable. Many people are victims of the *New Year's resolution phenomenon*—they are destined to fail because they set goals that are impossible to attain. It is important to start with a goal that is only moderately different from your present behavior. Instead of attempting to quit smoking, for example, you might set an initial goal of smoking 5 fewer cigarettes per day.

Step 2: Monitoring Target Behavior

In order to provide a reference point for determining your progress, it is important to determine your *baseline* by keeping track of your current behavior. Careful recordkeeping consists of tallying the frequency of the behavior in question (for example, the number of cigarettes smoked each day) and the circumstances surrounding the behavior. Record when the behavior occurred, where it occurred, and how you were feeling at the moment. This information will prove useful as you attempt to gain greater control over the behavior and eliminate it. Your baseline should be kept for about one week.

Step 3: Changing Setting Events

Stimuli that become strongly associated with a behavior are called *setting events*. Smoking, for example, often becomes conditioned to a variety of stimuli: waking up, socializing, watching TV, the end of a meal, studying, driving. Many people engage in a habit as conditioned responses to these stimuli without even being aware that they are doing so. A first step in eliminating undesirable behavior is to gain control over its setting events. Instead of attempting to quit smoking altogether, for example, restrict your smoking to one place in your house or dorm. Doing so has an additional benefit: it eliminates other reinforcers for your behavior. The absence of the TV, or that delicious cup of coffee, will make smoking less enjoyable.

Step 4: Establishing Effective Consequences

Many behaviors are governed by their environmental consequences. In order to increase your chances of success at self-modification, make a contract to reward your successful behavior with an event that is highly reinforcing to you. Choosing these reinforcers takes some thought. They might include listening to music, watching TV, reading, playing a favorite sport, buying an album or article of clothing. The important thing is to identify specific reinforcers for goal attainment. One popular quit-smoking technique is the establishment of a "ciggy-bank." Each day the successful nonsmoker places into a jar the amount of money saved by not purchasing cigarettes.

Step 5: Consolidating Gains

Many attempts at behavior change fail several months later when the person discontinues the self-modification program. Sooner or later, one does have to forgo self-recording, controlling setting events, and reinforcement. The trick is to gradually wean yourself from the program. If you have been recording and reinforcing on a daily basis, stretch it out so that you do so only every third, and then every fourth, day. Gradually fade the program. If you ever feel you may slip up, don't hesitate to return to the full program immediately. At this point in time you might also consider setting a new goal to be attained by using self-modification.

Using this program, select a personal target behavior that you would like to eliminate or establish. Follow the steps outlined above and see if self-modification is helpful for you, as it has been for many others.

WHERE TO LOOK FOR MORE INFORMATION

Rachman, S. J., and Wilson, G. T. (1980). *The effects of psychological therapy*, 2nd ed. New York: Pergamon Press.

A thorough and critical evaluation of various types of psychotherapy.

Finding the Hidden Freud. (1981, November 30). *Newsweek*.

A readable analysis of the influence of Sigmund Freud on contemporary theorists and therapists.

Feldman, L. B. Styles and strategies of family therapy. *Psychological Bulletin*, 10, pp. 16–27.

A description of several techniques used by family therapists.

Yudofsky, S. C. (1981, May). ECT: Shocking depression. *Science News*.

A recent review of what we know, and have yet to learn, about electroconvulsive therapy.

Williams, R. L., and Long, J. D. (1979). *Toward a self-managed life style*, 2nd ed. Boston: Hougton-Mifflin.

A practical and interesting discussion of the application of behavior modification to personal problems.

ANSWERS

PROGRESS TEST 1

Multiple-Choice Questions

1. b (p. 485)	5. d (p. 466)	9. b (pp. 479–480)
2. d (p. 463)	6. c (p. 468)	10. d (p. 481)
3. a (p. 463)	7. a (p. 478)	11. a (p. 486)
4. d (pp. 463–464)	8. b (p. 479)	12. a (p. 488)

Matching Items

1. e (p. 474)	5. g (p. 465)	9. c (p. 490)
2. k (pp. 469–470)	6. f (p. 467)	10. i (p. 484)
3. b (p. 470)	7. a (p. 472)	11. j (p. 478)
4. d (p. 474)	8. h (p. 462)	

PROGRESS TEST 2

Multiple-Choice Questions

1. c (p. 465)	5. a (p. 470)	9. d (p. 473)
2. a (p. 472)	6. b (p. 470)	10. c (p. 474)
3. c (p. 465)	7. d (p. 470)	11. c (p. 488)
4. b (p. 467)	8. a (p. 473)	12. c (p. 489)

Matching Items

1. e (p. 465)	5. d (p. 488)	9. a (p. 487)
2. i (p. 473)	6. c (p. 481)	10. g (p. 487)
3. f (pp. 482–483)	7. j (p. 486)	11. h (p. 462)
4. b (p. 484)	8. k (p. 486)	

CHAPTER 18

Health

CHAPTER OVERVIEW

In an effort to more fully understand the causes of illness, the behavioral and medical sciences have begun merging into a new field called *behavioral medicine*. The field of health psychology represents psychology's contribution to the prevention and treatment of illness. Chapter 18 discusses several health issues, including the effects of stress on the body, pain and its control, how people react to illness, the promotion of health through adequate nutrition, and the management of stress.

You will probably find that the most difficult material in chapter 18 is in the section called "Stress and Illness," which presents a great deal of information concerning the physiological effects of stress on the body. You might work through the Chapter Review section of the study guide several times, filling in the answers mentally until you do the final review. You should also be sure to provide complete answers to the Guided Study for this section of the chapter, both as you actively read the material, and then during your review.

GUIDED STUDY

The text chapter should be studied one section at a time. Before you read, preview each section by skimming it, noting headings and boldface items. Then read the appropriate section objectives from the following outline. Keep these objectives in mind, and as you read the chapter section, search for the information that will complete each one. You may wish to write out answers for each objective as soon as you finish reading that section of the chapter.

1. Explain the "systems theory" perspective of behavioral medicine.

Stress and Illness (pp. 497–507)

2. Describe the nervous system and hormonal response of the body to stress.

3. Outline the sequence of stages and physiological reactions in the general adaptation syndrome.

4. Discuss the major findings of studies of the health consequences of cataclysmic events and personal life changes.

5. Contrast the Type A and Type B behavior patterns and explain why Type A behavior is considered to be an independent risk factor for heart disease.

6. Contrast the physiological reactivity of Type A and Type B persons to stressful situations.

7. Define psychophysiological illness.

8. Describe how the immune system defends the body against illness and infection.

9. Explain how stress affects the body's immune system.

10. Discuss whether it is possible to condition the immune system.

Pain and Its Control (pp. 507–509)

11. Describe how pain differs from other bodily senses.

12. Explain the gate-control theory of pain and describe several techniques of pain control.

Reactions to Illness (pp. 509–514)

13. Discuss several factors that influence whether we notice physical symptoms of illness, and how we interpret them.

14. Discuss the factors that influence whether people seek medical treatment for their symptoms.

15. Describe the findings of animal studies on the effects of uncontrollable shock.

16. Discuss the health consequences of loss of control and the patient role of individuals.

CHAPTER REVIEW

When you have finished reading the chapter, complete the sentences that follow. Using your hand or a strip of paper, cover the correct answers in the margin and complete each sentence. Verify your answer

17. Discuss the factors that influence the tendency of patients to adhere to treatment instructions.

Health Promotion (pp. 514–521)

18. Contrast the cognitive and biochemical effects of high-carbohydrate and high-protein diets.

19. Discuss research findings concerning the following issues.

a. Why people start smoking

b. Why people continue smoking

c. Whether smoking-treatment programs are effective

20. Discuss the effectiveness of exercise as a stress-management technique.

21. Describe how a biofeedback system works.

22. Explain the relaxation response and how relaxation has been used to modify Type A behavior.

23. Discuss evidence that social support can serve as a buffer to stress.

by uncovering the correct one. As you proceed, evaluate your performance for each chapter section. *Do not continue with the next section until you understand why each margin term is the correct answer.* If you need to, review or re-read the appropriate chapter section in the textbook before continuing.

1. Today, half the mortality from the ten leading causes of death can be traced to people's _____.

behavior

2. List several of the behaviors that have been linked to the leading causes of death.

_____

_____

_____

_____

_____

_____

_____

smoking, excessive alcohol consumption, maladaptive responses to stress, nonadherence to doctor's orders, insufficient exercise, use of illicit drugs, poor nutrition

3. The new field that integrates psychological and medical knowledge relevant to health and disease is _____

_____ .

behavioral medicine

4. According to the systems theory, illness or well-being depends on the _____ of many interdependent systems.

interaction

5. The subfield of psychology related to behavioral medicine is called _____ psychology.

health

6. A century ago, the leading causes of death were diseases such as

_____ , _____ ,

_____ , and _____ .

influenza, pneumonia diphtheria, tuberculosis

7. Today's major diseases _____ (are/are not) caused by infectious germs.

are not

Stress and Illness (pp. 497–507)

8. The process by which environmental events threaten or challenge a person is called _____ .

stress

9. In the 1920s, physiologist Walter _____ began studying the effect of stress on the body.

Cannon

10. He discovered that the hormone _____ is released into the bloodstream in response to stress.

adrenaline or epinephrine

11. This hormone is released by the _____ region within the _____ glands in response to stimulation by the _____ nervous system.

medulla
adrenal
sympathetic

12. List several bodily effects of stimulation of this branch of the nervous system and the release of stress hormones.

_____

_____

_____

_____

_____

_____

_____

_____

increased heart rate and respiration, blood diverted from the skin and digestive organs toward muscles, fat released from the body's stores

13. Cannon referred to these responses as preparing the body for _____ or _____ .

fight; flight

14. In one experiment, Hans Selye found that injections of an ovary tissue extract caused three effects: (a) enlargement of the

_____ cortex, (b) shrinkage of the _____ gland, and (c) formation of _____ in the stomach.

adrenal
thymus
ulcers

15. Selye found that other stressors, such as shock and surgery, had physiological effects that were very _____ (similar/ different).

similar

16. Selye referred to the body's response to stress as the _____ _____ _____.

general adaptation syndrome

17. During the first phase—the _____ _____—the person is in a state of _____ due to the sudden arousal of the _____ nervous system.

alarm reaction

shock

sympathetic

18. The second stage of reaction is the stage of _____.

resistance

19. List the bodily responses that occur during this stage.

_____
_____
_____
_____

temperature, blood pressure, heart rate, and respiration increase

20. The third phase of reaction is the stage of _____.

exhaustion

21. During this stage, the _____ nervous system may become active in order to calm the body.

parasympathetic

22. During this stage, a person is especially susceptible to _____, _____ damage, or even _____.

diseases; tissue death

23. One type of stress that research has focused on includes the effects of combat, accidents, natural disasters, and other _____ life events.

cataclysmic

24. In one study, researchers found that following the eruption of Mount Saint Helens, there was an increase in the number of emergency room visits, deaths, and stress-related _____ in a nearby community.

illness

25. Research studies have found that people who have recently been widowed, fired, or divorced are _____ (more/less) vulnerable to illness.

more

26. A person's total score on a life stress scale generally _____ (is/is not) an accurate predictor of his or her future health.

is not

27. List several reasons that this may be so.

_____
_____
_____
_____
_____
_____
_____
_____
_____
_____

most people do not experience major crises; one's perception of the event may be more important than the event itself; the scale includes positive events; other factors such as one's personal hardiness may be equally important

28. The leading cause of death in North America is

_____ _____ _____ .

coronary heart disease

29. This disease results from a _____ of the blood vessels that supply the heart.

narrowing

30. Before the present century, death from this disease was _____ (more/less) frequent.

less

31. List several factors that increase the risk of heart disease.

_____
_____
_____
_____
_____
_____

smoking, obesity, family history of heart disease, high fat diet, physical inactivity, elevated blood pressure and cholesterol level

32. Taken together, these factors _____ (do/do not) account for most instances of heart disease.

do not

33. In the 1950s, Friedman and Rosenman discovered that white women were _____ (more/less) susceptible to heart disease than their husbands.

less

34. This was true even though their diets and those of their husbands were _____ (the same/different).

the same

35. The finding that black women have the same incidence of heart disease as their husbands rules out a difference in

_____ as an explanation for the male-female difference.

hormones

36. Friedman and Rosenman discovered that accountants experience an increase in _____ levels and blood _____ speeds during tax season.

cholesterol
clotting

37. List the behavioral characteristics of a Type A person.

_____

_____

_____

_____

competitive, hard-driving, impatient, time-conscious, super-motivated, aggressive, easily angered

38. People who tend to be more easygoing than Type A persons are labeled _____ _____.

Type B

39. Type A people are _____ (more/less) susceptible to coronary heart disease than Type B people.

more

40. The Type A characteristic that is most strongly linked with coronary disease is _____ _____.

aggressive reactivity

41. Type A persons also tend to engage in other coronary-prone behaviors, including:

_____

_____

_____

smoking, drinking more caffeinated drinks, getting less sleep

42. In relaxed situations, Type A persons _____ (do/ do not) differ from Type B persons in physiological reactivity.

do not

43. An experiment by Williams showed that when Type A men were challenged, their output of the hormones _____, _____, and _____ was _____ (greater/less) than that of Type B men.

epinephrine
norepinephrine; cortisol
greater

44. These hormones may increase the buildup of _____ in the artery walls.

plaques

45. The hardening of the arteries that may result is called _____.

atherosclerosis

46. When a person is angered, blood flow is diverted away from the internal _____.

organs

47. The liver is responsible for removing _____ and _____ from the blood.

cholesterol
fat

48. This finding may explain why _____ (Type A/B) persons have elevated levels of these substances in the blood.

Type A

49. The term that refers to physical symptoms with psychological causes is _____.

psychosomatic

50. Today, experts refer to such symptoms as _____ illnesses.

psychophysiological

51. Examples of such illnesses are _____, _____, and _____.

hypertension
ulcers; headaches

52. Such illnesses are not associated with any known _____ disorder, but appear to be linked to _____.

physical
stress

53. The body's system of fighting disease is the _____ system.

immune

54. This system consists of two types of white blood cells: the _____ _____, which fight infections, and the _____ _____, which attack foreign substances.

B lymphocytes
T lymphocytes

55. The disorder in which the immune system fails to function normally is _____ _____ _____ _____.

Acquired Immune
Deficiency Syndrome

56. When stress increases the levels of epinephrine, norepinephrine, and cortisol, there is a(n) _____ (increase/decrease) in the number of lymphocyte cells.

decrease

57. This results in a(n) _____ (increase/decrease) in disease resistance.

decrease

58. One study showed that stressed rodents that had been inoculated with tumor cells were _____ (more/less) resistant to cancer than unstressed rodents.

less

59. Experiments by Ader and Cohen demonstrate that the functioning of the body's immune system _____ (can/cannot) be affected by conditioning.

can

Pain and Its Control (pp. 507–509)

60. The least understood bodily sense is _____.

pain

61. A sensation of pain in an amputated leg is referred to as the _____ _____ sensation.

phantom limb

62. This phenomenon indicates that pain is not just a property of the senses, but also of the _____.

brain

63. The pain system _____ (does/does not) have one specific type of physical energy.

does not

64. The body _____ (does/does not) have specialized receptor cells for pain.

does not

65. Melzack and Wall have proposed a theory of pain called the _____-_____ theory.

gate-control

66. This theory proposes that pain signals may be blocked by a neurological _____ in the _____ _____.

gate; spinal cord

67. The gate may be opened by activation of _____ (small/large) nerve fibers and closed by activation of _____ (small/large) fibers.

small

large

68. Melzack and Wall explain psychological influences on pain by proposing that the gate may be closed by information originating in the _____.

brain

69. The Lamaze method combines the pain control techniques of _____, _____, and _____-_____.

relaxation; distraction
counter-stimulation

Reactions to Illness (pp. 509–514)

70. Most people _____ (are/are not) very accurate at diagnosing their physical state.

are not

71. In one experiment, joggers on a wooded course ran _____ (faster/slower) than joggers on a track.

faster

72. This finding demonstrates that when attention is diverted by the external environment, _____ cues may not be noticed.

bodily

73. Ruble and Brooks-Gunn found that women who believed females are more emotional during their premenstrual phases tended to remember premenstrual instances that _____ (confirmed/disconfirmed) their beliefs.

confirmed

74. Research has demonstrated that women's physical and mental skills _____ (do/do not) fluctuate greatly with menstruation.

do not

75. When a large group of people incorrectly attribute symptoms to a disease, the result is referred to as a mass _____ illness.

psychogenic

76. In terms of medical treatment, _____ (men/women) report more symptoms, visit physicians more often, and use more drugs.

women

77. This suggests that males pay less attention to their _____ (internal/external) state than do women.

internal

78. Experiments with animals have shown that those who experience electric shocks that are _____ (controllable/uncontrollable) are the most vulnerable to illness.

uncontrollable

79. In animals and humans a loss of control is followed by a drop in immune responses and a rise in the level of stress _____.

hormones

80. Taylor refers to patients who are cooperative, unquestioning, and undemanding as playing the _____-_____ role.

good-patient

81. Patients who are demanding and uncooperative may experience harmful effects from their hostility; these individuals are playing the _____-_____ role.

bad-patient

82. Researchers have found that the stress of treatment can be reduced by allowing patients to be _____ (more/less) active participants in their treatment.

more

83. Studies of patients about to undergo surgery have found that it is _____ (more/less) stressful for doctors to provide realistic information than false reassurance.

less

84. Recent studies have reported that as many as _____ of all patients do not consistently follow their doctor's instructions.

half

85. To increase patient adherence to treatment instructions, medical instructions should provide immediate _____ for compliant behavior.

incentives

Health Promotion (pp. 514–521)

86. It is _____ (more/less) economical to prevent disease than to treat it.

more

87. Certain foods may affect a person's mood and behavior by influencing the formation of _____ .

neurotransmitters

88. The neurotransmitter serotonin is synthesized from the amino acid _____ .

tryptophan

89. This amino acid is increased by meals that are high in _____ .

carbohydrates

90. When serotonin levels are raised, a person feels more _____ , _____ , and less sensitive to _____ .

relaxed; sleepy
pain

91. Concentration and alertness may be improved by meals that are low in _____ but have a high _____ content.

carbohydrate
protein

92. Most people with high blood pressure have higher-than-normal intake of _____ , but lower-than-normal intake of _____ .

salt
calcium

93. Traffic deaths, liver disease, and cancer have been linked to the consumption of _____ .

alcohol

94. Thirty percent of cancer and heart disease deaths in the United States are linked to _____ .

smoking

95. Most people begin smoking during _____ .

early adolescence

96. Social learning theory suggests that many people begin smoking in order to increase their _____ .

social acceptance

97. By terminating an aversive state, smoking provides a person with a powerful _____ reinforcer.

negative

98. Physiologically, nicotine triggers the release of _____ and _____ , which reduces appetite and increases _____ .

epinephrine
norepinephrine; alertness

99. Nicotine also calms anxiety due to the release of _____ and _____ .

acetylcholine
beta-endorphin

100. In the long run most programs to help people quit smoking _____ (are/are not) very effective.

are not

101. Junior high students who were taught to cope with peer pressure and advertisements for smoking were _____ (more/less) likely to begin smoking than students in a control group.

less

102. Recent studies have demonstrated that depression and anxiety can be reduced by _____ _____.   aerobic exercise

103. Neal Miller found that rats could learn to control their _____ _____ when they were rewarded with brain stimulation.   heart rates

104. A system for recording a physiological response and providing feedback concerning it is called _____.   biofeedback

105. Cardiologist Herbert Benson has promoted the healthful effects of meditation through a technique he refers to as the _____ _____.   relaxation response

106. Benson found that experienced meditators are able to decrease their _____ _____, _____ _____, and oxygen consumption.   blood pressure
heart rate

107. Friedman found that modifying Type A behavior in a group of heart attack survivors _____ (reduced/did not influence) the rate of recurrence of heart disease.   reduced

108. Other researchers have found that life events may be less disturbing in people with a good sense of _____.   humor

109. Another buffer against the effects of stress is _____ support.   social

110. Pennebaker found that persons who bear grief alone have _____ (more/fewer) health problems than those who confide in others.   more

---

FOCUS ON PSYCHOLOGY:
EXERCISE, STRESS, AND MUSIC

Recently, there has been a great deal of discussion about the effectiveness of aerobic exercise as a stress-management technique. In addition to promoting psychological feelings of relaxation, aerobic exercise also seems to provide physiological benefits. When the body is physically stressed, as during aerobic exercise, the level of *endorphins*—chemicals believed to be part of the body's natural system of analgesia—is believed to increase dramatically. Some athletes even argue that they have become addicted to the pleasurable effects of these physiological changes. The so-

called runner's high is one example of this phenomenon.

Several researchers have questioned the role of endorphins in exercise. In a recent study at the University of North Carolina, scientist and former All-American swimmer Robert McMurray had two groups of subjects exercise until exhaustion on a motorized treadmill. The subjects were asked to continue as long as they could, periodically reporting how tired they were. Before the study began, one group was injected with naloxone, a drug that prevents endorphins from working by blocking their neural receptor sites. The second group of volunteers was injected with a placebo. If endorphin production allows the body to tolerate the pain of strenuous exercise, the naloxone group should have become exhausted sooner and found the exercise more strenuous than the placebo group. In fact, there was no difference in how long the two groups continued to exercise, or in how strenuous they reported the task to be. Although McMurray believes that people may become dependent on the feelings associated with exercise, he attributes this to a psychological addiction, or the effects of other chemical changes, such as an increase in adrenaline.

Other researchers have found that endorphin levels in the body vary with how stressful a situation is *perceived* to be. In one study, well-trained long-distance runners were asked to work out two times on a motorized treadmill, once with and once without taped music being played. The speed and elevation of the treadmill was controlled so that for each athlete the *physical* exertion required in the two conditions was the same. All the athletes reported that the workout seemed less strenuous when they were listening to music. Physiologically, their bodies corroborated this perception. Endorphin levels were significantly lower in the music condition than in the no-music condition. The results of this study demonstrate the importance of attitude, or psychological perception, in determining physiological response to a stressful situation. In what practical ways could the findings of this study be applied to other stressful situations?

References: R. G. McMurray, D. S. Sheps, and D. M. Guinan. (1984). Effects of naloxone on maximal stress testing in females. *Journal of Applied Physiology, 56*(2), pp. 436–440. R. J. Trotter. (1984, May). Maybe it's the music. *Psychology Today*, p. 8.

PROGRESS TEST 1

Circle your answers to the following questions and check them with the answer key at the end of the chapter. Be sure to consult the appropriate pages of the text to understand the correct answer for any missed question.

1. The interdisciplinary field that integrates behavioral and medical knowledge relevant to health and disease is:

a. health psychology.
b. holistic medicine.
c. behavioral medicine.
d. osteopathic medicine.

2. The stress hormones epinephrine and norepinephrine are released by the
_____ gland, in response to stimulation by the _____
branch of the nervous system.
a. pituitary; sympathetic
b. pituitary; parasympathetic
c. adrenal; sympathetic
d. adrenal; parasympathetic

3. During which stage of the general adaptation syndrome is a person especially vulnerable to disease?
a. alarm reaction
b. stage of resistance
c. stage of exhaustion
d. stage of adaptation

4. The leading cause of death in North America is:
a. lung cancer.
b. colon cancer.
c. accidents.
d. coronary heart disease.

5. The component of Type A behavior that is most predictive of coronary disease is:
a. time urgency.
b. competitiveness.
c. high motivation.
d. anger.

6. The effect of the hormones epinephrine, norepinephrine, and cortisol is to:
a. lower the level of cholesterol in the blood.
b. promote the buildup of plaque on the coronary artery walls.
c. divert blood away from the muscles of the body.
d. reduce stress.

7. Which of the following diseases specifically results from suppression of the body's immune system?
a. arthritis
b. AIDS
c. coronary heart disease
d. cancer

8. In one experiment, rats developed an aversion to water when, after drinking, they were injected with a drug that suppressed the immune system. Later, some of the animals died. This experiment demonstrates that the animals:
a. could not survive the dehydration from not drinking.
b. had been conditioned to suppress their own immune systems.
c. developed an allergic reaction to the drug.
d. were not able to tolerate the stress of the injection.

9. According to the gate-control theory, neural activity in the _____ nerve fibers tends to _____ the neural gate.
a. short; open
b. small; close
c. long; open
d. large; close

10. In laboratory experiments, animals that experienced _____ shocks were the most vulnerable to disease.
a. frequent
b. infrequent
c. avoidable
d. unavoidable

11. Research has demonstrated that, for a patient's well-being, it is better for a doctor to be:
a. evasive in answering questions about the patient's condition.
b. reassuring in answering questions, even if the person's condition is grave.
c. realistic in answering questions about the patient's condition.
d. harsh, in order to impress the patient with the importance of treatment.

12. Studies have demonstrated that meals that are high in _____ promote relaxation because they raise levels of _____ .
a. carbohydrate; serotonin
b. carbohydrate; cortisol
c. protein; serotonin
d. protein; cortisol

13. Research has shown that when people are asked to confide troubling feelings to another person, they:
a. usually refuse to do so truthfully.
b. experience a sustained increase in blood pressure until the experiment is finished.
c. first become physiologically tense, then more relaxed after confiding their problem.
d. typically deny having any problems.

14. Research suggests that _____ influences often lead a person to start smoking, while _____ influences are more important in explaining why people continue to smoke.
a. biological; social
b. social; biological
c. biological; cognitive
d. cognitive; biological

15. Which of the following is true concerning exercise?
a. Exercise can reduce depression and anxiety.
b. Exercise can lower blood pressure.
c. Workers who exercise regularly have fewer medical claims than do sedentary workers.
d. All of the above are true.

FOCUS ON PSYCHOLOGY:
TYPE A OR B

For each of the following questions, circle the one answer that is true for you. Every individual is different, so there are no right or wrong answers.

1. Which do you usually do when you are under pressure or stress?
a. Do something about it immediately.
b. Plan carefully before taking any action.

2. How fast do you usually eat?
a. Usually the first one finished.
b. A little faster than average.
c. About the same speed as everybody else.
d. More slowly than most people.

3. When you listen to someone talking, and s/he takes too long to get to the point, do you feel like rushing them?
a. Yes, frequently.

b. Yes, occasionally.
c. Almost never.

4. How do most people consider you?
a. definitely hard-driving and competitive.
b. probably hard-driving and competitive.
c. probably more relaxed and easy-going.
d. definitely more relaxed and easy-going.

5. In school, do you ever keep two projects going at the same time by shifting back and forth from one to the other?
a. No, never.
b. Yes, but only in emergencies.
c. Yes, regularly.

6. Compared to others, how do you approach life?
a. Much more seriously.
b. A little more seriously.
c. A little less seriously.
d. Much less seriously.

7. If you tell someone that you will meet them somewhere at a definite time, how often do you arrive late?
a. Once in a while.
b. Rarely.
c. I am never late.

8. Which best describes the events that fill your everyday life?
a. Problems needing solution.
b. Challenges needing to be met.
c. A rather predictable routine.
d. Not enough things to keep me busy.

9. How was your temper when you were younger?
a. Fiery and hard to control.
b. Strong, but controllable.
c. No problem.
d. I almost never got angry.

10. How would your best friend rate your general level of activity?
a. Too slow. Should be more active.
b. Above average. Is busy much of the time.
c. Too active. Needs to slow down.

This survey is a modified version of the Jenkins Activity Survey, a test of Type A behavior developed by David Jenkins. To score your test, give yourself one point each time your answer agrees with these: (1) a, (2) a or b, (3) a, (4) a or b, (5) c, (6) a, (7) c, (8) a or b, (9) a or b, (10) c. There is, of course, no precise cutoff, but if you are a good judge of yourself, the higher the score, the more likely it is you have Type A tendencies.

PROGRESS TEST 2

Progress Test 2 should be completed during a final chapter review. Do so after you thoroughly understand the correct answers for the Chapter Review and Progress Test 1.

1. The field of health psychology is concerned with:
a. the prevention and treatment of illness.
b. the promotion of health.
c. the improvement of health care systems.
d. all of the above.

2. In order, the sequence of stages in the general adaptation syndrome is:
a. alarm reaction, stage of resistance, stage of exhaustion.
b. stage of resistance, alarm reaction, stage of exhaustion.
c. stage of exhaustion, stage of resistance, alarm reaction.
d. alarm reaction, stage of exhaustion, stage of resistance.

3. Research on life change scales has shown that a person's total score:
a. generally predicts future health with great accuracy.
b. generally does not predict future health accurately.
c. is greater if one is a female than if one is a male.
d. is strongly related to ethnic background.

4. Which of the following is *not* characteristic of the Type A behavior pattern?
a. impatience
b. competitiveness
c. low job motivation
d. easily angered

5. Which of the following is true?
a. Even when relaxed, Type A persons have higher blood pressure than Type B persons.
b. When stressed, Type A persons show greater output of epinephrine, norepinephrine, and cortisol than Type B persons.
c. When stressed, Type B persons show greater output of epinephrine, norepinephrine, and cortisol than Type A persons.
d. Type A persons tend to sleep more than Type B persons.

6. Genuine illnesses that are caused by stress are called:
a. psychophysiological illnesses.
b. hypochondriacal illnesses.
c. psychogenic illnesses.
d. psychotropic illnesses.

7. The disease and infection-fighting cells of the immune system are the:
a. B lymphocytes.
b. T lymphocytes.
c. both a and b.
d. antigens.

8. One effect of stress on the body is to:
a. suppress the immune system.
b. facilitate the immune system response.
c. increase disease resistance.
d. none of the above.

9. The phantom limb sensation indicates that:
a. pain is a purely sensory phenomenon.
b. each person's experience of pain is individual.
c. pain involves the brain's interpretation of neural activity.
d. all the above are true.

10. In response to unavoidable shock, levels of stress hormones _____ and immune responses are _____ .
a. decrease; suppressed
b. increase; suppressed
c. decrease; increased
d. increase; increased

11. Concerning patient adherence to treatment instructions, which of the following is *not* true?
a. Patients often fail to follow instructions because they do not understand them.
b. Patient compliance is affected by the doctor's credibility and attractiveness.

c. The vast majority of patients follow their doctor's instructions consistently.
d. The tendency to comply is influenced by the patient-doctor relationship.

12. Jack has an important psychology exam in the morning. In an effort to improve his concentration and alertness, he orders a meal that is high in _____ and low in _____ for dinner.
a. carbohydrate; protein
b. carbohydrate; fat
c. protein; carbohydrate
d. protein; fat

13. Teenage smokers tend to be perceived by other teenagers as:
a. social isolates.
b. foolish for destroying their health.
c. tough and sociable.
d. none of the above.

14. Which of the following is true concerning smoking-treatment programs?
a. Most are effective in the long run.
b. Hypnosis is more effective than behavior modification.
c. Treatment programs are more effective with women than with men.
d. Most participants eventually resume smoking.

15. Which of the following takes place during biofeedback training?
a. The person gains voluntary control over a physiological state.
b. The person is given sensory feedback for a subtle bodily response.
c. The autonomic nervous system is conditioned.
d. All of the above take place.

SAMPLE ESSAY QUESTIONS

1. Outline the sequence of stages in the general adaptation syndrome and describe the bodily changes that take place during each stage.

2. Describe the effects of stress on the immune system.

3. Discuss several factors that influence patient adherence to treatment instructions.

4. Explain the gate-control theory of pain.

5. Discuss several techniques for managing stress.

PROJECT:
RELAXATION THROUGH AUTOSUGGESTION

The text points out the beneficial effects relaxation training has been shown to have in Type A and other persons. A relaxed state has also been shown to improve performance in a variety of situations, from taking exams to sports. The following exercise can be used to prepare for any activity that requires being relaxed. It can also be used several times a week as part of a general program of stress management. You may find that your concentration will be improved if you tape-record the following instructions. Read them in a slow, even-paced monotone, with sufficient pauses to allow yourself to carry out the instructions.

Sit or lie down in a comfortable position. Close your eyes. Beginning with the top of your head, you are going to completely relax your entire body. Imagine that your scalp and forehead are so relaxed that the skin loses its elasticity and begins to melt, spreading deep relaxation wherever it goes. Relax your facial muscles completely. Relax your jaw so that there is not even enough muscle tone to keep your mouth closed. Let the relaxation spread down your neck to your shoulders. Let the tension leave, first from your right shoulder, now from your left. As the relaxation spreads down your arms, let them go limp. Allow the relaxation to spread to your hands. Feel the tension leave each of your fingers. Now relax your chest and upper body. As you do so, feel the muscles lose their ability to maintain posture. Allow your stomach to relax completely. Your entire upper body should now be completely relaxed and free of tension. Let the wave of relaxation now spread to your lower body. Relax your left thigh. Now let the tension leave the right thigh. Allow the relaxation to spread to your lower left leg. Now your lower right leg. Finally, allow the last remaining tension to leave your body through your toes. Now that you are completely relaxed, use the following instructions to begin controlling your breathing.

Inhale to the count of one; exhale to the count of two, three. Repeat this breathing pattern five times. Now inhale to the count of one, two; exhale to the count of three, four, five, six. Repeat this breathing pattern five times. Continue this breathing pattern for another ten to fifteen minutes. As you breathe, mentally begin repeating to yourself "I am calm." (You may wish to allow the tape to continue to run, signaling the end of this quiet period at the appropriate time.)

If you find that it is difficult to tell if your muscles are relaxed, try a technique that is used in LaMaze training. Pick a muscle group in your body (your face, stomach, or fist are good choices). Clench this muscle as tightly as you can. Feel the tension. Hold it a few seconds. Now relax the muscle and notice the difference in sensations. Tense it once more. Now relax it. With practice, you should become capable of detecting muscular tension anywhere in your body.

Reference: D. B. Ellis. (1984). *Becoming a master student*, 4th ed. Rapid City, SD: College Survival, Inc.

WHERE TO LOOK FOR MORE INFORMATION

Schwartz, G., and Weiss, S. (1977). What is behavioral medicine? *Psychosomatic Medicine, 36,* pp. 377–81.
   A description of the new field of behavioral medicine by one of its pioneers.

Krantz, D. S., Grunberg, N. E., and Baum, A. (1985). Health psychology. *Annual Review of Psychology, 36.*
   Three health psychologists review recent accomplishments in their field.

Benson, H. (1984). *Beyond the Relaxation Response: How to Harness the Healing Power of Your Personal Beliefs.* New York: Times Books.
   A short, popular book on stress management by a noted biofeedback researcher.

Garr, D. (1981, September). The healing brain. *Omni.*
   This article discusses the brain's influence on the immune system and resistance to diseases such as cancer.

ANSWERS

PROGRESS TEST 1

1. c (p. 495)
2. c (p. 498)
3. c (p. 499)
4. d (p. 501)
5. d (p. 502)

6. b (p. 503)
7. b (p. 504)
8. b (pp. 505–506)
9. d (p. 508)
10. d (p. 504)

11. c (p. 513)
12. a (p. 514)
13. c (p. 521)
14. b (p. 515)
15. d (pp. 517–518)

PROGRESS TEST 2

1. d (p. 496)
2. a (pp. 498–499)
3. b (p. 500)
4. c (p. 502)
5. b (p. 503)

6. a (p. 504)
7. c (p. 504)
8. a (p. 504)
9. c (p. 508)
10. b (p. 504)

11. c (p. 513)
12. c (p. 514)
13. c (p. 515)
14. d (p. 516)
15. d (p. 518)

PART SEVEN

SOCIAL
BEHAVIOR

CHAPTER 19

Social Influence

CHAPTER OVERVIEW

Chapter 19 demonstrates the powerful influence of social situations on the behavior of individuals by discussing research studies on conformity, compliance, attitudes, persuasion, and group influence. These social principles help us to understand how individuals are influenced by advertising, political candidates, and the various groups to which they belong. Although social influences are powerful, we need to remember the role of individuals in choosing and creating the social situations they are influenced by.

There is not a great deal of terminology for you to learn in this chapter; your primary task is to absorb the findings of the many research studies discussed. The author of the text has provided one effective way of organizing these findings: Each topic (persuasion, conformity) can be rephrased as a question, such as "What situational factors promote conformity?" The research findings (individual feelings of incompetence and insecurity, group status and size) may then form the basis of your answers.

You may find some sections particularly difficult, because the findings are somewhat abstract or counter-intuitive. You should devote extra time to these sections. You should also write careful answers to the objectives and sample essay questions in this study guide.

GUIDED STUDY

The text chapter should be studied one section at a time. Before you read, preview each section by skimming it, noting headings and boldface items. Then read the appropriate section objectives from the following outline. Keep these objectives in mind, and as you read the chapter section, search for the information that will complete each one. You may wish to write out answers for each objective as soon as you finish reading that section of the chapter.

Explaining Our Own and Others' Behavior
(pp. 528–529)

   1. Explain the fundamental attribution error.

Conformity and Compliance (pp. 529–537)

   2. Describe how Sherif studied suggestibility and the findings of his studies.

   3. Describe Asch's method of investigating the effects of group pressure on an individual.

   4. Identify several situational factors that promote individual conformity to group pressure.

5. Explain the differences between normative and informational social influence.

6. Describe the obedience studies conducted by Milgram.

7. Identify the social conditions that promote obedience to authority.

8. Discuss three ways in which social and personal control interact.

Attitudes and Actions (pp. 537–541)

9. Discuss whether attitudes guide actions. Identify those circumstances in which attitudes and actions tend to correspond.

10. Discuss the effects of a person's actions on his or her attitudes.

11. Explain and contrast cognitive dissonance theory and self-perception theory.

Persuasion (pp. 541–545)

12. Discuss the importance of the attractiveness and credibility of the communicator in persuasion.

13. Discuss how the nature of a message influences its persuasiveness.

14. Discuss how the medium of communication and the audience's background influence persuasion.

Group Influence (pp. 545–551)

15. Explain social facilitation and discuss how arousal interacts with task difficulty in influencing an individual's behavior.

16. Define social loafing and deindividuation; identify the social circumstances in which each tends to occur.

17. Discuss the effects of crowding on behavior, including that of prison populations.

18. Explain group polarization and groupthink; identify their effects on behavior.

19. Discuss the importance of minority influence on majority opinion.

CHAPTER REVIEW

When you have finished reading the chapter, complete the sentences that follow. Using your hand or a strip of paper, cover the correct answers in the margin and complete each sentence. Verify your answer by uncovering the correct one. As you proceed, evaluate your performance for each chapter section. *Do not continue with the next section until you understand why each margin term is the correct answer.* If you need to, review or re-read the appropriate chapter section in the text before continuing.

Explaining Our Own and Others' Behavior (pp. 528–529)

1. Social psychologists refer to explanations of behavior as _____.

attributions

2. Most people tend to _____ (overestimate/underestimate) the extent to which people's actions are influenced by social situations.

underestimate

3. This tendency is called the _____ _____ _____.

fundamental attribution error

4. When a person is explaining his or her *own* behavior, this tendency is _____ (stronger/weaker).

weaker

Conformity and Compliance (pp. 529–537)

5. The term that refers to the tendency to adjust one's behavior to coincide with an assumed group standard is _____.

conformity

6. The psychologist who studied social influences on suggestibility is
_____Sherif_____ .

Sherif

7. These studies made use of the _____autokinetic_____ phenomenon, in which a stationary spot of light appears to move.

autokinetic

8. When the group of subjects repeatedly estimated the apparent movement of the light, their estimates tended to
_____converge_____ (converge/diverge).

converge

9. The psychologist who studied the effects of group pressure on conformity is _____Asch_____ .

Asch

10. Identify the situational factors that promote conformity.

_____

_____

_____

_____

_____

_____

_____

_____

_____

_____

conformity is promoted when a person is made to feel incompetent or insecure; when the group has three or more people; when the group is unanimous; when the group is high in status; when the person is observed by others in the group; and when the person has been socialized to respect social standards

11. One reason people comply with social pressure is to gain approval or avoid rejection; this is called _____normative_____
_____social_____ _____fluence_____ .

normative social influence

12. Other people can also provide a person with useful information: this type of influence is called _____informational_____
_____social_____ _____influence_____

informational social influence

13. The classic social psychology studies of obedience were conducted by _____Milgram_____ .

Milgram

14. When ordered by the experimenter to shock the "learner," most subjects _____complied_____ (complied/refused).

complied

15. Identify the social conditions in which obedience was greatest in Milgram's experiments.

_____

_____

obedience was greatest when the victim was

_____
_____
_____
_____
_____
_____
_____
_____
_____
_____
_____

at a distance; the
person giving the
orders was nearby and
a legitimate authority;
the authority was
supported by a
prestigious institution;
and when there were
no models of other
people defying the
experimenter's commands

16. When subjects were asked to administer the test while another person delivered the shocks, compliance was ___increased___ (reduced/increased).

increased

17. Identify three ways in which social and personal control of situations interact.

a. _____
_____
_____

b. _____
_____

c. _____
_____

The same situation
will affect different
people in different ways.
We choose the situations
that influence us.
We help create the
situations that influence us.

18. An individual's tendency toward nonconformity when being coerced by another person is called ___reactance___.

reactance

Attitudes and Actions (pp. 537–541)

19. A person's predisposed belief about something is called a(n) ___attitude___.

attitude

20. It is commonly assumed that attitudes guide an individual's ___action___.

actions

21. During the 1960s, many research studies _____ (challenged/supported) this assumption.

challenged

22. List three circumstances in which attitudes tend to predict actions.

a. _____
_____

when other influences
are minimized

b. _____ when the attitude is
_____ specific to the behavior

c. _____ when we are fully
_____ aware of our attitudes

23. Attitudes that come to mind quickly are _____ more
(more/less) likely to guide behavior than those that do not.

24. A set of behaviors expected of someone in a given social position is
called a(n) ___role___. role

25. After playing a role, actors often find their actions
___more___ (more/less) believable than they did before. more

26. When people are induced into performing actions that violate their
true attitudes, these attitudes are often _____ weakened
(strengthened/weakened).

27. People are motivated to justify their actions to themselves as a way
of relieving hypocritical feelings; this statement reflects the
___cognitive___ ___dissonance___ theory. cognitive dissonance

28. This theory was proposed by ___Festinger___. Festinger

29. Dissonance arises when two of a person's thoughts are
___inconsistent___. inconsistent

30. This theory predicts that people induced (without coercion) to
behave contrary to their true attitudes will be motivated to reduce the
resulting dissonance by changing their ___attitudes___. attitudes

31. The theory that suggests that an individual's personal attitudes are
inferred from self-observation of behavior is
___self___-___perception___ theory. self-perception

32. This theory was proposed by ___Bem___. Bem

33. If a person is rewarded for doing something he or she already
enjoys, the enjoyment may be decreased; this is the
___overjustification___ effect. overjustification

34. This phenomenon cannot be explained by the
___cognitive___ ___dissonance___ theory. cognitive dissonance

35. Which theory best explains what happens when a person's actions
and attitudes are inconsistent? ___cognitive___
___dissonance___ cognitive dissonance

36. The theory that best explains behavior in situations where people

are unsure of their attitudes is ___self p___-
___perception___ theory.

self-perception

Persuasion (pp. 541–545)

37. Social psychologists have studied four factors that influence persuasion: the _____, the _____, the _____, and the _____.

communicator; message
medium; audience

38. For matters of personal preference, an _____ communicator tends to be more persuasive than one who is not.

attractive

39. For factual matters, the communicator's _____ becomes more important.

credibility

40. Identify several behaviors that increase a communicator's credibility.

_____

_____

_____

_____

looking the person straight
in the eye; speaking fairly
rapidly; arguing against
one's self-interest

41. When a communicator is not highly credible, the message is most persuasive when it differs from the audience's existing opinions by a(n) _____ (moderate/extreme) amount.

moderate

42. With well-informed audiences, messages are most effective if they present _____ (one/both) side(s) of an issue.

both

43. When both sides of an argument are separated by a time gap, the side presented _____ (first/second) usually has the advantage.

second

44. For audiences that are not deeply involved in an issue, a message is more persuasive if it _____ (is very logical/arouses emotion).

arouses emotion

45. Messages presented in the mass media are most effective for issues that are relatively _____.

minor or unfamiliar

46. In general, face-to-face messages are _____ (more/less) effective than those in the mass media.

more

47. Techniques that make people think about a message are more effective when the audience's initial reaction to the message is _____ (agreement/disagreement).

agreement

48. Individuals are most sensitive to persuasion when their attitudes _____ (are/are not) well defined.

are not

Group Influence (pp. 545–551)

49. The tendency to perform a task better when other people are present is called _____ _____ .

social facilitation

50. This tendency is greatest for tasks that are _____ (simple/difficult).

simple

51. Arousal from the presence of others enhances the responses that are the most _____ (likely/unlikely) in a given situation.

likely

52. Ingham found that people worked _____ (harder/less hard) in a team tug-of-war than they had in an individual contest.

less hard

53. This phenomenon has been called _____ _____ .

social loafing

54. The feeling of anonymity an individual may develop within a group is called _____ .

deindividuation

55. The buffer zone people maintain around their bodies is called _____ _____ .

personal space

56. Researchers have found that the reactions of people in crowded situations are often _____ (lessened/amplified).

amplified

57. List several findings of the effects of crowding on prison populations.

_____

_____

_____

_____

_____

_____

increased rates of death, illness, suicide, disciplinary infraction, and psychiatric commitment; higher blood pressure

58. Over time, the initial differences between groups usually _____ (increase/decrease).

increase

59. This phenomenon is called _____ _____ .

group polarization

60. When the desire for group harmony overrides realistic thinking in individuals, _____ has occurred.

groupthink

61. Groupthink is promoted by _____ , _____ - _____ , and group _____ .

conformity
self-justification
polarization

62. A minority opinion is more forceful in swaying the majority if the minority position is presented in a manner that is _____ (consistent/inconsistent).

consistent

FOCUS ON PSYCHOLOGY:
SOCIAL FACILITATION IN COCKROACHES

Social facilitation demonstrates that the mere presence of other people often has an arousing and motivating effect on behaviors that are well learned. In contrast, performance on more difficult tasks may be impaired by the presence of an audience. Zajonc, Heingartner, and Herman (1969) wondered if social facilitation would apply to other species as well. To test their hypothesis, they conducted a study using the venerable cockroach as a subject. The experiment took advantage of the fact that cockroaches are *photophobic*—they do not like bright light. Two mazes were constructed. In the first maze, the roach had to run straight down an alley in order to escape a bright light. In the second maze, the task was more difficult. In order to escape the light, the roaches had to learn to make a left or right turn. Since the two mazes differed in difficulty (at least from the experimenters' viewpoint), the presence of an audience of four other cockroaches was predicted to have opposite effects in each. The results confirmed the predictions: In the "easy" maze, the roaches tended to reach the goal box more quickly when other roaches were present than when there was no audience. In the "difficult" maze, however, the roaches reached the goal more rapidly when no audience was present.

Source: R. Zajonc, A. Heingartner, and E. Herman. (1969). Social enhancement and impairment of performance in the cockroach. *Journal of Personality and Social Psychology, 13,* pp. 83–92.

PROGRESS TEST 1

Circle your answers to the following questions and check them with the answer key at the end of the chapter. Be sure to consult the appropriate pages of the text to understand the correct answer for any missed question.

1. When explaining the behavior of other people, we often underestimate the importance of social influences. This phenomenon is called:
  a. attributional underestimation.
  b. the fundamental attribution error.
  c. social underestimation.
  d. the social-situational attribution error.

2. In his study of obedience, Milgram found that:
  a. most subjects refused to shock the learner even once.
  b. most subjects complied with the experiment until the shocks reached a painful level.
  c. most subjects complied with all the demands of the experiment.
  d. women tended to be more compliant than men.

3. According to the cognitive dissonance theory:
  a. dissonance occurs when a person is coerced into doing something disagreeable.
  b. dissonance occurs when two people are in disagreement.
  c. dissonance occurs more during adolescence than during adulthood.
  d. dissonance occurs when a person, without coercion, does something disagreeable.

4. Which of the following statements is true?
  a. Minority opinion almost never influences that of the majority.
  b. Groupthink is more likely when the group members frequently disagree.
  c. Groupthink can be prevented by an open-minded leader who welcomes all opinions.
  d. A minority opinion that frequently changes can be very effective in changing the opinion of the majority.

5. The psychologist who studied suggestibility using the autokinetic phenomenon was:
  a. Sherif.   **c.** Milgram.
  b. Asch.   **d.** Festinger.

6. If you are giving a speech to an audience that disagrees with you, which of the following should you do to try and change attitudes?
a. Speak loudly and with passion.
b. Present both sides of the argument.
c. Present only your side of the argument.
d. Try to make the audience afraid.

7. In Asch's studies of conformity, conformity increased when:
a. the group included three or more people.
b. the group had high status.
c. individuals were made to feel insecure.
d. all of the above were true.

8. One reason people comply with social pressure is to avoid rejection or to gain approval; this is called:
a. informational social influence.
b. the fundamental attribution error.
c. normative social influence.
d. deindividuation.

9. During his army basic training, Jack would sometimes do things "just to be different." Jack's behavior demonstrates:
a. deindividuation.
b. reactance.
c. normative social influence.
d. groupthink.

10. Which theory suggests that people infer their attitudes from their own actions?
a. attribution theory
b. cognitive dissonance theory
c. self-perception theory
d. arousal theory

11. In selecting an actor for a television advertisement, a clothing manufacturer would be advised to select an actor who is:
a. highly credible.
b. very attractive.
c. highly intelligent.
d. of the opposite sex of potential users of the product.

12. Which of the following behaviors would be most likely to be subject to social facilitation?
a. running speed
b. proofreading a long paragraph for grammatical errors

c. typing accuracy
d. playing a difficult piece on a musical instrument

13. The phenomenon in which individuals lose their identity and normal restraints when part of a group is called:
a. groupthink.
b. cognitive dissonance.
c. reactance.
d. deindividuation.

14. Which of the following is the most predictable effect of crowding on behavior?
a. irritability
b. an increase in the intensity of most reactions
c. an increase in altruistic behavior
d. Crowding has no predictable effect on behavior.

15. Jane and Sandy were best friends as freshmen. After belonging to different sororities for four years, they found that they had less in common with each other than with the other members of their own sororities. This tendency of groups to become progressively different is called:
a. group polarization.
b. groupthink.
c. deindividuation.
d. the normative social influence.

FOCUS ON PSYCHOLOGY:
RAT CITY

The effects of crowding on behavior have been studied in several ways. In one classic study, Calhoun (1962) confined five pregnant wild rats in an enclosure that measured one-quarter of an acre. The rats were provided with ample food, water, and nesting materials. For the next 27 months, Calhoun watched the population quickly grow, estimating that it could reach 5,000 or more. However, due to increased fighting and diminished parental care, many of the rat pups died and the population stabilized at about 150 animals.

In a second series of studies, Calhoun confined groups of 80 rats in a 10- by 14-foot room that was divided into four smaller pens. This number was about twice that which the room could comfortably accommodate. Calhoun prevented the crowded population from growing further by removing any infants that survived past weaning. Despite having adequate food, water, and nesting materials, the rats exhibited many behavioral abnormalities over the 16-month observation period. Normally fastidious housekeepers, the rats spent very little time building or maintaining their nests under these conditions. Sexual behavior was also abnormal. Males frequently mounted and attempted to mate with other males. In several instances, infant rats were mounted. Parental disinterest and neglect became common. In one group, 80 percent of the infants died before they reached weaning age. Some of the animals became so aggressive that "at times it was impossible to enter a room without observing fresh blood spattered about the room from tail wounds." Calhoun coined the term *behavioral sink* to refer to the abnormal behaviors that developed under these conditions. Calhoun estimates that a behavioral sink will occur in a population when the density is approximately twice that which the available resources can support.

Although studies of the effects of crowding on human behavior do not paint such a bleak picture, many people do associate crowded conditions and urban density with crime and aggression. How do you feel? Do the results of Calhoun's studies surprise you? How applicable do you feel they are to human behavior?

PROGRESS TEST 2

Progress Test 2 should be completed during a final chapter review. Do so after you thoroughly understand the correct answers for the Chapter Review and Progress Test 1.

1. The board members of Acme Truck Company are so afraid of going against the boss's ideas and breaking the "team spirit" that they often conceal their true opinions; this group is a victim of:
a. group polarization.
b. normative social influence.
c. informational social influence.
d. groupthink.

2. When subjects in an experiment were told that a young woman had been instructed to act friendly or unfriendly to them, most attributed the actor's behavior to:
a. the situation.
b. both the situation and the actor's personal disposition.
c. the actor's personal disposition.
d. There was no consistency in attribution.

3. Which of the following group characteristics is important in promoting conformity in individuals?
a. whether an individual's behavior will be observed by others in the group
b. whether the individual is male or female
c. the size of the room the group is meeting in
d. the age of the members of the group

4. After Marilyn Monroe committed suicide, there was an increase in suicide in the United States. This has been attributed to the social influence of:
a. conformity.
b. suggestibility.
c. compliance.
d. all of the above.

5. An army captain orders a village destroyed. Which of the following would promote the greatest compliance with the orders?
a. The orders were delivered over a walkie-talkie.
b. The soldiers are to destroy the village by attacking on foot.
c. The orders are delivered in person.
d. After hearing the orders, two soldiers balk and are verbally reprimanded.

6. As a new member, Bill often looks to his fraternity brothers during meetings when he is unsure how to act. This group influence is called:
a. informational social influence.
b. normative social influence.
c. reactance.
d. group polarization.

7. Which of the following is true?
a. Attitudes and actions almost never correspond.
b. Attitudes predict behavior about half of the time.

c. Attitudes and behavior almost always correspond.

d. Attitudes predict behavior when other influences (such as group pressure) are minimal.

8. When Lynn first joined the sorority, she felt awkward during rituals and sorority functions. After she has been a member for some time, she will probably:
a. feel more awkward.
b. feel awkward, but learn to hide these feelings.
c. begin resenting the group.
d. begin to adopt to her role and feel more comfortable.

9. Which of the following situations should produce the greatest cognitive dissonance?
a. A soldier is forced to carry out disagreeable orders.
b. A student who loves animals has to put one to sleep in order to complete a biology project.
c. As part of an experiment, a subject is directed to deliver a shock to another person.
d. A student volunteers to debate an issue, taking the side he personally disagrees with.

10. Which of the following is important in persuasive communication?
a. the credibility of the communicator
b. whether the message is delivered on television or in person
c. whether the communicator presents one or both sides of the issue
d. all of the above

11. A somewhat questionable authority on sleep attempts to convince a skeptical audience that they can do with less sleep than they currently believe they need. The speaker will probably produce the greatest attitude change by advocating a position that is:
a. extremely different from the audience's.
b. not too different from the audience's.
c. attributed to a legitimate authority on the subject.
d. based on instilling fear in the audience.

12. An individual may work harder when alone than as a member of a group. This phenomenon is called:
a. social loafing.   c. reactance.
b. social facilitation.   d. polarization.

13. The buffer zone people maintain around their bodies is called:
a. mobile territory.
b. the intimate zone.
c. the social buffer.
d. personal space.

14. Concerning minority influence on the opinion of the majority, which of the following is true?
a. Minorities very rarely influence group opinions.
b. A consistent minority opinion is more effective than one that wavers.
c. Minorities are most effective when they express their opinions loudly, and with anger.
d. A minority influence is more effective when the majority opinion has never been questioned.

15. When people are rewarded for doing what they already enjoy, their enjoyment may actually decrease. This phenomenon is called:
a. cognitive dissonance.
b. the overjustification effect.
c. deindividuation.
d. the self-perception effect.

SAMPLE ESSAY QUESTIONS

1. Discuss the importance of the communicator, the message, the medium, and the audience in persuasive communication.

2. Discuss how groups influence behavior. Include a consideration of group polarization, groupthink, deindividuation, and social facilitation.

3. Explain and contrast cognitive dissonance theory and self-perception theory. How do these theories account for the ways in which actions influence attitudes?

4. Describe Solomon Asch's studies of conformity. Under what circumstances is the tendency to conform increased?

5. Describe Milgram's procedure for studying obedience. Summarize the major findings of these studies.

As the text indicates, each person maintains a buffer zone, or mobile territory, around his or her body. Edward Hall (1966) formalized a method of analyzing personal space called **proxemics**. According to Hall, there are four basic distances relevant to personal space.

Intimate: extending from contact to about 18 inches
Personal: extending to about 4 feet
Social: extending from 4 to 12 feet
Public: distances greater than 12 feet

The distance another person stands from you may be considered appropriate or an uncomfortable "invasion," depending on your relationship and cultural background. People from the Middle East, for example, tend to stand much closer to one another than do the English and North Americans, who find such close quarters extremely uncomfortable. Conversations between two individuals from different cultures can lead to misunderstandings. The tendency of an American to back away from an Arab, for example, might be considered a social insult.

You can easily measure these distances using a technique called the *intrusion method.* This method is based on the tendency of people to feel uncomfortable or to withdraw when another person is standing too close. Using chalk or pieces of tape, measure and mark two lines on the floor that are exactly 12 feet apart. Invite several friends and acquaintances to be your subjects. You should select people with varying degrees of relationship to one another, from total strangers to close friends or roommates. Have one person stand at the starting line. Ask a second volunteer to begin slowly approaching from the 12-foot mark, stopping when the first subject reports feeling that the other is uncomfortably close. Using a tape measure, measure the distance between the two and record it. Have several others with different degrees of relationship to the first subject repeat the procedure. If you can, test students who have different cultural backgrounds. Using the table below, determine the average minimum distance that was tolerated for each category of relationship.

Questions to Consider

1. Did your measured distances conform to those reported in previous studies?

2. If you tested students from other cultures, did the results differ from those for American students?

3. What factors other than the cultural background of the participants would you expect to influence personal space?

Minimum Distances Tolerated Between Various Individuals

Subject	Strangers	Acquaintances	Friends	Intimate Friends
1.				
2.				
3.				
4.				
5.				
average:				

WHERE TO LOOK FOR MORE INFORMATION

Aronson, E. (1984). *The social animal.* San Francisco: W. H. Freeman.
    A very readable social psychology textbook.

Calhoun, J. (1962). Population density and social pathology. *Scientific American, 206,* pp. 139–48.
    Calhoun discusses his research on the effects of overcrowding on colonies of rats.

Festinger, L. (1957). *A theory of cognitive dissonance.* Stanford, Calif.: Stanford University Press.

Festinger's original formulation of this influential theory.

Myers, D. G. (1984). *Social psychology.* New York: McGraw-Hill.

An excellent social psychology text by the author of this introductory psychology text.

ANSWERS

PROGRESS TEST 1

1. b (p. 528)	6. b (p. 543)	11. b (p. 542)
2. c (p. 534)	7. d (p. 531)	12. a (p. 545)
3. d (p. 540)	8. c (p. 532)	13. d (p. 547)
4. c (p. 550)	9. b (p. 536)	14. b (p. 548)
5. a (p. 530)	10. c (p. 540)	15. a (p. 549)

PROGRESS TEST 2

1. d (p. 549)	6. a (p. 532)	11. b (p. 543)
2. c (p. 528)	7. d (p. 537)	12. a (p. 546)
3. a (p. 532)	8. d (p. 549)	13. d (p. 547)
4. b (p. 530)	9. d (p. 540)	14. b (p. 550)
5. c (p. 535)	10. d (pp. 542–545)	15. b (p. 541)

CHAPTER 20

Social Relations

CHAPTER OVERVIEW

Chapter 20 discusses the two-sided aspects of social relations: aggression and altruism, prejudice and attraction, conflict and peacemaking. The topics are addressed in terms of their social, cognitive, and biological roots and the steps that might be taken to prevent the further development of undesirable social relations in the world. The chapter concludes with a discussion of the social traps that engender the nuclear arms race, along with techniques that have been shown to promote conflict resolution between groups—techniques that foster cooperation, communication, and conciliation.

In comparison to other chapters, Chapter 20 has relatively few terms that you must memorize. Your major task will be to understand and remember the findings of the numerous experiments that are discussed. This is especially true in the section on aggression. The sections on prejudice and conflict should also be studied with extra care, since they contain rather complex examples and concepts. You should find this chapter quite interesting to study, however, since it discusses topics of considerable relevance to your everyday life. You may find it helpful to devote most of your study time for this chapter to one or more forms of recitation. Mentally, verbally, and in writ-

ing, carefully answer each of the chapter objectives and sample essay questions.

GUIDED STUDY

The text chapter should be studied one section at a time. Before you read, preview each section by skimming it, noting headings and boldface items. Then read the appropriate section objectives from the following outline. Keep these objectives in mind, and as you read the chapter section, search for the information that will complete each one. You may wish to write out answers for each objective as soon as you finish reading that section of the chapter.

Aggression (pp. 555–566)

1. Discuss whether aggression is an instinctive drive.

2. Explain the importance of genetic, neural, and biochemical factors in aggression.

3. Evaluate the role of aversive events and learning in the expression of aggression.

4. Identify and discuss three ways in which the learning of aggression might be counteracted.

5. Discuss whether violence on television promotes aggression.

6. Discuss the effects of pornography on aggression and how attitudes toward sexual assault have changed in recent years.

Altruism (pp. 566–571)

7. Explain the bystander effect and the sequence of decisions that must be made in order to prevent it.

8. Identify the circumstances in which a person is most likely to offer help to a person in need.

9. Compare and contrast the social exchange and sociobiological theories of altruistic behavior.

Prejudice (pp. 571–576)

10. Distinguish prejudice, stereotypes, and discrimination.

11. Identify and explain the social and emotional roots of prejudice.

12. Identify and explain the cognitive roots of prejudice.

Attraction (pp. 576–580)

13. Discuss the influence of proximity, physical attractiveness, and similarity in attraction to another person.

14. Compare and contrast the ingredients of romantic love and companionate love.

Conflict and Peacemaking (pp. 580–588)

15. Explain the non-zero-sum game and how it models a common social trap that fosters conflict.

16. Explain the tragedy of the commons.

17. Discuss how each of the following social influences promote conflict and discourage its resolution.

a. mirror-image perceptions

b. the self-serving bias

c. the fundamental attribution error

d. stereotypes

e. group polarization and groupthink

18. Discuss the findings of research studies concerning cooperation and conflict resolution.

19. Explain the GRIT model of communication and conciliation in conflict resolution.

CHAPTER REVIEW

When you have finished reading the chapter, complete the sentences that follow. Using your hand or a strip of paper, cover the correct answers in the margin and complete each sentence. Verify your answer by uncovering the correct one. As you proceed, evaluate your performance for each chapter section. *Do not continue with the next section until you understand why each margin term is the correct answer.* If you need to, review or re-read the appropriate chapter section in the textbook before continuing.

Aggression (pp. 555–566)

1. Aggressive behavior is behavior that _____ to hurt or destroy.

intends

2. Two theorists who proposed that aggression is instinctive are _____ and _____.

Freud; Lorenz

3. Freud believed that aggression reflected an individual's redirected _____ instinct.

death

4. Behaviors classified as instinctive are _____ and characterize an entire _____.

innate (unlearned)

species

5. Today, most psychologists _____ (do/do not) believe that human aggression is instinctive.

do not

6. In humans, aggressiveness _____ (does/does not) vary greatly from culture to culture.

does

7. That there are genetic influences on aggression can be shown by the fact that many species of animals have been _____ for aggressiveness.

bred

8. The region of the brain that triggers aggressive behavior when stimulated is the _____ .

amygdala

9. The aggressive behavior of animals can be manipulated by altering the levels of the hormone _____ .

testosterone

10. When this level is _____ (increased/decreased), aggressive tendencies are reduced.

decreased

11. One drug that diminishes natural restraints against aggression is _____ .

alcohol

12. When people are frustrated, their tendencies toward aggression may be increased. This is an expression of the _____-_____ theory.

frustration-aggression

13. List several stimuli that have been shown to provoke aggression.

_____

_____

_____

foul odors; heat smoke

14. List three ways in which the learning of aggression might be counteracted.

a. _____

_____

_____

b. _____

_____

_____

c. _____

_____

_____

by teaching children how to interpret media violence
by using rewards to socialize boys the way girls are socialized
by teaching parents how to nurture more positive behavior

15. Eron and Huesmann found that children were less influenced by watching television violence if they had been taught that it portrays the world _____ .

unrealistically

16. List some characteristics of parents of delinquent youngsters that may contribute to their children's aggressiveness.

_____

_____

_____

_____

_____

_____

_____

they tend to be unaware of where their children are; they do not effectively discipline them for antisocial behavior; they rely on spanking as a method of dealing with problems

17. In 1983, the average American household had the television on _____ hours a day.

seven

18. The consensus of researchers is that violence on television _____ (does/does not) promote aggressive behavior.

does

19. This effect is probably due to three factors: being _____ by the violence depicted, weakened _____ against violent acts, and the tendency of viewers to _____ .

aroused
inhibitions
imitate

20. Watching television also _____ viewers to violent acts.

desensitizes

21. In 1970, the President's Commission reported that pornography _____ (does/does not) promote antisocial behavior.

does not

22. The findings of more recent studies _____ (agree/disagree) with those of the President's Commission.

disagree

23. Recent experiments have revealed that there has been a(n) _____ (decrease/increase) in the acceptance of myths about rape.

increase

24. After seeing violent movies for several days, male subjects judged a rape victim as _____ (more/less) worthless and her physical injury as _____ (more/less) severe compared to a control group.

more
less

25. Zillmann and Bryant found that after regular exposure to sexually explicit films, students recommended _____ (shorter/longer) sentences for a rapist than did a control group.

shorter

26. Most unreported rapes _____ (are/are not) committed by strangers.

are not

27. Men who have committed rape are more likely to believe that females actually _____ rape.

provoke

Altruism (pp. 566–571)

28. An unselfish regard for the welfare of others is called _____.

altruism

29. In Takooshian and Bodinger's study in which a burglary was staged in full view of others, a surprisingly _____ (small/large) number of passersby stopped to question the "burglars."

small

30. In a series of staged emergencies, Latané and Darley found that a bystander was _____ (more/less) likely to help if other bystanders were present.

less

31. This phenomenon has been called the _____ _____.

bystander effect

32. According to Darley and Latané, people will help only if they first _____ the incident, then _____ it as an emergency, and finally _____ _____ for helping.

notice; interpret
assume responsibility

33. When people who overheard a seizure victim calling for help thought others were hearing the same plea, they were _____ (more/less) likely to call for help than when they thought no one else was aware of the emergency.

less

34. Identify the circumstances in which a person is most likely to offer help during an emergency.

_____
_____
_____
_____
_____
_____
_____
_____
_____
_____
_____

after having observed
someone else helping;
when not in a hurry;
when the person
appears to need and
deserve help; when
the person needing
help is similar to the
helper; when the
helper is feeling guilty;
when the helper is not
preoccupied and is in
a good mood

35. The theory proposing that social behavior aims to maximize rewards and minimize costs is the _____ _____ theory.

social exchange

36. According to this theory, people are most likely to help those who can _____ favors in the future.

reciprocate

37. Rules of accepted social behavior are called _____.

norms

38. One such rule tells us to reciprocate to those who have helped us; this is the _____ norm.

reciprocity

39. Another is that we should help those who need our help; this is the _____ _____ norm.

social responsibility

40. According to sociobiologists, altruism may have a _____ basis.

genetic

41. According to this viewpoint, a person should tend to be _____ (more/less) altruistic toward close relatives than to distant ones, because of the greater proportion of shared _____.

more

genes

42. Altruistic acts among animals _____ (have/have not) been demonstrated.

have

Prejudice (pp. 571– 576)

43. An unjustifiable negative attitude toward a group is called _____.

prejudice

44. Prejudiced beliefs are called _____.

stereotypes

45. These beliefs often predispose actions that are _____.

discriminatory

46. Allport has shown that prejudice is fostered in those possessing money, power, and prestige as a means of _____ social inequalities.

rationalizing (justifying)

47. Prejudice is also fostered by the _____ _____—a tendency to favor groups to which one belongs.

ingroup bias

48. People who have experienced failure or been frustrated are _____ (more/less) likely to criticize another person.

more

49. The theory suggesting that prejudice derives from attempts to blame others for one's own frustration is called the _____ _____.

scapegoat theory

50. Research on information processing suggests that prejudice may also derive from _____—an attempt to simplify the world by classifying people into groups.

categorization

51. One by-product of this phenomenon is that people tend to _____ (overestimate/underestimate) the similarity of those within a group.

overestimate

52. Another factor that fosters the formation of group stereotypes is the tendency to _____ from vivid or memorable cases.

overgeneralize

53. The belief that people get what they deserve—that the good are rewarded and the bad punished—is expressed in the _____ _____ phenomenon.

just-world

54. In one study, people learned to echo another person's thoughts; Milgram referred to such people as _____.

cyranoids

55. In Milgram's study, the teachers' impressions of a child echoing Milgram's thoughts were constrained by their _____ about the child.

preconceptions

Attraction (pp. 576–580)

56. The most powerful predictor of whether two individuals will be attracted to one another is _____.

proximity

57. When people are repeatedly exposed to unfamiliar stimuli, their liking for those stimuli _____ (increases/decreases).

increases

58. This phenomenon is called the _____ _____.

mere exposure effect

59. When people were shown regular and mirror-image photographs of their own faces, they preferred the _____ photographs.

mirror image

60. Our first impression of another person is most influenced by the person's _____.

attractiveness

61. List several characteristics that attractive individuals are judged to possess.

_____

_____

_____

_____

_____

attractive people are judged to be happier, more sensitive, successful, and socially skilled

62. Attractive people _____ (are/are not) more likely to make a good impression during job interviews.

are

63. A person's attractiveness _____ (is/is not) strongly related to self-esteem.

is not

64. Relationships in which the partners are very similar are _____ (more/less) likely to last.

more

65. List several things that friends and couples are more likely than strangers to share.

_____

_____

_____

_____

_____

attitudes, beliefs, interests, age, religion, race, education, intelligence, smoking behavior, economic level

66. A person's liking for another _____ (is/is not) influenced by the extent to which their attitudes are similar.

is

67. Hatfield and Walster (1981) have distinguished two types of love: _____ love and _____ love.

romantic; companionate

68. According to the two-factor theory, emotions have two components: _____, and a _____ label.

arousal; cognitive

69. When college men were placed in an aroused state, their feelings toward an attractive woman were more _____ (positive/negative) than those of men who had not been aroused.

positive

70. Companionate love is promoted by _____—mutual sharing and giving by both partners.

equity

Conflict and Peacemaking (pp. 580–588)

71. A perceived incompatibility of actions or goals is referred to as _____.

conflict

72. Lifton coined the term _____ _____ to refer to the defensive process in which a person's feelings are numbed during a disaster.

psychic numbing

73. Two destructive social processes that contribute to the arms race are _____ _____ and _____-_____ perceptions.

social traps
mirror-image perceptions

74. When the "non-zero-sum game" is played, most people fall into the social trap by mistrusting the other player and pursuing their own _____-_____.

self-interest

75. The "tragedy of the commons" refers to situations in which people pursue their personal interests at the expense of a _____ resource.

shared (communal)

76. Leaders of the United States and USSR see _____ images of each other as evil and untrust-worthy.

mirror

77. The tendency of people to accept credit for their good deeds and to justify their bad deeds is called the _____-_____ _____.

self-serving bias

78. The arms race is fostered by the _____ _____ _____—a tendency of each country to attribute the other's actions to an aggressive disposition.

fundamental
attribution error

79. Also contributing to the biased thinking that fosters the arms race are preconceived attitudes, or _____, and the tendency of each nation to develop _____ and see its own actions as moral.

stereotypes
groupthink

80. Conflict resolution is most likely in situations characterized by _____, _____, and _____.

cooperation
communication; conciliation

81. In most situations, establishing contact between two conflicting groups _____ (is/is not) sufficient to resolve conflict.

is not

82. In Sherif's study, two conflicting groups of campers were able to resolve their conflicts by working together on projects in which they shared _____ goals.

superordinate

83. Osgood has advocated a strategy of conciliation called GRIT, which stands for _____ and _____ _____ in _____ reduction.

Graduated; Reciprocated
Initiatives; Tension

84. The key to this method is each side's offering of a small _____ gesture in order to increase mutual trust and cooperation.

conciliatory

FOCUS ON PSYCHOLOGY:
A LESSON IN PREJUDICE

Firsthand experience is a hard but effective way to develop an understanding of the devastating effects that prejudice can have on people, and how easily members of the ingroup can become prejudiced toward others. In a dramatic demonstration of these points, Jane Elliot conducted a study with a group of third-grade children. The experiment began when the teacher announced that brown-eyed people were more intelligent and generally superior to blue-eyed people. Several classroom rules were established. Blue-eyed children had to sit at the back of the classroom and wait at the end of the line for recess, lunch, and other activities. The brown-eyed children were given virtually all classroom privileges. At first some of the children resisted, because many intergroup friendships existed. But the members of each group quickly became socialized to the new group norms. The brown-eyed children began to act as if they were superior; some became quite vicious and nasty in their interactions with their blue-eyed classmates. The blue-eyed children also adopted roles. They began to do poorly in their lessons and refer to themselves with negative terms such as bad and stupid. Intergroup friendships were broken and replaced with hatred. After three very unpleasant days the experiment was terminated when the teacher announced to the class what she had done. Most of the children were relieved to be able to drop their brown- or blue-eyed roles and to be reassured that all of them were equal.

Elliot's study effectively demonstrates the extent to which a number of social and cognitive factors influence prejudice, stereotyping, and discrimination. Based on your reading of Chapter 20, can you identify these factors? Are there any examples of these phenomena on your campus? How might they be counteracted?

PROGRESS TEST 1

Circle your answers to the following questions and check them with the answer key at the end of this chapter. Be sure to consult the appropriate pages of the text to understand the correct answer for any missed question.

1. Aggression is defined as behavior that:
a. hurts another person.
b. intends to hurt another person.
c. is hostile, passionate, and produces physical injury.
d. is all the above.

2. Which of the following is true?
a. Although all cultures are aggressive, aggression is most likely a result of learning, not instinct.

b. Since aggressiveness varies from culture to culture, it is probably not instinctive.
c. Since every known culture is somewhat aggressive, there probably is an aggressive instinct in humans.
d. Although violence occurs in every culture, most violent acts are not by definition aggressive.

3. Research studies have found a positive correlation between aggressive tendencies in animals and levels of the hormone:
a. estrogen.   **c.** noradrenaline.
b. adrenaline.   **d.** testosterone.

4. According to Eron and Huesmann, how might the learning of aggression be counteracted?
a. by teaching children how to interpret media violence
b. by socializing both boys and girls as girls are usually socialized
c. by teaching parents how to nurture more positive social behavior
d. All the above tend to counteract the learning of aggression.

5. Research studies of the effects of pornography have indicated that the acceptance of rape myths, such as the idea that women encourage rape:
a. is increased by exposure to pornography.
b. is not changed after exposure to pornography.
c. is decreased in men by exposure to pornography.
d. is decreased in both men and women by exposure to pornography.

6. The greater the number of people present during an emergency, the less likely it is that anyone will help. This phenomenon is called the:
a. altruistic effect.
b. deindividuation effect.
c. Good Samaritan effect.
d. bystander effect.

7. Which of the following is associated with an increased tendency of a bystander to offer help in an emergency situation?
a. being in a good mood
b. feeling guilty

c. observing others helping

d. all the above

8. Which of the following best expresses the sociobiological theory of altruistic behavior?

a. Altruism toward strangers should never occur.

b. Self-sacrificing behaviors are never favored by natural selection.

c. Some forms of altruism help perpetuate our genes.

d. People help others because of a genetically based moral obligation.

9. Psychologists who study the tendency of people to categorize their worlds in terms of "us and them" would argue that prejudice results from:

a. a basic process by which children are socialized.

b. a stable personality trait.

c. a natural tendency toward ingroup bias.

d. all the above.

10. The tendency of people to assume that those who suffer deserve their fate is expressed in the:

a. just-world phenomenon.

b. phenomenon of ingroup bias.

c. fundamental attribution error.

d. cyranoid effect.

11. The mere exposure effect demonstrates that:

a. familiarity breeds contempt.

b. opposites attract.

c. birds of a feather flock together.

d. familiarity breeds fondness.

12. In one experiment, college men were physically aroused and then introduced to an attractive woman. Compared to men who had not been aroused, these men:

a. reported more positive feelings toward the woman.

b. reported more negative feelings toward the woman.

c. did not differ in their feelings toward the woman, since the arousal was not attributed to her.

d. reported that the woman seemed less intelligent.

13. The deep affection that is felt in long-lasting relationships is called _____

love; this feeling is fostered in relationships in which:

a. mature; there is equity between the partners.

b. mature; traditional male-female roles are maintained.

c. companionate; there is equity between the partners.

d. companionate; traditional male-female roles are maintained.

14. Which of the following is the usual outcome when the "non-zero-sum game" is played?

a. Both sides lose by mistrusting each other and pursuing their own self-interests.

b. Both sides win by mistrusting each other and pursuing their own self-interests.

c. One side dominates the other.

d. The two sides eventually cooperate.

15. Which of the following strategies would be most likely to foster positive feelings between two conflicting groups?

a. Force them to sit down together and work out their differences.

b. Segregate the groups from each other.

c. Have one representative from each group visit the other and field questions.

d. Have the groups work together on a shared, superordinate goal.

FOCUS ON PSYCHOLOGY:
THE SUICIDE-PILL OPTION

How do you feel about the following article by Jason Salzman, student at Brown University and founder of Students for Suicide Tablets?

Brown University students overwhelmingly passed a referendum on our student-council election ballot last fall, asking our infirmary "to stockpile suicide pills for optional use by students only after a nuclear war." I call on college students across the country to put the same measure up for a vote at their schools.

I get four types of reactions when I propose that students adopt a suicide-pill referendum: (1) It's nothing but a crazy joke. (2) It's an offensive idea that does more harm than good. (3) It's worth supporting. (4) What it says is irrelevant; it's not worth the time to listen to the idea.

The suicide option emphasizes people's belief that surviving nuclear war is a dangerous illusion. If it is believed that a nuclear war will be won by the side with the most survivors or by the side which can rebuild the fastest, then waging a nuclear war becomes a realistic, not theoretical, idea. Opting for suicide pills would debunk the "nuclear winners" hypothesis.

Similarly, nuclear war is often associated with words such as "victory," "survival," and "recovery." The suicide-pill program links more appropriate words to nuclear war, such as "death" and "suicide."

On an even more theoretical level, the suicide-pill program is a logical way to stabilize the arms race. It would demonstrate to the Soviet Union that people in the United States are absolutely serious about preventing nuclear war. By denying the instinctive desire for life after nuclear war, we would be making the strongest possible statement for peace and disarmament.

Perhaps one of the best reasons is also the most simple: life after nuclear war, if possible, would be undesirable. As the phrase goes, "the living will envy the dead."

Now, about those students who will not even listen to the idea. Sometimes I try to catch their attention by asking them, "Do you think you can survive a nuclear war?" Students have replied with something like this, "If I can make it through college I can survive anything." Although clearly spoken in jest, this response illustrates an unspoken mind-set. Asked about survival, the first thing these students think about is college. In many ways this is understandable. It is hard to realize that political problems, including the threat of nuclear weapons, can be almost as immediate as what's right in front of us. It is easy to forget that the bombs could start falling from the sky before your next exam starts.

Source: "My turn: The suicide-pill option," *Newsweek On Campus,* March 1985.

PROGRESS TEST 2

Progress Test 2 should be completed during a final chapter review. Do so after you thoroughly understand the correct answers for the Chapter Review and Progress Test 1.

1. Which theorist argued that aggression was a manifestation of a person's "death instinct" redirected toward another person?
a. Wilson
b. Freud
c. Lorenz
d. Lagerspetz

2. Research studies of selective breeding suggest that aggressive behavior:
a. may have a genetic basis.
b. is primarily a learned rather than genetically determined behavior.
c. cannot be increased through breeding.
d. is both (b) and (c).

3. Which of the following is true regarding the relationship between alcohol and aggressive behavior?
a. As a stimulant, alcohol makes a person feel unusually strong.
b. Alcohol triggers increased activity in the amygdala of the brain.
c. Alcohol diminishes natural restraints against aggression.
d. No consistent relationship has been found between aggression and alcohol.

4. Which of the following is true concerning the effects of television violence on aggressive behavior?
a. Most researchers agree that violent television does promote aggression.
b. No significant relationship has been demonstrated.
c. Watching violent television diminishes an individual's aggressive tendencies.
d. Violent television influences boys more than girls.

5. Research studies have shown that frequent exposure to sexually explicit films:
a. may promote the attitude that women encourage rape.
b. diminishes the attitude that rape is a serious crime.
c. may increase men's aggressive behavior against women.

d. may produce all the above effects.

6. Research studies of the bystander effect indicate that the presence of other people in an emergency situation often:
a. prevents people from even noticing the situation.
b. prevents people from interpreting an unusual event as an emergency.
c. results in a diffusion of responsibility among those present.
d. leads to all the above.

7. Which of the following best expresses the social exchange theory of altruistic behavior?
a. People help others because they have been taught that doing so is a moral obligation.
b. People help others out of a sense of guilt or pity.
c. People help others on the chance that they will later reciprocate.
d. People rarely help others unless they are related to them.

8. People with power and status may become prejudiced as a result of the tendency:
a. to justify the social inequalities between themselves and others.
b. in those with less status and power to be resentful toward them.
c. in those with less status and power to be less capable.
d. to feel proud and boastful of their achievements.

9. Which of the following tends to foster prejudice?
a. People tend to blame others for their own failures.
b. People form stereotypes of others in order to simplify a complex world.
c. People have a tendency to favor their own group and to exclude others.
d. All the above foster prejudice.

10. Which of the following factors is most important in determining whether two people will like each other?
a. their similarity in age
b. their racial and religious backgrounds
c. their similarity in physical attractiveness
d. their physical proximity

11. Jim and Sue are on a blind date. Which of the following factors will probably be most influential in determining whether they like each other?
a. their personalities
b. their intelligence
c. their social skills
d. their physical attractiveness

12. Which of the following is true?
a. Birds of a feather flock together.
b. Opposites attract.
c. Familiarity breeds contempt.
d. Absence makes the heart grow fonder.

13. The tendency of people to become indifferent or unfeeling after a disaster is called:
a. deindividuation.
b. the tragedy of the commons.
c. psychic numbing.
d. groupthink.

14. Which of the following is an example of the commons dilemma?
a. John saves gas by taking the emission control device off his car.
b. After having been raped, Jill campaigns against anti-abortion legislation.
c. To demonstrate his allegiance to a fraternity, Bill steals the mascot of another fraternity.
d. Kathy copies from another student's paper during an exam.

15. Which of the following best characterizes the GRIT technique of conciliation?
a. Each side stands firm; mutual respect prevents further escalation of the problem.
b. The two sides engage in a series of reciprocated conciliatory acts.
c. The two sides agree to have their differences settled by a mediator.
d. The two sides agree to have their differences resolved by a competition between representatives from each group.

SAMPLE ESSAY QUESTIONS

1. Discuss whether television violence and pornography promote aggression.

2. Identify and explain the social, cognitive, and emotional roots of prejudice.

3. Discuss the bystander effect in terms of why it occurs, and the circumstances in which bystander intervention *is* likely to occur.

4. Explain the social traps that promote conflict.

5. Discuss the physiological influences on aggressiveness.

PROJECT:
STEREOTYPING AND PREJUDICE

Most people have certain prejudices and stereotypes—unjustifiable negative attitudes and beliefs toward various groups and their members. This exercise may help you gain insight into your own attitudes and how they influence your behavior.

For each of the groups noted below, list two or three adjectives you believe to be characteristic of its members. If you have no particular reaction to a group, do not feel compelled to come up with one; leave a blank. Try to be candid and honest as you fill in the table. After listing each group's characteristics, decide whether your overall impression of the group is positive (+) or negative (−), and so indicate in the appropriate column.

Group	Characteristics	Overall Impression (+ or −)
Americans		
Blacks		
Jews		
Japanese		
Chinese		
Irish		
Italians		
Mexicans		
Iranians		

Questions to Consider

1. Did you find that you hold many negative stereotypes toward these groups?

2. Do you believe your stereotypes are accurate descriptions of individual members of these groups?

3. In what ways do you think your stereotypes affect the way you act toward individual members of these groups?

4. How can you account for the development of your personal stereotypes? Are they the result of overgeneralization from a negative experience with a member of one of the groups? Are they a reflection of the ways in which you were socialized?

5. How might you go about changing your own stereotypes, or those of a friend?

WHERE TO LOOK FOR MORE INFORMATION

Donnerstein, E., and Linz, D. (1984, January). Sexual violence in the media: A warning. *Psychology Today.*

Popular "slasher" movies are shown to desensitize viewers to violence.

Elliott, J. (1977). The power and pathology of prejudice. In P. G. Zimbardo and F. L. Ruch (eds.), *Psychology and life, 9th ed.* Glenview, Ill.: Scott, Foresman.

A group of third-grade children learn about prejudice firsthand.

Freedman, J. L. (1984). Effect of television violence on aggressiveness. *Psychological Bulletin, 96,* pp. 227–46.

A prominent social psychologist reviews the evidence that television violence promotes aggression in viewers.

Snyder, M. (1982, July). Self-fulfilling stereotypes. *Psychology Today.*

The author demonstrates how prejudice is maintained by the interactions of those holding the prejudicial attitudes and their victims.

ANSWERS

PROGRESS TEST 1

1. b (p. 555)
2. b (p. 556)
3. d (p. 557)
4. d (pp. 559–560)
5. a (p. 563)

6. d (p. 567)
7. d (p. 568)
8. c (p. 570)
9. c (p. 573)
10. a (p. 575)

11. d (p. 577)
12. a (p. 580)
13. c (p. 580)
14. a (p. 584)
15. d (p. 586)

PROGRESS TEST 2

1. b (p. 556)
2. a (p. 557)
3. c (p. 558)
4. a (p. 561)
5. d (p. 563)

6. d (p. 568)
7. c (p. 570)
8. a (p. 572)
9. d (pp. 574–575)
10. d (p. 577)

11. d (p. 577)
12. a (p. 579)
13. c (p. 581)
14. a (p. 584)
15. b (p. 588)

APPENDIX A

Statistical Reasoning in Everyday Life

CHAPTER OVERVIEW

A basic understanding of statistics has become a necessity today: Statistics are tools that help psychologists and ordinary people to interpret the vast quantities of information they are confronted with on a daily basis. This appendix discusses two fundamental uses of statistics: describing data and generalizing from instances.

Organizing data into frequency distributions is an effective method of summarizing large amounts of information. In describing the average, or central tendency, of a distribution, the mean, median, and mode may be computed. The range and standard deviation allow the determination of whether the scores in a distribution are uniformly spaced or spread out. The correlation coefficient is a measure of the extent to which two scores are related.

In addition to being useful tools for describing data, statistical techniques help the psychologist to generalize from sample instances to populations, and to determine whether such generalizations are statistically significant.

In studying this chapter, you must concentrate on learning a number of procedures and understanding several underlying principles in the science of statistics. The computational procedures are all in the sec-

tion called "Describing Data," and include the mean, median, mode, range, and standard deviation. Make sure you are also able to construct a frequency distribution and frequency diagram from a distribution of scores. Most of the conceptual material is covered in the section called "Generalizing from Instances." You should be able to discuss four important principles concerning populations and samples, as well as the concept of significance in testing differences.

GUIDED STUDY

The text chapter should be studied one section at a time. Before you read, preview each section by skimming it, noting headings and boldface items. Then read the appropriate section objectives from the following outline. Keep these objectives in mind, and as you read the chapter section, search for the information that will complete each one. You may wish to write out answers for each objective as soon as you finish reading that section of the chapter.

Describing Data (pp. 593–600)

1. Explain how frequency distributions, histograms, and percentile ranks are used in describing data.

2. Differentiate the three measures of central tendency and explain how to compute each.

3. Differentiate the range and standard deviation and explain how to compute each.

4. Explain the concept of the normal curve and describe its characteristics.

5. Explain what the correlation coefficient measures and the difference between positive and negative correlations.

6. Discuss the concept of the illusory correlation.

7. Explain the phenomenon of regression toward the average.

Generalizing from Instances (pp. 600–604)

8. Explain the difference between a population and a sample.

9. Discuss the principle: "Representative samples are better than biased samples."

10. Discuss the principle: "Random sequences may not look random."

11. Discuss the principle: "More cases are better than fewer."

12. Discuss the principle: "Less variable observations are better than more variable."

13. Explain the concept of statistical significance.

CHAPTER REVIEW

When you have finished reading the chapter, complete the sentences that follow. Using your hand or a strip of paper, cover the correct answers in the margin and complete each sentence. Verify your answer by uncovering the correct one. As you proceed, evaluate your performance for each chapter section. *Do not continue with the next section until you understand why each margin term is the correct answer.* If you need to, review or re-read the appropriate chapter section in the text before continuing.

Describing Data (pp. 593–600)

1. For descriptive purposes, statistics are useful in _____ and _____ data.

organizing; interpreting

2. A table or graph that depicts the number of individual scores occurring at each level of some measure is called a _____ _____.

frequency distribution

3. A bar graph that depicts a frequency distribution is called a _____.

histogram

4. The percentage of scores in a distribution that fall below an individual score is that score's _____ _____.

percentile rank

5. A pioneer in the use of statistics and medical reform was _____ _____.

Florence Nightingale

6. The three measures of central tendency are the _____, the _____, and the _____.

mean; median
mode

7. The most frequently occurring score in a distribution is called the _____.

mode

8. The median is the score at the _____ percentile.

fiftieth

9. The mean is computed as the total _____ of scores divided by the _____ of scores.

sum
number

10. The three measures of central tendency may all be different in a distribution that is not _____.

symmetrical

11. The measures of variation include the _____ and the _____ _____.

range
standard deviation

12. The range is computed as the _____
_____
_____.

difference between the highest and lowest scores in a distribution

13. The range provides a(n) _____ (crude/accurate) estimate of variation, because it _____ (is/is not) influenced by extreme scores.

crude
is

14. The standard deviation _____ (is/is not) a more accurate measure of variation than the range.

is

15. Unlike the range, the standard deviation _____ (does/does not) take into consideration information from each score in the distribution.

does

16. List the four steps in computing the standard deviation.

a. _____
_____
_____

b. _____

c. _____
_____

d. _____

Square the deviation between each score and the mean.
Sum these deviations.
Divide this sum by the number of scores.
Take the square root of this sum.

17. The bell-shaped distribution that often describes large amounts of data is called the _____ _____.

normal curve

18. In this distribution, approximately _____ _____ percent of the individual scores fall within one standard deviation on either side of the mean.

68

19. Within two standard deviations on either side of the mean in a normal distribution fall _____ percent of the individual scores.

95

20. A graphed plot that depicts the relationship between two sets of scores is called a _____.

scatterplot

21. A measure of the direction and extent of relationship between two

sets of scores is called the _____   correlation coefficient
_____ .

22. Numerically, the correlation coefficient ranges from _____ to _____ .   +1.00; −1.00

23. When the correlation between two sets of scores is positive, the scores _____ (increase/decrease) in proportion to one another.   increase

24. When the correlation between two sets of scores is 0.00, the scores _____ (are/are not) related.   are not

25. When the correlation between two sets of scores is negative, as one increases, the other _____ .   decreases

26. The tendency to perceive a correlation when none exists is called _____ _____ .   illusory correlation

27. When we believe a relationship exists between two things, we are most likely to recall instances that _____ (confirm/disconfirm) our belief.   confirm

28. Although the correlation coefficient is useful in seeing relationships between things, it does not give information about _____ and _____ relationships.   cause; effect

29. Illusory correlation can also lead to the illusion that we have control over _____ events.   chance

30. That average results are more typical than extreme results is expressed in the phenomenon of _____ _____ _____ .   regression toward the average

Generalizing from Instances (pp. 600–604)

31. All the cases in a total group make up a _____ .   population

32. List four important principles in generalizing from samples to populations.

a. _____
_____
_____

b. _____   Representative samples are
_____   better than biased samples.
     Random sequences may
     not look random.
c. _____   More cases are better than
_____   fewer.

d. _____
_____
_____
_____

Less variable observations are better than more variable observations.

33. People have a tendency to _____ from unrepresentative but vivid cases.

generalize

34. A random sample is one in which each person in the population has: _____
_____

an equal chance of being selected

35. Small samples provide a _____ (more/less) reliable basis for generalizing than large samples.

less

36. The expected standard deviation among a group of sample means is called the _____ _____
_____ _____
_____ .

standard error of the mean

37. Averages based on a large number of cases are _____ (more/less) reliable than those based on only a few cases.

more

38. Averages are more reliable when they are based on scores with low _____ .

variability

39. When people perceive little variability in individual instances, they are _____ (more/less) likely to generalize from them.

more

40. Tests of statistical _____ are used to estimate whether observed differences are reliable.

significance

41. List the circumstances in which the difference between two sample averages is likely to be statistically significant.

_____
_____
_____
_____
_____
_____
_____
_____
_____
_____

when the samples are reliable estimates of their populations; when each is based on a large number of observations that have a small standard deviation; when the difference between the two averages is large

42. If a difference is statistically significant, it means that it is not likely to be the result of _____ variation.

chance

Our lives are so dependent upon statistics, from interpreting daily weather forecasts to evaluating the results of the latest political poll, that it is difficult to imagine functioning without them. Statistics is a relatively young science, however. Its history can be traced only as far back as the seventeenth century. In 1654, a gambler named Antoine Gombard sought the advice of the noted French mathematician Pascal concerning a hypothetical gambling dilemma. Gombard posed the following problem. Suppose five individuals are in the middle of a poker game, when it becomes necessary to stop the play. How should the prize money be divided among the players if the game cannot be completed? How would you solve this dilemma? Do each of the players have an equal chance of winning?

Consideration of this problem led Pascal to the study of probabilities. In order to solve the problem, it was necessary to determine the likelihood of any given player winning a canceled hand if it could be continued until completion. Gombard and Pascal's mutual interest in gambling and other games of chance led to a lengthy correspondence. Out of this correspondence, and their consideration of other problems, the new science of statistics emerged. That statistics was created as a solution to a particular problem exemplifies the familiar saying, "Necessity is the mother of invention."

PROGRESS TEST 1

Circle your answers to the following questions and check them with the answer key at the end of the chapter. Be sure to consult the appropriate pages of the text to understand the correct answer for any missed question.

Multiple-Choice Questions

1. Jack found that his score on the psychology exam was the highest in his class. His percentile rank for this score is:
a. 99.
b. 100.
c. 95.
d. not determinable from the information given.

2. What is the mean of the following distribution of scores: 2, 3, 7, 6, 1, 4, 9, 5, 8, 2?
a. 5
b. 4
c. 4.7
d. 3.7

3. What is the median of the following distribution of scores: 1, 3, 7, 7, 2, 8, 4?
a. 1
b. 2
c. 3
d. 4

4. What is the mode of the following distribution: 8, 2, 1, 1, 3, 7, 6, 2, 0, 2?
a. 1
b. 2
c. 3
d. 7

5. Compute the range of the following distribution: 9, 14, 2, 8, 1, 6, 8, 9, 1, 3.
a. 10
b. 9
c. 8
d. 13

6. Compute the standard deviation of the following distribution: 3, 5, 6, 2, 4.
a. 1
b. $\sqrt{2}$
c. $\sqrt{10}$
d. 4

7. If two variables are negatively correlated, it means that:
a. as one increases, the other decreases.
b. as one increases, the other increases.
c. there is no relationship between them.
d. knowing one, you cannot predict the other.

8. Jane usually averages 175 in bowling. One night her three-game average is 215. Over the next several weeks of bowling, her bowling average will probably:
a. return to about the level of her average.
b. continue to increase.
c. vary erratically.
d. be unpredictable, given the above information.

9. In a normal distribution, what percentage of

scores fall between $+2$ and -2 standard deviations of the mean?

a. 50%
b. 68%
c. 95%
d. 99.7%

10. If x and y are positively correlated, which of the following is true?

a. There is a cause-effect relationship between x and y.
b. As x increases, y decreases.
c. Knowing x, one can predict y.
d. None of the above is true.

11. In generalizing from a sample to the population, which of the following is important?

a. The sample is representative of the population.
b. The sample is large.
c. The scores in the sample have low variability.
d. All of the above are important.

12. When a difference between two groups is "statistically significant," it means that:

a. the difference is statistically real, but of little importance practically.
b. the difference is probably the result of sampling variation.
c. the difference is not likely to be due to chance variation.
d. all of the above are true.

Matching Items

Match each term with its corresponding definition.

_____ **1.** histogram
_____ **2.** median
_____ **3.** population
_____ **4.** sample
_____ **5.** mode
_____ **6.** range
_____ **7.** standard deviation
_____ **8.** scatterplot
_____ **9.** mean
_____ **10.** measures of central tendency
_____ **11.** measures of variation

a. mean, median, and mode
b. difference between highest and lowest scores
c. arithmetic average of a distribution
d. range and standard deviation
e. all the cases in a group
f. the most frequently occurring score
g. a subset of scores from a group
h. a bar graph depicting a frequency distribution
i. middle score in a distribution
j. a graphed cluster of dots depicting the values of two variables
k. square root of the average squared deviation of scores from the mean

FOCUS ON PSYCHOLOGY:
COULD A MONKEY HAVE WRITTEN THIS STUDY GUIDE?

It has been said that given enough time, a monkey randomly striking the keys of a typewriter could theoretically turn out the great American novel. What is the actual probability of this occurring?

In this study guide there are approximately 200,000 characters—letters, numbers, and spaces. The keyboard of the microcomputer used to type it has 63 keys. Therefore, at any given point in time, the monkey would have a 1 in 63 chance of striking the correct key. Sounds plausible, you say? To complete the entire study guide, our diligent ape would have to strike the correct key 200,000 times in succession. The probability of this occurring is computed as $1/63 = 0.016$ raised to the power of 200,000. To develop a feeling for how remote this probability is, 0.016 raised to the power of 2 is equal to 0.000256; 0.016 raised to the 20th power is equal to .000000000000000000000000000000000000121. Raised to the power of 200,000, the probability is so small that the decimal point is followed by more zeros than there are characters in this entire book.

Suggested by A. F. Grasha. (1963). *Practical applications of psychology*, 2d ed. Boston: Little, Brown.

PROGRESS TEST 2

Progress Test 2 should be completed during a final chapter review. Do so after you thoroughly understand the correct answers for the Chapter Review and Progress Test 1.

Multiple-Choice Questions

1. A bar graph that depicts a frequency distribution is called a(n):
a. scatterplot.
b. normal curve.
c. coefficient plot.
d. histogram.

2. What is the mean of the following distribution of scores: 2, 5, 8, 10, 11, 4, 6, 9, 1, 4?
a. 2
b. 10
c. 6
d. 15

3. The tendency for extreme scores to fall back toward the average is called:
a. illusory correlation.
b. regression toward the average.
c. the standard deviation.
d. representability.

4. Which score falls at the fiftieth percentile of a distribution?
a. mean
b. median
c. mode
d. standard deviation

5. Which statistic is the average amount by which the scores in a distribution vary from the average?
a. standard deviation
b. range
c. median
d. mode

6. The most frequently occurring score in a distribution is the:
a. mean.
b. median.
c. mode.
d. range.

7. When two variables are positively correlated, which of the following is true?
a. As one increases, the other decreases.
b. As one increases, the other increases.
c. There is a cause-effect relationship between them.
d. All of the above are true.

8. In a normal distribution, what percentage of scores fall between -1 and $+1$ standard deviation units of the mean?
a. 50%
b. 68%
c. 95%
d. 99%

9. What is the standard deviation of the following distribution: 3, 1, 4, 10, 12?
a. 10
b. 15
c. $\sqrt{18}$
d. 4

10. A graph that depicts the relationship between two sets of scores is called a:
a. histogram.
b. scatterplot.
c. frequency distribution.
d. bar graph.

11. Joe believes that his basketball game is always best when he wears his old gray athletic socks. Joe is a victim of the phenomenon called:
a. regression toward the average.
b. the availability heuristic.
c. illusory correlation.
d. the gambler's fallacy.

12. If a difference between two samples is *not* statistically significant, which of the following can be concluded?
a. The difference is probably not a true one.
b. The difference is probably not reliable.
c. The difference could be due to sampling variation.
d. All of the above are true.

True–False

_____ 1. A percentile score of 60 means that most of the scores in the distribution fall above it.

_____ 2. In almost all distributions, the mean, median, and the mode will be the same.

_____ 3. When a distribution has a few extreme scores, the range is more misleading than the standard deviation.

_____ 4. If increases in the value of variable x are accompanied by decreases in the value of variable y, the two variables are negatively correlated.

_____ 5. Over time, extreme results tend to fall back toward the average.

_____ 6. If a sample was selected randomly, it cannot be representative of the population from which it was drawn.

_____ 7. Averages that have been derived from scores with low variability are more reliable than those derived from scores that are more variable.

_____ 8. If a difference between two groups is due to sampling variation, it cannot be statistically significant.

_____ 9. Small samples are less reliable than large samples for generalizing to the population.

SAMPLE ESSAY QUESTIONS

1. Identify the three measures of central tendency and explain how each is computed.

2. Explain how the range and standard deviation are computed and what these measures tell us about distributions.

3. Discuss what a correlation between two sets of scores does and does not mean.

4. Identify and discuss four important principles in generalizing from samples to populations.

5. Discuss the concept of statistical significance, including what it means and the circumstances under which a difference between two samples is likely to be significant.

PROJECT:
COMPUTING THE CORRELATION COEFFICIENT

The correlation coefficient is an indication of the degree of relationship between two variables (referred to as X and Y). Although a strong correlation between X and Y does not imply that one caused the other, it does mean that if you know the value of a particular X, you can predict what its Y equivalent is likely to be. The correlation coefficient ranges from 0 to 1, with numbers close to 1 indicating stronger relationships. In the following example, a procedure for describing these relationships—called the _Pearson product moment correlation coefficient_ (symbolized by the letter r)—is outlined. Work the example, then apply the formula to the problem that follows.

Computation of Correlation Coefficient

In this example, a teacher wishes to determine the relationship between the average number of hours per day each of her students watches television (variable X) and the number of hours each devotes to studying (variable Y). The data for 10 students are given in Table A.1 on page 303.

The formula for r is given below, along with the procedure for computing each term in the equation. Make sure you understand how each of the values for the sample problem was derived.

$$r = \frac{N\Sigma XY - \Sigma X \Sigma Y}{\sqrt{[N\Sigma X^2 - (\Sigma X)^2][N\Sigma Y^2 - (\Sigma Y)^2]}}$$

N = the number of XY pairs (students): (10)

ΣX = the sum of scores for variable X: ($1 + 4 + 2 + 2 + 3 + 1 + 5 + 6 + 2 + 3 = 29$)

ΣY = the sum of scores for variable Y: ($4 + 1 + 2 + 3 + 1 + 5 + 4 + 1 + 3 + 2 = 26$)

ΣXY = the sum of each variable X score multiplied by its variable Y equivalent:
($1 \times 4 = 4$) + ($4 \times 1 = 4$) + ($2 \times 2 = 4$) + ($2 \times 3 = 6$) + ($3 \times 1 = 3$) + ($1 \times 5 = 5$) + ($5 \times 4 = 20$) + ($6 \times 1 = 6$) + ($2 \times 3 = 6$) + ($3 \times 2 = 6$) = 64

ΣX^2 = the sum of each variable X score squared (multiplied by itself):
($1 \times 1 = 1$) + ($4 \times 4 = 16$) + ($2 \times 2 = 4$) + ($2 \times 2 = 4$) + ($3 \times 3 = 9$) + ($1 \times 1 = 1$) + ($5 \times 5 = 25$) + ($6 \times 6 = 36$) + ($2 \times 2 = 4$) + ($3 \times 3 = 9$) = 109

Table A.1. Data Regarding Television Watching and Studying

Student	Hours Watching TV (variable X)	X²	Hours Studying (variable Y)	Y²	XY
1	1	1	4	16	4
2	4	16	1	1	4
3	2	4	2	4	4
4	2	4	3	9	6
5	3	9	1	1	3
6	1	1	5	25	5
7	5	25	4	16	20
8	6	36	1	1	6
9	2	4	3	9	6
10	3	9	2	4	6
Totals	29	109	26	86	64

ΣY^2 = the sum of each variable Y score squared (multiplied by itself):
$(4 \times 4 = 16) + (1 \times 1 = 1) + (2 \times 2 = 4) + (3 \times 3 = 9) + (1 \times 1 = 1) + (5 \times 5 = 25) + (4 \times 4 = 16) + (1 \times 1 = 1) + (3 \times 3 = 9) + (2 \times 2 = 4) = 86$

$(\Sigma X)^2$ = the sum of scores for variable X squared (multiplied by itself):
$(29 \times 29 = 841)$

$(\Sigma Y)^2$ = the sum of scores for variable Y squared (multiplied by itself):
$(26 \times 26 = 676)$

$$r = \frac{(10 \times 64) - (29 \times 26)}{\sqrt{[(10 \times 109) - 841] \times [(10 \times 86) - 676]}}$$

$$= \frac{640 - 754}{\sqrt{[1090 - 841] \times [860 - 676]}}$$

$$= \frac{-114}{\sqrt{[249 \times 184]}}$$

$$= \frac{-114}{\sqrt{45816}}$$

$$= \frac{-114}{\sqrt{214.05}}$$

$$= -0.533$$

Based on a correlation coefficient of -0.533, the teacher would have to conclude that, for this sample of students, there is a negative (or inverse) correlation between the amount of time spent watching television and studying. This means that, as the number of hours of watching television increases, there is a corresponding decrease in the amount of time spent studying.

Correlation Problem

The president of DATACOMP computers wants to know whether some of her salespeople are getting too old to keep up with the productivity of their younger competitors. In order to help her make the decision, she asks her sales manager to determine whether the number of years of sales experience is correlated with annual computer sales. These data are given in the table below.

Table A.2. Data Regarding Sales Experience and Annual Sales

Employee number	Years With DATACOMP (variable X)	X²	Total Sales (10s of thousands) (variable Y)	Y²	XY
1	3		15		
2	7		22		
3	4		19		
4	1		6		
5	6		16		
6	11		26		
7	2		11		
8	2		7		
9	1		9		
10	3		13		
Total					

From the data in the table, plot a frequency distribution and compute the Pearson product moment correlation coefficient.

Using the axes below, plot a frequency distribution.

Based on your frequency distribution, does there appear to be a relationship between X and Y? If so, is the relationship positive or negative?

Now compute the correlation coefficient by completing Table A.2 and filling in the information requested in the work sheet and formula below.

Work Sheet for Correlation Problem

$$r = \frac{N\Sigma XY - \Sigma X \Sigma Y}{[N\Sigma X^2 - (\Sigma X)^2][N\Sigma Y^2 - (\Sigma Y)^2]}$$

N = _____

ΣX = _____

ΣY = _____

ΣXY = _____

$(\Sigma X)^2$ = _____

$(\Sigma Y)^2$ = _____

$\Sigma X \Sigma Y$ = _____

r = _____

The solution to this problem is provided in the Answers section at the end of the chapter. Based on your computations, what do you conclude is the relationship between experience and annual sales?

WHERE TO LOOK FOR MORE INFORMATION

There are a number of excellent general introductions to the science of statistics; two are listed below:

Huff, D. (1954.) *How to lie with statistics*. New York: Norton.

Shaughnessy, J. J., and Zechmeister, E. B. 1985. *Research methods in psychology*. New York: Knopf.

ANSWERS

PROGRESS TEST 1

Multiple-Choice Questions

1. a (p. 594)
2. c (p. 596)
3. d (p. 596)
4. b (p. 596)

5. d (p. 597)
6. b (p. 597)
7. a (p. 598)
8. a (pp. 599–600)

9. c (p. 597)
10. c (p. 598)
11. d (pp. 601–603)
12. c (p. 604)

Matching Items

1. h (p. 594)
2. i (p. 596)
3. e (p. 601)
4. g (p. 601)

5. f (p. 596)
6. b (pp. 596–597)
7. k (p. 597)
8. j (pp. 597–598)

9. c (p. 596)
10. a (p. 596)
11. d (pp. 596–597)

PROGRESS TEST 2

Multiple-Choice Questions

1. d (p. 594)
2. c (p. 596)
3. b (pp. 599–600)
4. b (p. 596)

5. a (p. 597)
6. c (p. 596)
7. b (p. 598)
8. b (p. 597)

9. c (p. 597)
10. b (pp. 597–598)
11. c (p. 599)
12. d (p. 604)

True–False

1. F (p. 594)
2. F (p. 596)
3. T (pp. 596–597)

4. T (p. 598)
5. T (pp. 599–600)
6. F (p. 601)

7. T (p. 603)
8. F (p. 604)
9. T (p. 602)

CORRELATION PROJECT

$$N = 10$$
$$\Sigma X = 40$$
$$\Sigma Y = 144$$
$$\Sigma XY = 747$$
$$(\Sigma X)^2 = 1600$$
$$(\Sigma Y)^2 = 20736$$
$$\Sigma X \Sigma Y = 5760$$

$$r = \frac{(10)(747) - (5760)}{\sqrt{[(10)(250) - (1600)][(10)(2458) - (20736)]}}$$

$$= \frac{7470 - 5760}{\sqrt{[2500 - 1600][24580 - 20736]}}$$

$$= \frac{1710}{\sqrt{[900][3844]}}$$

$$= \frac{1710}{\sqrt{3459600}}$$

$$= \frac{1710}{1860}$$

$$r = 0.91927$$